Small Time Operator

How to Start Your Own Small Business, Keep Your Books, Pay Your Taxes And Stay Out of Trouble!

by Bernard B. Kamoroff, C.P.A.

BELL
SPRINGS
Publishing

Laytonville & Willits, California

Please Read:

I have done my very best to give you useful and accurate information in this book, but I cannot guarantee that the information is correct or will be appropriate to your particular situation. Laws, procedures and regulations change frequently and are subject to differing interpretations. It is your responsibility to verify all information and all laws discussed in this book before relying on them. Nothing in this book can substitute for legal advice and cannot be considered as making it unnecessary to obtain such advice. In all situations involving local, state or federal law, obtain specific information from the appropriate government agency or a competent person.

You Can Keep This Book Up To Date:

This edition of Small Time Operator is current as of the date shown below. Every January, we publish a one-page Update Sheet for Small Time Operator, listing changes in tax laws and other government regulations, referenced to the corresponding pages in the book. If you would like a copy of the Update Sheet, send a self-addressed, stamped #10 envelope (business size) and $1.00 to Small Time Operator Update, Box 1240, Willits, CA 95490.

Published by
BELL SPRINGS PUBLISHING
Box 1240, Willits, California 95490
(707) 459-6372

22nd Edition, 51st Printing, March 1997
Library of Congress Catalog Number 97-92986
ISBN: 0-917510-14-3

Printed by Consolidated Printers, Berkeley, California.
Cover illustration by Bruce McCloskey.
Cover layout by Jeanne H. Koelle, Koelle & Gilbert, Willits, Ca.
Illustrations, cartoons and song lyrics used with permission
of copyright holders.

Small Time Operator is a trademark of Bell Springs Publishing.

PRINTED ON RECYCLED PAPER

Quantity Purchases:
We offer substantial discounts on bulk sales to organizations,
schools, professionals, and businesses. For more information
call (707) 459-6372.

Many thanks to:

Jim Hayes for your original idea. To Jim Robertson for your encouragement and for suggesting the title. To Robert Greenway for helping to launch the company. To the business people who allowed me to interview them: Joe Campbell, Lara Stonebraker, Charles Dorton, Jan Lowe, Kathy Ward Eisman, Bob Mathews, Pat Ellington, Mike Simon, Nick Mein, Mike Snead, Mike Madson and Key Dickason. To the people who generously shared their expertise: Paul Paul and Mary Lai (insurance), Dave Raub and Tony Mancuso (corporations), Joe Sachs (SBA), Larry Jacobs (taxes), John Bobbitt (marketing), Lance Hoffman, Don McCunn and Leigh Robinson (computers), Joanie Mitchell and Michael McCaffrey (import/export). To my tireless editor Andy Blasky: this book would not be half as well written without him. To my illustrators Bruce McCloskey, Kitty and Will Emerson, and my dad David Kamoroff for drafting the ledgers. To the people who helped design and produce the book and get it out there: Hal Hershey, Sharon Miley, Dick Ellington, J'Ann Forgue, Sharon Kamoroff, Peter and Paul deFremery, Jeanne Koelle, John Fremont, and Cindy Frank. To the people who had faith in me and supported the project when it was just a manuscript and a dream: Lance and Kathy Hoffman, Beth Hackenbruch, Jerry Eisman, Richard Benson and Paul and Laura Klipfel. To my long lost friend H. Berry. And especially to Sharon, the Sweet Yodelady.

This book is dedicated to John Muir, The Mechanic.

In this world, a person must either be anvil or hammer.

—Longfellow

BE YOUR OWN BOSS

You can be your own boss. All it really requires is a good idea, some hard work, and a little knowledge. "A little knowledge" is what this book is all about. *Small Time Operator* will show you how to start and operate your own small business.

Small-Time Operator is a technical manual, a step-by-step guide to help you set up the "machinery" of your business, the "business end" of your business, and keep it lubricated and well maintained. It is written in everyday English so anyone can understand it. You will not need a business education or an accounting dictionary to grasp the concepts or do the work. *Small Time Operator* is also a workbook that includes bookkeeping instructions and a full set of ledgers, especially designed for small businesses.

Many people think that businessmen and businesswomen all come out of business school, kind of like Chevys coming out of a G.M. assembly plant. This just isn't true. I know many people in business, and most of them had no formal business education, and little or no experience.

Some new small business owners are people who just got tired of the nine-to-five life, tired of working for someone else, and who decided to go into business for themselves.

Some are people—hard working, talented people—who lost their jobs due to corporate "downsizing" and "restructuring", the latest big-business euphemisms for eliminating jobs and cutting back services. Every corporate employee now knows that the words "job" and "security" no longer go together.

And many new small business people are still holding onto their jobs, but starting a little part-time, sideline business, probably at home, to bring in some extra income, or to make a little money at something that started out as a hobby, or to experiment with their business ideas and learn the ropes before going at it full-time.

Small Time Operator comes out of my experience during the past twenty years as a consultant and accountant for small businesses, businesses started from scratch by inexperienced people, and from operating two of my own small businesses. I've learned from successes and I've learned from mistakes, my own and others'. Now I hope to teach you what I've learned.

Small Time Operator will show you things to do and things not to do. But like any book, it can't do more than that. You've got to go ahead and do it yourself. Bilbo Baggins said, "One should always begin at the beginning." That's where you are now. Other people, many others, now run their own small businesses. You can too.

The journey of a thousand miles begins with a single step.
—Lao Tsu

Contents

Section One
GETTING STARTED

Trying seems to be a start for getting things done
You get to know the right way by doing it wrong
And when you cross a bridge over shallow water
Does it always mean you're afraid to get wet
When you ought to?

—Barbara Pack

A Small Time Operator: A True Story

When I first met Joe Campbell several years ago, he was working as a switchman for Southern Pacific. He liked working on the railroad. Didn't love it, but it was a job.

Joe's hobby and one of his great pleasures in life was electronics. He especially enjoyed assembling electrical gadgets from kits, repairing old stereos and VCRs, playing with anything that had wires and resistors. In the process of building and experimenting, Joe also acquired a good theoretical and technical knowledge of radio and electronics. It was not long before he'd built himself a few test meters and started repairing the neighbors' TVs. He used to offer to fix my stereo for free, just to get the experience.

Gradually, Joe's hobby developed into a business. He moved slowly at first, a step at a time. He set up a small workshop in a spare bedroom and began taking in paying business on evenings and weekends. Joe was a good repairman, he didn't charge very much, and he gave his customers fast service. And Joe's business grew. He soon found himself with more business than he could handle in his spare time. He started working less hours for the railroad, then quit altogether and set up a small repair shop of his own.

Joe is a success, but not just because he makes his own living. Joe has shaped his life around his interests. He enjoys his work, and his customers recognize and appreciate the personal interest he takes in what he's doing. Joe "made it" because he worked hard to develop his interests and because he had the ambition to learn his trade. It *never* just comes naturally. Prior experience? He had none. A business background? None. Money? He saved a few hundred dollars to spend on test gear and parts, not much more.

The most important lesson to learn from Joe, I feel, is that you can start out easily and simply. You don't have to make the Big Plunge, selling everything you own and going into debt. More than two-thirds of all new businesses are started as part-time or weekend ventures, started by people still holding onto a job while they experiment with their new business. So, start slowly, try it out and learn as you go. You'll get there.

Things worked well for Joe. But if they had not—if he really did not have it in him to be in business for himself, or if he just picked the wrong thing at the wrong time—he could easily have stopped anywhere along the way with little or no loss. And maybe try it again sometime.

What Kind of Business?

Joe's repair shop is an example of what is commonly called a "service" business. He *does* something for his customers and they pay him for his services. You can also support yourself by selling something (sales) or by making something (manufacturing). Many businesses combine several of these aspects, such as sales and service.

A service business is the easiest to set up. It requires the smallest initial investment and the simplest bookkeeping. It is also the easiest kind of business to operate out of your home. On the other hand, you will have to be competent at the service you offer. More than any other business, service will require some experience. The owner of a service business is also more likely to be subject to state licenses and regulations.

If you do something well—fixing things, painting or decorating, writing or editing, cutting hair, operating a computer—these are but a few possibilities for your own service business. And if you are good at something, you might consider teaching those skills to others. Be imaginative. Don't ignore your own resources.

Find a need and fill it.
*   —Lettered on a cement truck, Oakland, Ca.*

A sales business can take many different forms: retail, wholesale, storefront, mail order, direct sales, network marketing, on-line sales, or some other approach. Your own sales business allows you to select and handle merchandise that reflects your own interests and tastes, and the interests and needs of your community. Most sales businesses will require inventory (stock on hand) which means a bigger investment than a service business. You are more likely to need a storefront to display your goods and attract customers. You will have to keep inventory records. Bookkeeping is a little more complex. Sales businesses, however, offer more flexibility than service. Service people are often limited by their training and experience. With sales, as your interests change and as the fashions change, it is easy for your sales business to change with them.

Manufacturing, for many small businesses, means crafts: leather, clothing, pottery, jewelry and furniture to name a very few. Crafts offer, probably more than any other business, an opportunity for the craftsperson to do what he or she enjoys for its own pleasure, and get paid for it, too. But again, you have to be good at what you're doing. Nobody wants an ugly necklace or a chair that falls apart. And more than with a sales or service business, you may have a harder time finding a steady and reliable market for your product. But if you have imagination and talent, you might discover that what you think of as your hobby can become your source of income.

Conventional manufacturing often requires a large investment in machinery. But you would be surprised how many successful manufacturing businesses started out in some inventor's garage with homemade, experimental equipment, on a surplus-store budget.

Mike Madsen owns Mike Madsen Leather, manufacturer and seller of hand-made leather goods: "Look around, figure out what you want to do, and then try to sum up your business in one sentence or a paragraph at the most. No more than that or you haven't done it. And then concentrate on doing just that. Realize that business is just like life in a lot of ways, and you take things step by step. You don't become a big business overnight. You build it little by little every day you walk into the building. You get started through your own will and determination and have a little fun at it.

"You can learn an awful lot by observation. Anyone in a small business should try to visit other people who are in similar businesses. When I was in Argentina I went to seven leather factories. They're very willing to show you something when you're not in direct competition, and they're kind of pleased to show off their business. But if you and I lived in the same city, you might be less willing to show your manufacturing process to a future competitor.

"Small business is the backbone of this country. Big businesses provide main-line products, but it's small business that provides all the little things that make your life interesting. I think it's also the kind of people who are in small business, those of a pioneering spirit. We built a country on pioneering spirit. That's just what being in a small business is, being a pioneer."

Can You Do It?

You don't have to be an expert in the line of business that you're thinking of going into, but you do have to be willing to learn. There are people who actually try to start a certain business because it's a "sure thing," a "guaranteed" big seller, and they know absolutely nothing about the field. Some of these people are, of course, real hustlers, but there are also a lot of honest dopes in this group. They think that a little money and some good intentions are all they need to get started. And most of them soon wind up with neither their money nor any intention of ever being in business again.

I've known a lot of people in business, some who made it, some who didn't. And while nobody has a guaranteed secret for success, I believe that there are a few basic characteristics that you've got to have or be willing to develop if you're going to start a business, *any* business.

The first and most important characteristic, I feel, is a clear head and the ability to organize your mind and your life. The "absent-minded professor" may be a genius, but he will never keep a business together. In running a small business, you are going to have to deal with many different people, keep schedules, meet deadlines, organize paperwork, pay bills, and the list goes on. It's all part of every business. So if balancing your checkbook is too much for you, or you just burned up your car engine because you forgot to check the oil, maybe you're not cut out for business. The work in a small business is rarely complicated, but it has to be done and done on time. Remember, this is going to be *your* business. It's all up to you.

A second important characteristic is the ability to read carefully. Most of your business transactions will be handled on paper, and if you don't pay attention to what you're doing, you could miss out. You may receive special orders for your product. You will be billed by your suppliers in all kinds of ways, sometimes offering discounts if you are prompt in paying. You will have to fill out a lot of government forms. Government agencies cannot exist without forms, and the instructions for these forms are sometimes tricky. If you mess up, these agencies have the most aggravating way of casually telling you that you have to do it all over again.

A third important trait is, if not a "head for numbers," at least a lack of fear of numbers. Tax accountants get rich off of people who look at a column of six numbers and panic. It doesn't have to be that way. The math involved in running a small business is mostly simple arithmetic, addition, subtraction, some multiplication.

Is all of this too much for you? Still feel you have a good product or a good service to sell but, Oh! all this paperwork… If you are alone in your venture, short of hiring a bookkeeper or finding a partner, there is no alternative. You're gonna have to learn to do it. Very often, however, the future business owner with no business moxie is blessed with a wife or husband who has all those fine traits and is just itchin' to be part of it all.

Beyond the numbers, if you plan to operate a retail store, a service business, or any other business where you will be in regular contact with the public, you should be a person who likes to deal with people. Are you friendly and outgoing, pleased to talk about your products—and the weather, the ball scores, and the latest neighborhood gossip? Do you like selling, solving people's problems, listening to complaints, answering the same questions over and over again? Do you look forward to running a store five, six or even seven days a week, keeping regular hours, stocking shelves, doing repetitive tasks every day?

There are many fine people, potentially excellent business people, who are not the outgoing type, who would never survive behind the counter, and who certainly shouldn't be running a retail operation. And fortunately, there are many businesses that don't require these personality traits. Mail-order, manufacturing, some service businesses, businesses where you don't face the public every day, businesses where you know all your customers, businesses where you do custom work for only a few people: these businesses do not rely so much on your personality, and they won't require that you constantly act and dress a certain way.

Mike Madsen, Mike Madsen Leather: "You talk to people who are outside of business, they don't understand it. You talk to somebody who's on a fixed income or working on a salary or an educator or a student, they don't understand what being in business is all about. They're not risk takers. They're not striving to make a whole number of things work simultaneously. They go to work in the morning or go to school and have a prescribed routine and they get off at five o'clock, and they go home and their business is done. But if you're in business for yourself, you don't turn off the switch when you go home. You're constantly thinking about it."

Your Idea—and the Market

Every person who has ever started a business, I imagine, thought he or she had a good idea. It's the smart person, and the rare person, who tries to find out the most important thing: do other people think it's a good idea? The majority of new businesses fail because the majority of new business owners never looked past their own desires and dreams, gave no real forethought to their ventures—no "market research," which is just a fancy term for "look before you leap."

Do people really want what you have to sell? Can you find these people and convince them that they should buy from you instead of from someone else—someone else who may have a better product, a better price, a better location, a good reputation?

Research is everything. You've got to find where you fit into the puzzle.
—Mikal Ali, Sidestreet Inc.,
greeting card manufacturer.

No matter how good your business idea is, you still must have a market—someone who is willing to buy your product or pay for your services. Talk to your friends; they're consumers. How many of them would buy what you have to sell? Then look around your community. Does your product or service fit the social, economic and ethnic make-up of the area? Will your product appeal to these people? Can they afford it?

How many other businesses in the area are doing the same thing? How well are they doing? What would it be like to compete with them? A new business always starts at a disadvantage. Try not to duplicate services already available, unless you have good reason to believe you can attract customers away from existing businesses.

Mike Simon, Metric Motors Auto Repair: "There are some people who want to work for themselves, and they're not going to be happy working for anybody else. And then other people don't like the responsibility. They want to go in and work their 9 to 5 and not have to worry about it when they go home. It takes a certain kind of person to run your own business, to accept the responsibilities and be thinking abut it all the time. The first two years I worked, I worked seven days a week from 7 in the morning until 7 at night. And now I take Sundays off. But I wouldn't have it any other way. I could have made more money working for somebody else, but I'm happy with the way it is. And I think in the future it will be to my advantage. As for the guy who's working 9 to 5, I'll be better off than he is. Of course, he thinks he's better off than I am."

DESIGNER
PRETZELS
THEY COST MORE BUT
AREN'T YOU WORTH IT?

P. Steiner

BEFORE YOU ACT

Let's say you've decided on an idea for a new business. Now comes the most important step:

Ponder. Think. Relax.

Let the idea simmer for a week or two and see how it feels then. Picture yourself as the owner-operator of the business you have in mind. Does it still sound like a good idea? Can you make it on an unpredictable income? Is it time to take control of your career, and your life?

BUSINESS LOCATION

For retail stores, retail service businesses, restaurants, and other businesses where customers come to you, location is critical. A bad neighborhood, a street that's hard to find, a location away from other shops, a location where it's difficult to park, a store too far away from the kind of customer you seek—any of these factors can easily lead to business failure, quickly. Do not underestimate the importance of the business location. Do not settle for a poor location. Do not compromise.

Many people want to locate in their own neighborhood, but is it a good business area? How many people shop in your neighborhood? Is there adequate parking? Is there already a similar business in the area? It's smart to locate near complimentary, not competing businesses.

Before you rent a storefront, find out why it's vacant in the first place. Try to locate the former tenant and ask him why he moved. Talk to other shopkeepers in the area and learn as much as you can about the area and its shoppers. A nearby supermarket or discount store, particularly a store people shop at once or twice a week, is usually a plus because it will draw a lot of people to your area. Be wary if there are several unoccupied buildings for rent. Besides being a general sign of a poor business area, vacant buildings make poor neighbors. Shoppers tend to stay away from them, and from you.

Spend a full day or two observing the area. A steady stream of pedestrians passing your door is the biggest single help a store can get. Avoid side streets, even if they are right around the corner from a main shopping street. Most shoppers will not go out of their way, even a few feet, to check you out. And get a first floor location. Second floor shops are less accessible, less visible, and less inviting. Customers who don't know you will not make that commitment, will not walk up a flight of stairs.

A location on a street that many people use going to and from work will make you even more visible, especially a street with no more than a 30-35 mph speed limit. If people are whizzing by at 45 mph, you're just a blur in the rear view mirror. Being close to a well known landmark will also help because it is a point of reference people can easily remember.

For businesses that don't rely on customers coming to the door—manufacturers, wholesalers, workshops, mail-order operators, many service businesses—the location is no longer of critical concern. You can find a place suitable to your own needs: close to home, inexpensive, close proximity to your suppliers and the services you require, easy access for deliveries and pick-ups.

In many cities, small businesses are finding excellent facilities in old and formerly run-down industrial areas of town. Real estate developers are buying abandoned commercial buildings, fixing them up, dividing them into smaller offices, shops, and warehouse spaces; and renting at prices much lower than the busy shopping areas.

Incubators

Some developers are creating what they call "executive suites" and "business incubators". These facilities provide, in addition to a location, shared support services such as secretaries, management counselors, conference rooms, office equipment, truck docks, and other amenities. As the term implies, incubators are often first-step locations for new businesses. After a few years, you no longer need nor care to pay for many of the support services. You are ready to be on your own. You've been hatched, so to speak.

Most incubators are privately owned, profit-making ventures; but some are publicly funded and supported. The U.S. Small Business Administration (the SBA) works with a lot of public and private business incubators across the country. Contact a local SBA office for more information.

The Building

Before you sign a rental agreement, be sure the building is right for you. Is it large enough,

or is it perhaps too large? Will it require extensive remodeling? Can you afford it? Make sure the roof doesn't leak. Test the heating and air conditioning. How expensive will it be to heat and cool the building? Check out exterior lighting around sidewalks and parking areas. How good is the building security?

Learn all you can about the other tenants. If their behavior and activities annoy your customers, you may lose business. Ask neighbors how they feel about the location. Are people hanging out on the corner? Will that affect your business?

Have the store examined by the local building inspector and, if you plan to serve food, by the health inspector. You don't want to learn after you've moved in that you must spend a thousand bucks to bring the premises up to code. Don't rely on the previous tenant or the landlord for this information. Building violations are often ignored or just not noticed by the inspectors, until a new business moves in.

Is the building wheelchair accessible? Many businesses must comply with the Americans with Disabilities Act (ADA). Find out before you move in if someone is going to require you to redesign the entrance.

Zoning

Before you sign a lease, check with the local zoning department to make sure the building is zoned for your use. Find out about any special requirements, such as off-street parking or sign limitations. Don't rely on the landlord for this information. Just because a similar business previously occupied the same building without zoning problems, it is no guarantee you'll have no problems. The old business may have been there before current zoning laws were in effect (called "grandfathering") or maybe they had a special arrangement or variance that may or may not be transferred to you.

If there are zoning problems, don't give up right away. Zoning officials often have authority to negotiate variances, to make exceptions to the rules. Be sure to get any variance in writing.

The Lease

Can you get a suitable lease? Without a lease, the landlord can, with little or no notice, evict you or arbitrarily raise the rent to any amount he pleases. Don't count on oral agreements with a landlord. Get a written lease that covers all the details, options, and who's responsible for what. Never assume *anything*.

There is no such thing as a "standard lease". Every provision in a lease is negotiable, and you should read and understand every word. You may have to live with it for years.

How many years will the lease run? Is it renewable, will the rent increase, and by how much? Can you get out of the lease if your business fails or if you want or need to move? Can you sublet? If you sell the business, can you transfer the lease to the new owner? If the landlord sells the building, will you be at the mercy of the new owner, or will the old lease legally be binding on the new owner? Can you get a protection clause in which the landlord agrees not to rent adjacent space to a competitor? Can you get first refusal if adjacent space becomes available?

Who is responsible for repairs, maintenance, janitorial and garbage? How quickly will a problem be fixed? Who is responsible for damage due to fire, or a broken water pipe or any other calamity? Are there restrictions on parking, or signs, or hours of use?

"As far as I'm concerned, location is everything." Lara Stonebraker owns Cunningham's Coffee, a retail store: "That can make or break a business. If you don't already have an established reputation, nobody will go looking for you in some obscure place. You have to be where there is a lot of foot traffic, and you have to be located next to some other established business that already has a clientele you can draw on.

"The corner is obviously the best choice, and you usually have to pay more rent for it. The middle of the block is less desirable because there isn't as much visibility or parking. Parking can be a great problem. I've known a lot of very fine businesses to fail because people would just get exasperated not being able to find a parking space and never go in them.

"One of the things we did at every location we looked at was spend a day just sitting around, hanging around, and watching the traffic flow, the patterns of the way people walk, where they stopped, and how many people came in and out of different stores in order to assess the desirability of that location.

"Talk to the building inspector and the health inspector and find out what the building and health codes are for your particular business. We made the mistake of seeing them after we signed the lease and then discovered that we had to put in just a load of improvements that rightfully should not have been our responsibility. That was a tremendous amount of money which will just be lost. They don't check old businesses, but they check every new one. You apply for a permit, you have to get a business license, then they know what kind of business it is and they send out their people. If you're doing any kind of reconstruction inside and any electrical work, the plumber has to get a permit, the electrician has to get a permit—you can't get away from it."

Joe Campbell owns Resistance Repair, a stereo repair shop. He recently moved his shop away from a high foot traffic area to a more remote part of town:

"In a service business, especially a technical service business, customers don't have the slightest idea how to determine even the most rudimentary things about their equipment. If it doesn't work, they don't have the means of determining what is wrong. So you get an incredible amount of people who come in and just go on and on, like an old Kenmore on the spin cycle, about some problem which is extremely minor and usually is a hookup problem. They've just got it hooked up wrong, which means they didn't read their instruction book. But it's very hard to convince them of that, and they all want detailed explanations.

"If you're in a high foot traffic area, you get the guy who's going to the restaurant next door for lunch, and as he walks out he thinks, `Ah, there's a stereo repair shop. I'll stop in here and ask this guy about my problem...' and he comes in and there's 20 minutes gone. You get people who come in and say, `I need your recommendation of the 15 best stereos you can buy, and why.' Just enormous time and energy sinks. Those people don't spend money. The kind of people who spend money are the people who walk in the door with stereos under their arms, and say, `Fix this mother, it doesn't work, and call me when it's ready.'

"My traffic was never off the street. It was from referrals from other stereo shops. I took around cards and there was such a big demand for a reasonable, good repair shop that they'd send people by. You don't need those twerks who walk in off the street. You need the people who have the confidence in you and, by reputation, know that they can dump it in your hands. Now, when somebody walks through that door they've either got a stereo under their arm or they're picking one up. If they're there to pick it up, that means when they leave you're going to have money in the cash register. If they're coming in the door with one, that means two weeks later you're going to have money in the cash register. Those are the only two reasons you want that front door to open."

Rural Businesses

It's a dream many people have, to move to the peace and quiet of the countryside and start a relaxed, prosperous little business. Unfortunately, a large percentage of these rural shops fail. The main reason? There are not enough people and there is not enough money in rural communities to support anything but the most basic businesses.

A tropical fish store is not going to survive in West Pork Chop, Oklahoma. Nor will a gourmet coffee shop, an art gallery or a leather crafts workshop. The business just isn't there. Service businesses, repair shops, trades, have the best chance of survival in a rural area. But even these will have to compete with established locals who know everyone in town and have all the business.

When you have a particular area in mind, get to know the area and its residents first before you try to set up a business. Ideally, you should live there a while, and then try to judge what product or service the people need. Most country people are not wealthy; they don't spend money on things they have no use for.

Many successful rural businesses simply do not depend on local customers. They "export" their products and services out of the area. Manufacturing and crafts businesses have retail accounts in nearby metropolitan areas. Mail order businesses, publishers, designers, and some professionals and consultants can do all their business via the mail, phone, fax and computer.

Lara Stonebraker, Cunningham's Coffee: "If you don't enjoy what you're doing, it's going to be very obvious to the customers. It will be obvious in your attitude. I find it very exciting, and I also find it a great challenge to try to make the business profitable. That's why I look at all the angles to decrease expenses and bring in more income. I want to prove can do it. I don't just want a business, I want a booming business."

FINANCING: How Much Do You Need?

How much money you need depends a lot on the type of business you are starting and the type of person you are. If you are willing to work hard, to make a few sacrifices, to live on canned beans for a while, you can start a successful business for little or no investment.

Every service business I know started with almost no money. I started my accounting practice with a $30 adding machine and 500 business cards. My friend Joe Campbell started Resistance Repair with $500 worth of test equipment. Another friend's computer programming service was started with $50 in supplies. Self-employed carpenters, mechanics and repair people often start with their box of tools, period.

If you start a crafts business, you will need, besides your tools, materials to make your product. But you do not have to stock a large supply of inventory, and if you hunt around you can always find good deals on remnants and close-out materials. All of the craft business owners interviewed for this book started their businesses with less than $1,000 initial investment.

A retail store requires a good stock of inventory, which will cost at least a few thousand dollars, often a good deal more. A retail business can sometimes save on initial inventory costs by taking goods on consignment, as in a custom dress shop, or by having only samples on hand and taking orders for the goods.

In addition to the money you need to get started, you will probably need "working capital" to operate the business until it becomes profitable. The money *always* seems to keep going out long before it starts coming in.

Mike Simon owns Metric Motors, a repair shop: "I started with basically nothing and built from that. I had a box of hand tools and some heavy equipment, jacks and things like that, nothing very impressive. If I had to have a tool, I'd buy it and then I'd have it. I guess I have about $3,000 worth of equipment now. A lot of garage owners buy $20,000 worth of equipment right at the start and don't have the clientele to pay it off. I'd say starting out small would be a very smart thing to do. Find some place that's not expensive to rent, like this place. Don't put a lot of money into tools or inventory and try to keep your costs down to a minimum until you can build your business up."

Lara Stonebraker's coffee store: "The worst thing you can do is start a retail business on a shoestring. If you're undercapitalized, your store will not be impressive when you open because it will be empty. There's nothing worse than walking into an empty store. It's bound to fail because it embarrasses people. If you don't have your shelves just crammed with stuff, and if you don't have an attractive, prosperous looking store, you might as well forget it. And you really ought to have not only enough money to open the doors, but enough to run the business for the first six months, because you'll be running it at a loss for sure."

START-UP CAPITAL:
Financing A New Business

There are three typical financing arrangements for new businesses: (1) Self-financing: you put up your own money. (2) Debt financing: you borrow money. (3) Equity financing: you take on a partner or a stockholder, an individual who acquires an ownership interest in your business in exchange for start-up money.

Self-Financing

Just about every new business is at least partly self-financed, and many are 100% self-financed. A lot of new business owners simply cannot find anyone to loan them money or to invest in their untested and obviously risky ventures. Many new business owners simply do not *want* outside financing and the risk and pressure of having to pay off a loan, and do not want to worry about, or share the profits with, a partner or co-owner.

Debt Financing (Loans)

When someone lends you money, you promise to pay it back, usually with interest. Most business loans are also personal loans; you, the owner of the business, personally guarantee the loan, and you must repay the loan whether your business succeeds or not, out of your personal non-business assets if necessary. This is quite different from "equity financing" where you acquire a partner or an investor who only gets paid back if the business succeeds.

Most loans to new businesses come from relatives, friends, and acquaintances. Conven-tional bank loans are very difficult to get for first-time business people. People who know you, and possibly people they know, are much more likely to help finance your venture than an extra-cautious, policy-laden bank. You just have to ask around. Quite often, someone you know or someone you can be introduced to has some extra money, and might be willing to take a chance on your business if they like you and your idea and the terms of the financing.

There are no real standards when it comes to this kind of informal financing. People lending you money will most likely want a better interest rate than they would get at a bank. Often they already have a good idea of the rate they would like to get. The repayment terms are entirely between you and the lender.

Private loans should be in writing and should include the names and addresses of the lender and borrower, the amount, the date the loan was given, the interest rate, and the pay-back terms. This is especially important for loans from relatives, so it is very clear that this is a loan and not a gift. If you are unable to repay the loan, the lenders can take a bad-debt tax write-off without risk that the IRS will try to say the loan wasn't really a loan, but a non-deductible family gift.

Most loans are paid back over a period of months or years, with equal periodic payments. Some loans are repaid all at once at the end of the loan period. Again, the terms are entirely up to the lender and borrower. You may want a clause allowing you to pay off the loan early without penalty if you, the borrower, so desire.

The loan agreement should be prepared in duplicate, a copy for the lender and a copy for the borrower. Both parties should sign and date both copies. If the agreement is kept simple, you can write it up yourself. If the agreement gets complicated, with late-payment penalties, collateral, provisions for death of one of the parties, etc., you will probably want professional help drafting the agreement. Find out if your state requires a notary's endorsement, filing or registering the loan papers, or other requirements. Your state's Secretary of State office, the county clerk or the city hall clerk can probably give you information.

When the loan is paid off, have the lender write "Paid in full" on all copies, sign and date them, and return them to you. If the loan is filed with the state or county, the final pay-off (or "reconveyance") should also be recorded.

Bank Loans

Bank loans are hard to get. The banks are less willing than ever to take chances on new and untested businesses and new and untested entrepreneurs. Many new businesses are looking for very small loans (small, that is, by bank standards), and banks don't make any money on those. It's a lot of time and paperwork, not to mention the risk, for very little return.

Banks, however, do sometimes make small business loans, and a bank just may make one to you—if you can convince the bank that your business has a good potential for success, that you are competent and reliable, and that you have a good plan to repay the loan.

Not all banks are alike, so try several. A young progressive bank is more likely to be interested in you and your needs than staid old First Conservative, Est. 1833. The bank's advertising may indicate its willingness to do business with you.

When you meet a banker, come well prepared. Bring a resume that includes your general and educational background and your prior experience. Read the chapter on business plans at the end of this section, and create one. Bring a personal financial statement and a statement projecting income and expenses of your business for the first six months or year. The chapter "Profit And Loss Analysis" in the Bookkeeping section will help you prepare the projections.

If you have done business with or obtained a loan from a particular bank, that bank is a good place to start. When a bank knows you, knows something of your willingness and capability to repay a loan, it will be more willing to give serious consideration to your ideas. If you know influential people in the community, have them put in a word for you. The old saw, "It's who you know" goes a long way in *all* business dealings.

The bank will expect you to have some of your own money invested in your business, typically a third to half of the starting capital.

You will most likely need collateral, security to give the bank in exchange for a loan. The bank may want a mortgage on equipment or even a second mortgage on your home. This is called a "secured" loan, the only kind usually available to new businesses. "Unsecured" loans, ones that don't require collateral, are usually available only to successful, proven businesses who are long time bank customers.

But, stop! Are you ready to risk your home or other valuables on your new business? When you borrow money for your business, you are *personally* liable to pay it back. If the business fails, you will be required to repay the loan from your personal funds. In taking out a loan, you are making a big personal commitment. Be sure you are not getting yourself in over your head.

Other Possible Loan Sources

A surprising number of people finance their new businesses with their personal credit cards. This of course is an expensive method, given the high interest rates most cards charge.

If there is a credit union where you work, they may be more receptive than a bank. If you own stocks and bonds, ask your broker about borrowing against the securities. If you have a retirement plan from a job or another business, you may be able to borrow from the plan or get the funds out of the plan. If you own a life insurance policy and have been making payments for at least a few years, you can probably borrow on the "cash value" of your policy.

The company that sells you your equipment may also "loan" you money in the form of credit. Most manufacturers have financing plans allowing you to buy your equipment on the installment basis. Commercial finance companies also offer short-term loans for purchase of equipment.

Your wholesalers or suppliers may also extend short-term credit. But if you are new to the world of business, you may have to operate C.O.D. (cash on delivery) with your suppliers until you are a little better established.

Some communities have "revolving loan" or "seed loan" funds for local businesses. Check with the Chamber of Commerce or City Hall.

Small Business Administration (SBA) Loans

The U.S. Small Business Administration has several loan programs for new and expanding "small" businesses. But by government definition, a "small" business is one with as much as

---

If you open them all the same day, they'll all be approved.
—Karen Behnke, Pacific Wellness Co, on using 17 credit cards to finance her new business.

$18 million in yearly sales and as many as 1,500 employees! There are a lot of big businesses in these small business programs.

SBA loans are not obtained directly from the SBA, although the SBA will assist you with questions and paperwork. You apply to a bank or some other agency that handles SBA loans. The lender then decides if it wants to approach the SBA. You may need to talk to more than lender before you find one interested in helping you.

To get an SBA loan, you will have to convince the SBA and the bank that you have the ability to operate a business successfully and that the loan can be repaid from the business earnings. SBA loans will require you to put up collateral, usually equipment or real estate.

SBA loans come with strings attached. The agency has a set of operating guidelines you must follow, which limits your freedom and flexibility somewhat. The SBA will periodically audit your books, which can be both a help and a nuisance.

The SBA is in a constant state of flux, with new loan programs being created, and others eliminated, almost every year. You may show up just as they create the perfect loan for you. The SBA does not give any grants: no free money.

An excellent source of help in applying for SBA loans are Small Business Development Centers. SBDCs work closely with the SBA and are usually affiliated with colleges and universities.

SBA's current loan programs include:

7(a) Program. The SBA's largest and best known loan program is called the 7(a) Program, the Loan Guarantee Plan. Under this program, a regular bank loans you money and the SBA guarantees up to 80% of the loan (75% if over $100,000). Only about 30% of these available loan funds go to new businesses. The bulk of the 7(a) money is lent to existing and expanding small businesses.

The maximum 7(a) loan guarantee is $750,000 with a 15-year (25 years for real estate) payback period. Maximum interest is 2¾% above prime. The banks set the actual terms and interest rates. You also pay a loan fee, 2% for loans of $100,00 or less, 3% to 4% for larger loans.

LowDoc. A loan guarantee program aimed primarily at new businesses, LowDoc (for "low documentation") loans go up to $100,000, with the SBA guaranteeing 80% of the loan. Fees are lower and paperwork is less than for 7(a) loans.

502, 503, 504 Programs. The 502, 503 and 504 Local Development Company Programs make loans to businesses in economically depressed areas, to purchase land, buildings or equipment, but only if the loans are used primarily to create jobs. Requirements and limits vary.

Export Working Capital Program. Export businesses can get loans, lines of credit, letters of credit and other financial assistance.

Micro-Loan Program. For new and very small businesses, the Micro-Loan Program is administered by SBA-approved non-profit organizations. This program provides loans from a few hundred dollars up to $25,000. Micro-loan interest rates tend to be much higher than other loans. Collateral is usually required.

Other Programs. SBA-backed loans are also available from Community Development Corporations (CDCs), which are usually non-profit, community-based organizations; and from Small Business Investment Companies (SBICs), which are licensed by the SBA. These organizations, in addition to giving loans, sometimes actually invest in small businesses (acquire an ownership interest) See the Venture Capital chapter.

There are 68 SBA offices in the country. Contact the one closest to you or write Small Business Administration, Washington, DC 20416.

Pat Ellington, Kipple Antiques: "There's no point in even going to a bank unless you can say, 'Well, we've been operating now for two years, and we've established a track record, and we want to expand. We've got our books, our balance sheets, we've got good references, some people do extend us credit.' I know that from my own experience. If you go there armed with a certain amount of paperwork, a certain kind of history, you'll have fewer problems dealing with them.

"I have mixed feelings about SBA loans. Sometimes they can be gotten easily, but it's sort of like by magic. And other times, no matter what you give them, no matter what sound business approach you give them, they're deaf to you. That's discouraging. It's like grantsmanship. There's a whole lot to applying, and if you don't have the art, you don't get the loan."

Loans To Yourself

For tax and bookkeeping purposes, there is no such thing as a loan to yourself (except for corporations). Any of your own money that you put into your business is considered personal funds. It is not taxable income, the repayment is not a tax deduction, you cannot pay yourself interest on the funds. As far as the IRS is concerned, loaning money to your own business is the same as taking money out of your right pocket and putting it in your left pocket. The reasoning behind this law will make more sense after you read the chapter, "Sole Proprietorship". Partners in partnerships come under the same law.

Corporations: If you incorporate your business, you can loan your business money and treat it as a regular loan. But you must be careful. Most states require corporations to have some amount of equity capital, called "minimum capitalization", money that you the owner invest in the corporation. Before you loan money to your corporation, make sure you aren't going to run afoul of your state's capitalization requirements. Talk to a good accountant.

Equity Financing

"Equity" means ownership. "Equity financing" is money put up by the owner or owners of the business. Self-financing is, in fact, equity financing, even though I gave it a separate category in this chapter.

Equity financing usually involves an investor who buys into your business, as a general or limited partner in a partnership with you, as a shareholder who owns part of the stock in your corporation, or as an investor-member in a Limited Liability Company. The investor is taking a risk on your business, just as you are. Like the typical lender, the typical investor is usually a friend, acquaintance or relative. Unlike a lender, however, the investor gets his or her money back only if the business succeeds. The owner of the business is usually not obligated to repay the investor out of personal non-business funds.

If you're determined to succeed, you can find a way around any obstacle, even money.
—Nancy Ridge, Ridge Tech Co.

How the investor and the business owner share in the profits is negotiable. A 50-50 split is common. I've known investors to accept as little as 30-35% of the profits; some may want a much bigger cut. Investments can be for a specified, limited time or for the life of the business.

Investments can be set up in a variety of ways, depending on how much the investor will or will not participate in the actual running of the business, how much liability exposure the investor wants, and how the business and the investment are legally structured. The investor might become a full partner in a regular partnership, a limited partner in a limited partnership, a stockholder in a corporation, a member of a Limited Liability Company (LLC), or perhaps some other arrangement. Most states have laws regulating investments and how to set them up legally. You will most likely need some professional help.

Limited Partnerships

Limited partners are not partners in the usual sense of the word. They are investors only. Their liability is limited to the amount of their investment. They are legally prohibited from participating in the management and operation of the business.

Don't confuse a limited partner with a regular business partner who invests money in the business. Limited partnerships are very different from regular (general) partnerships and are subject to much greater government scrutiny. Limited partnerships usually must be registered with the county or the state. A limited partnership must have at least one general partner (you, the owner) with full personal liability just like a sole proprietorship or general partnership.

Limited Liability Company (LLC)

Due to the many state restrictions on limited partnerships, some businesses wanting the kind of financing limited partnerships offer, are instead setting up Limited Liability Companies. LLCs are not as tightly regulated as limited partnerships, and they offer limited liability protection to the owner as well as the limited partners. Limited Liability Companies are covered in the Growing Up section.

Venture Capital

Venture capitalists are a different breed of investor than limited partners. Limited partners are usually friends and relatives. Venture capitalists are usually wealthy individuals who make their living as investors. Venture capitalists are usually only interested in businesses that have potential for huge growth and big profits within a few years, especially businesses on the cutting-edge of new technology. The typical small local business—sales, service, repair, crafts—will not be of interest to most venture capitalists.

When you get financing from a venture capitalist you will be taking on a partner who not only wants a percent of the profits but may even want ownership control (51% interest) of your business. You may be able to locate a venture capitalist through referral. Talk to other business people, your banker or an accountant.

A new breed of venture capitalist is the Community Development Corporation (CDC), which combines public interest with private business investment. Many CDCs are non-profit, community sponsored and operated organizations, and many receive government grants. Their goal, in addition to making money on their investments, is to encourage small-scale local enterprises and to expand local job markets. To locate a CDC, contact a regional Community Action Agency, SBA office, or state office of community affairs.

Venture capital is also available from Small Business Investment Companies (SBICs). SBICs are licensed by the Small Business Administration but they are privately organized and privately managed firms; they set their own policies and make their own investment decisions. The Small Business Administration often makes loans to SBICs so they can turn around and invest the money in your business. The SBA publishes a National Directory of SBICs. Write the SBA, Washington, D.C., 20416.

Herbert Heaton, a well known business counselor, once described venture capital financing as "selling out before starting." Author Bill Friday put it this way: "At best you will be taking on back seat drivers, and at worst you will get pushed to the back seat with an investor doing the driving." *Caveat emptor:* Buyer Beware.

A fool and his money are soon parted.
—*Anon., 16th Century*

I think what has made us successful is my fiscal caution. We have no debt. We borrowed no money. Everything is owned by the company. We buy equipment only if the cash is available.
—*Howard Moskowitz, HJM Computers*

LEGAL STRUCTURE

Every new business must decide if it will start as a sole proprietorship, partnership, corporation or Limited Liability Company (LLC). Most new one-person and husband-and-wife businesses start as sole proprietors, simply because sole proprietorships are the quickest, easiest and least expensive form of business to start.

If you don't incorporate and if you don't have a partner (other than your spouse), you are *automatically* a sole proprietor. The simple act of starting a business legally makes you a sole proprietor. The fact that you have or have not filed any forms, gotten any permits or licenses, notified any government agency or filed a tax return is not material.

If you have one or more partners (other than your spouse) and if you don't incorporate, you have legally started a partnership. It's automatic, just like the sole proprietorship. Partnerships are covered in the Growing Up section.

A husband and wife who start an unincorporated business together can be either a sole proprietorship or a partnership. It's their choice. Generally, unless a husband and wife prepare a partnership agreement and file a partnership tax return, the business is considered to be a sole proprietorship owned by one spouse. Even though both spouses are working in the business, even though both spouses may actually own the business, if they set up a sole proprietorship, they must pick one spouse to be the "official" owner of the business. The Husband and Wife chapter in the Appendix explains these options.

To become a corporation, nothing is automatic. You must file incorporation papers with your state department of corporations, prepare articles of incorporation and bylaws, issue state-approved stock certificates, and pay filing and registration fees and corporate franchise taxes. Corporations are covered in detail in the Growing Up section.

A Limited Liability Company (LLC) is similar to a partnership but with limited liability like a corporation. See the Growing Up section.

A business can start as a sole proprietorship or a partnership and incorporate (or become an LLC) at any later date. In fact, most small corporations started as unincorporated businesses and incorporated after they were successful and found a real need to incorporate.

SOLE PROPRIETORSHIP:
The Traditional One-Person Business

A one-person business that has not incorporated is known as a sole proprietorship. There are over 20 million small businesses in this country, and most of them are sole proprietorships. This form of business has flourished because of the opportunities it offers to be boss, run the business, make the decisions and keep the profits. A sole proprietorship is the easiest form of business to start up. Despite all the regulations, it is the least regulated of all businesses.

Sole proprietors may call themselves business men, business women, shop keepers, entrepreneurs, self employed, artists, craftspeople, artisans, trades people, direct, network or multi-level marketers, drop shippers, free agents, sales reps, manufacturers, inventors, employers, moonlighters, professionals, full-time, part-time, sideline, you name it. Legally, if you don't incorporate or form a partnership or an LLC, you are a sole proprietor; your business is a sole proprietorship.

Consultants, outside and independent contractors, professionals and freelancers should understand that they are also sole proprietors. I can't tell you how many times someone has come up to me and said, "I don't have a business, but I'm an independent consultant". Unless you are on someone else's payroll as an employee, you *do* have a business, you are a sole proprietor.

You, the owner of the business, the sole proprietor, are your own boss. You make or break your business, which may sound singularly appealing to those of you instilled with the entrepreneurial, pioneering spirit. But you also have sole responsibility as well as sole control. **You and your sole proprietorship are one and the same in the eyes of the law.** All business debts and obligations are the personal responsibility of the owner. Damages from any lawsuits brought

against the business can be taken from the personal assets of the owner. You should be fully aware of these legal aspects of the sole proprietorship. If you get your business into legal trouble or too far into debt, not only could you lose your business, you could lose your shirt.

The only way to avoid the unlimited personal liability of the sole proprietor is to incorporate or set up an LLC. Generally speaking, the debts, obligations, and legal liability of corporations and LLCs are limited to the assets of the business and are not the personal responsibility of the owner or owners (see the Growing Up section).

Paying Yourself a Wage

You, as the owner of a sole proprietorship, cannot hire yourself as an employee. This is a point of law often misunderstood by new business people. You cannot pay yourself a wage and deduct it as a business expense. You may withdraw (that is, pay yourself) as much or as little money as you want, but this "draw" is not a wage, you do not pay payroll taxes on it, and you cannot claim a business deduction for it. The profit of your business, which is computed without regard to your draws, is your "wage" and is included on your personal income tax return.

For example, if your business made a $30,000 profit last year, you personally owe taxes on $30,000. If you withdrew (paid yourself) less than $30,000—or, for that matter, if you didn't even take a penny out of the business—you still pay taxes on $30,000. If you withdrew more than $30,000, you still pay taxes only on $30,000. Owner's draw is covered in more detail in the Bookkeeping and Tax sections of the book.

The sole proprietorship itself does not file income tax returns or pay income taxes. You file a Schedule C, "Profit or Loss From Business," (or for some small businesses, a Schedule C-EZ) with your 1040 return, and pay personal income taxes on the profit. You also pay self-employment tax, which is Social Security/Medicare tax, in addition to income taxes. These taxes are covered in detail in the Tax section.

Mistakes are natural. Five-year-olds know this, but somehow we forget it when we enter into business.
—Author Tom Peters

LICENSES and PERMITS

The Lord's Prayer contains 56 words. Lincoln's Gettysburg Address has 268 words. The Declaration of Independence is 1,322 words long. Federal regulations governing the sale of cabbages are 26,911 words long.

When you open a new business, every government agency that can claim jurisdiction over you wants to get into the act. There are forms to file, permits and licenses to obtain, regulations and restrictions to understand and to heed. And, always, there are fees to pay.

Why all the government regulations? Why does water flow downhill? It's just the nature of government to regulate, license, permitize, officialize, "fees, fines and forms" you to death.

Some of the laws were passed to protect the consumer public from unscrupulous or incompetent business people. Some laws were created solely to provide additional revenues to the government. Some...well, who knows.

Most business licenses and permits are required and administered by local governments: the city if you live within city limits; possibly the county. Some businesses must also have state and federal licenses. This chapter will describe the different licenses and permits typically required by states and municipalities and those currently required by the federal government. Regulations, however, vary from city to city and state to state, and they are changing and multiplying all the time. You should make it your responsibility to contact state and local government agencies (anonymously if you prefer) to learn the current requirements and restrictions.

DBA : Doing Business As
(Fictitious/ Assumed Name Statement)

When a business goes by any name other than the owner's real name, the business is being operated under a "fictitious name" (also known as an "assumed name" or a "DBA"—doing business as). Country Comfort Carpentry, Johnson Plumbing, Ralph's Cleaners are all examples of fictitious names.

People doing business under a fictitious name are required to file a Fictitious Name Statement (or Assumed Name Certificate, or DBA, or whatever it's called in your state) with the county where your business is located. Filing a Fictitious

Name Statement prevents any other business in the county from using the same business name (with a few important exceptions, covered in the chapter Choosing A Business Name). In some states, the Fictitious Name Statement is registered at the state level rather than the county, and gives you state-wide name protection.

In addition to filing for the name, you may be required to publish the Fictitious Name Statement in a local newspaper, the theory being that the public has a right to know with whom they are doing business. The county clerk can provide you with a list of acceptable newspapers. Publication costs can be relatively low if your county has one of those newspapers that specialize in running legal notices (and little else). If not, small-time newspapers almost always charge less than large-circulation dailies.

You will be required to renew your fictitious name periodically, usually once every five years. In many states, the county notifies you when your renewal is due. If you forget to renew, someone else can step in and file for your business name and you will not be able to use it any more.

You usually don't have to register for a DBA if you use your real name as your business name, such as "Julia Smith." If, however, you are doing business as "Julia Smith Company" or "Julia Smith, Attorney at Law" or "Julia Smith's Bookstore," some (not all) states consider this to be a fictitious name, subject to regular DBA rules.

For specific requirements for your locality, contact the county clerk's office.

For more information on business names, see the chapter "Choosing a Business Name" in this section, and "Trademarks" in the Appendix.

Corporations: Unless you are operating under a name other than the official name of the corporation, you do not usually need to file a Fictitious Name Statement. But you should verify this, as local rules vary from state to state.

Partnerships: Partnerships must file a Fictitious Name Statement unless operating under the full names of all the partners.

Local Business Licenses

A local business license, if required, is merely a permit to do business locally. Most business licenses are simply a revenue-raising scheme, another tax imposed on business, offering no benefits to the business.

Some states, counties and/or cities require all businesses to get a business license. In many states, no licenses are required at all. Some localities require licenses only for certain types or sizes of businesses. Some cities require "home occupation permits" or similar special licenses only for home-based businesses.

Local business licenses can cost anywhere from $25 or $30 to as much as several hundred dollars, and usually must be renewed annually. The size of the business and the type of business often determines how much the license will cost. It might help to ask about the categories and fees, and see if you can define your business so it will fit into the least expensive category.

A few large cities impose "Business Registration Fees" and issue "Business Registration Certificates" in addition to any regular business license. These clever cities have basically created a second business license, and local businesses must purchase both.

In some states, the business license is a combined license, DBA and sales tax permit.

Bob Matthews, owner of Country Comfort Carpentry: "I never filed a DBA. I liked the name, and right on the checks and letterheads it says 'Country Comfort Carpentry' with my name immediately under it. I felt that's good enough. I never got a business license. I'm in a rural area, twenty miles from town. I feel that business licenses are a tax on people who work in town, to make them conform."

Other Local Permits

Your business may be required to conform to local zoning laws, building codes, health requirements, fire and police regulations. You may be required to get a "use permit" to operate your business in a new location.

I suggest that you contact your local government *before* you open your doors. If you do not get the proper permits or meet the local building codes, the city or county can shut you down.

Key Dickason is a partner in Major Dickason's Blend, a coffee store: "My partner is an honest, law-abiding person, and what he wanted to do is have everything A-OK. Then he found out that to put in

what the health inspectors required would cost about $1,200: a three-compartment sink, all of the walls smooth in the restrooms, a six-inch molding all around the bottom of the restrooms. The sink could not be in the location we wanted it, it had to be out in the storage room, the storage room had to be repainted. The main reason, well it's my opinion that the regulatory agencies are loaded with 'genus-clerks', and the only thing that they can see is the letter of the law.

"Genus is Latin for family. It's a biological term. I say it's a sub-species of Homo sapiens, and you run across this type of person all the time. When they come in and you're serving coffee, they look up in their book and they say, 'Oh, serving beverages. It's a restaurant.' Then they say that you have to comply with this regulation, and they cite book-and-verse.

"Now we've been in business a year and haven't done any of the things that they've recommended. We didn't do it because we didn't have the money. When the health inspector comes, he looks around, he says, 'Oh, the place is clean, it's nice', that's it. There's no pressure at all to comply with the written directive they gave us. If they plan to shut us down, then they'd say, 'You have 30 days to comply.' Well, then you do it.

"The laws are written for health reasons, for safety reasons. In the case of the health laws, it's to prevent people from getting sick from eating restaurant food. But if you're just serving coffee in paper cups, well it doesn't apply. But you take a genus-clerk and they enforce the law exactly. To the letter. You run into 'em everywhere. And the spirit of the law is to prevent illness. But, you see, they can't make that distinction."

Jim McFeely, commenting in Inc. Magazine: "When my partner and I asked the city of Grand Rapids what was needed to open a business, we were told we needed only two things: a business license and a sales tax license. We obtained the licenses and opened a downtown flea market. We advertised our grand opening by offering brand-name nail polish for 25¢ as well as a package of noodles for 25¢.

"On opening day we got nailed by city licensing for not having a license to sell paint (nail polish), by grocer licensing for not having a day-old variance, and by the fire marshall for not having $900 in fire extinguishers. Two men showed up and demanded to inspect the freight elevator, which hadn't run since 1935. Inspection fee: $285. We were deluged with forms for business activity taxes, interim business taxes and inventory taxes. When we hired a woman to mind the store, we got this huge form from the unemployment office that looked like a wallpaper sample book.

"There were just the two of us. We closed our business forever. One week later we were cited for failure to get a going-out-of-business license. A week after that, the mayor appeared on TV saying, "We have to seek new ways to attract business to downtown Grand Rapids".

Help From Local Government

Many cities, particularly smaller ones in economically depressed areas, are eager to help new businesses locate in their jurisdiction, especially businesses that will be hiring local people. They will help you through the red tape, and they are very likely to help if you have minor zoning or building code problems. Some cities even have a grant fund—free money!—to help local businesses. Ask at City Hall if they have any kind of economic development program or assistance.

State Licenses

Most sales and manufacturing businesses (unless they sell alcoholic beverages) and many service businesses do not need state licenses.

States have traditionally licensed doctors, nurses, lawyers, accountants, architects, engineers, contractors, real estate and insurance agents, and other professionals. In recent years, demand for consumer protection has brought about state licensing of dozens of additional occupations. Auto mechanics, stereo, TV and computer repair shops, marriage counselors, psychologists, pharmacists, barbers, bill collectors, funeral directors, pest control businesses, private investigators, plumbers, travel agents and tour operators, even dry cleaners, to name a few, are often licensed.

Occupational licenses are usually issued for one or two year periods and, as always, for a fee. Some of the occupational licenses require the licensee to pass a test. Some have education and experience requirements. Contact your state's agency for consumer affairs to inquire about possible licensing of your business. State offices are always located at the state capital and usually in the larger cities around the state.

Sales Tax

Unless you live in a state that does not have a sales tax, you will be required to collect sales tax from your customers and remit the tax to the state. States, counties and cities may all have a sales tax, but usually it is all reported and collected on one combined sales tax return.

Generally—and every state is different—retail goods (goods sold to the public; and goods sold to businesses for their own use, not for resale or manufacture) are subject to sales tax. Wholesale goods are exempt from sales tax.

Special note: Don't confuse "wholesale" with "discount". Wholesale refers to goods that are sold by one business to another, to re-sell or to go into a manufactured product. The ads in the papers that say "Wholesale to the Public", "Wholesale—Factory To You," or some other misuse of the word are actually referring to discount retail sales, subject to sales tax.

Services (what you charge for your time) are taxed in some states and not in others.

Many states tax prepared food (restaurants, etc.) but exempt groceries. Some states exempt shipping charges, newspapers, magazines, manufacturing equipment, and printing. Many states tax leased property and rentals.

Depending on the dollar volume of your business, you will have to prepare monthly, quarterly or annual sales tax returns, to report your sales and pay the taxes collected. Some states let you keep a portion of the sales tax you collect as a payment for the cost of collecting it.

Seller's (Reseller's) Permits

Every state that collects a sales tax issues "seller's permits" (also called reseller's permits, resale numbers, resale licenses, sales tax certificates or something similar), and every in-state business that sells goods (including repair parts) or taxable services must have one.

Some states will require a security deposit from you before issuing you a seller's permit, which is the state's way of guaranteeing that you will file your sales tax returns and pay what is owed. States sometimes allow you to put your deposit into a special interest-bearing bank account. After a year, paying your sales tax on time, you usually get your deposit back. In lieu of a deposit, most states will let you purchase a sales tax bond from an insurance company.

When a new business applies for a seller's permit, the sales tax people may ask you to estimate your taxable sales, and base the deposit on your estimate. Since you have no idea what your sales will be, no law requires you to be overly optimistic. Keep your sales estimate low, and you may avoid a deposit altogether.

Besides registering you as a seller, a seller's permit gives you the right to buy goods for resale, both finished products and the "raw materials" that go into products you manufacture, without paying sales tax to your supplier. Only goods that will be resold or manufactured in the normal course of business (and also goods used for display or samples) can be purchased tax-free. You may not use your seller's permit to make tax-free purchases of office supplies, furniture, equipment, or goods for personal, non-business purposes.

In some states, if you are a retailer and do pay sales tax on goods you later resell, you may be entitled to take a deduction on your sales tax return and get credit for the tax previously paid.

Businesses that sell wholesale goods to other businesses without charging sales tax must keep a record of all customers who make tax-free purchases. Your customers must give you their resale numbers before you can sell to them tax-free. States often provide forms for this purpose.

In states where services are exempt from sales tax, some businesses have problems over the definition of what is a service (not taxable) as opposed to a product (taxable). For example, is an expensive custom-designed computer program a taxable product or a non-taxable service? The same question applies to the work of freelance artists, graphic designers, typesetters, and the like. Be very careful to find out if your work is subject to sales tax. Sometimes the people in the sales tax office are unsure, so ask to see the rules in writing. A carefully worded contract or invoice that separately bills taxable and non-taxable items may be needed.

Out of State Sales

If you sell by mail-order (or telephone, fax or online), you do not collect sales tax on orders shipped out-of-state, and you do not need a sales tax permit from any state except your own.

If you have an office, warehouse or store in another state, or if you or your employees are regularly travelling through and selling in another state (what's called "nexus", a physical presence) you must abide by that state's sales tax laws, and you must file sales tax returns in that state, for *all* retail sales made to that state. If you sell only occasionally in another state, such as at a seminar or trade show, it is not considered nexus. You only have to collect sales tax on the sales made at those shows and remit the tax to that state (not to your home state).

If you sell or offer services on the Internet, many states are trying to find some way to tax your out-of-state Internet sales. No state has accomplished this yet, and no one is paying out-of-state sales taxes on Internet sales, but keep your eyes open.

Use Tax

Although a seller does not collect sales tax on out-of-state sales, in most states the buyer is supposed to *pay* sales tax on mail-order purchases from out-of-state vendors—not to the seller, but directly to the state where you, the buyer, reside (unless the purchases are for resale).

No, I'm not kidding. When you buy a computer or office supplies from an out of state company, your own state may want you to pay sales tax on the purchase. It is called a "use tax" (sometimes a "compensating tax"). This is not a well-known law, and, as you can imagine, it is not easy to enforce. Purchases originally made for resale but used for another purpose, such as personal use, are also subject to the use tax.

On your sales tax return, you will find a line where you calculate the use tax you owe, and pay it along with the sales tax you collected from your customers. Some states offer a small discount or rebate to help offset the bookkeeping costs of computing the use tax.

Other State Regulations

To find out about any other state requirements, contact the Secretary of State or Consumer Affairs office. Many states publish a booklet for new businesses, usually free, describing all of the state requirements. Here are a few:

Truckers, taxi cab operators, bus lines, and household movers must often register with the Public Utilities Commission. Businesses operat-

Form SS-4 — Application for Employer Identification Number

Form **SS-4**
(Rev. December 1993)
Department of the Treasury
Internal Revenue Service

Application for Employer Identification Number
(For use by employers, corporations, partnerships, trusts, estates, churches, government agencies, certain individuals, and others. See instructions.)

EIN
OMB No. 1545-0003
Expires 12-31-96

1 Name of applicant (Legal name) (See instructions.)
Sam Leandro

2 Trade name of business, if different from name in line 1
Music Photo Service

3 Executor, trustee, "care of" name

4a Mailing address (street address) (room, apt., or suite no.)
P.O. Box 1599

5a Business address, if different from address in lines 4a and 4b
640 Bell Springs Road

4b City, state, and ZIP code
Laytonville, CA 95454

5b City, state, and ZIP code
Laytonville, CA 95454

6 County and state where principal business is located
Mendocino, California

7 Name of principal officer, general partner, grantor, owner, or trustor—SSN required (See instructions.) ▶ 123-45-6789
Sam Leandro

8a Type of entity (Check only one box.) (See instructions.)
☒ Sole Proprietor (SSN) 123-45-6789

14 Principal activity (See instructions.) ▶ photographer

10 Date business started or acquired (Mo., day, year) (See instructions.)
June 14, 199

11 Enter closing month of accounting year. (See instructions.)
December

12 First date wages or annuities were paid or will be paid (Mo., day, year). **Note:** *If applicant is a withholding agent, enter date income will first be paid to nonresident alien. (Mo., day, year)* ▶ May 1, 199

Name and title (Please type or print clearly.) ▶ Sam Leandro, owner
Business telephone number (include area code)
(707) 984-6746

Signature ▶ Sam Leandro
Date ▶ April 1

For Paperwork Reduction Act Notice, see attached instructions.
Cat. No. 16055N
Form **SS-4** (Rev. 12-93)

---

ing factories or other potential air and water polluting equipment must often meet state Air and Water Resources Commission requirements. Employers may be subject to state wage and hour laws and occupational safety and health laws. States often have laws regulating finance charges imposed on customers. Repair shops may need bonds or proof of solvency. Telephone marketers must be registered in many states (I personally think they ought to be jailed).

Federal Identification Numbers

Your business will be required to identify itself on tax forms and licenses by either of two numbers: your Social Security number or a Federal Employer Identification Number (called "FEIN" or, more often, "EIN").

If you are a sole proprietor, a Social Security number is all the identification you need unless (1) you hire employees, or (2) you are required to file an excise tax return (covered in the Tax section), or (3) you purchase or inherit an existing business. Then you must have an EIN.

Some sole proprietors get an EIN even though not required to have one, because they do not want to give out their Social Security number to every government agency and corporate bureaucracy now requiring a business ID before they'll buy anything from you.

Partnerships, corporations and LLCs must have the federal EIN (and, in many states, state identification numbers as well) whether they hire employees or not.

As you can see, although the federal identification number is called an "Employer" Identification Number, the EIN is used by any business that needs (or wants) a federal ID number, whether the business has employees or not.

To get an EIN, file Form SS-4 with the IRS. They can mail or fax the EIN. No fee is charged.

If you are getting an EIN but will not be an employer, be careful how you fill out Form SS-4. Line 12 ("First date wages were paid or will be paid") should be marked "No employees—NOT APPLICABLE". If you put a date on Line 12, the IRS will assume you have employees, and will automatically send you payroll tax returns that you must fill out and return.

Also be careful how you fill out Line 13 (number of employees). If you have none, write "NONE". Remember, you are not an employee of your own business unless you incorporate. If you will have employees but don't yet know how many, estimate on the low side to avoid a premature avalanche of unnecessary IRS forms. One employee is enough.

Federal Licenses

Most small businesses do not need any federal licenses. The federal government licenses all businesses engaged in common-carrier transportation, radio and television station construction, manufacture of drugs, alcohol or tobacco products, preparation of meat products, manufacture or sale of firearms, and investment counseling. Contact the Federal Trade Commission, Washington, D.C. 20580, for specific requirements.

Mike Snead, Ms. Perc Leather: "Our business grew incredibly fast, and word of mouth helped us a whole lot. So did the fact that we were one of a kind at a time, sociologically, when that kind of business was ripe to own. The hand-made crafts, the craftsman-entrepreneur concept was brand new and it generated a lot of curiosity, and the curiosity generated sales. I don't know if that can happen now. It's no longer unique. As a matter of fact, it's pretty much the status quo, and I suspect it's going to be one of the things people will rebel against on their way to the next new thing. And whoever has some concept of what's coming next will be in the same position we were in."

Federal Trade Commission Rules

The Federal Trade Commission (FTC) has dozens of laws affecting all kinds of businesses. Some laws only apply to specific types of businesses. Some are for all businesses. To find out if your type of business is subject to specific FTC laws, write the FTC, Washington, D.C. 20580.

The laws discussed here are for a wide variety of businesses. These laws change regularly, new ones are added, old ones eliminated. Write the FTC before relying on this information:

Guarantees and warranties must comply with the Consumer Products Warranty Law. Some warranties must be made available to customers before they buy. Although the terms are often used interchangeably, warranty refers to the product itself (it will perform as promised for a given period of time), while a guarantee is a promise of customer satisfaction (the customer can get an exchange or refund even if the product lives up to its warranty).

Mail order & telephone-sales businesses (including fax and online sales) must comply with the Mail or Telephone Order Merchandise Rule: Sellers must ship merchandise within their stated time, or if no time is stated, within 30 days. If there is an additional delay, the seller must notify the buyer of the delay, and give the buyer an option, at seller's expense (such as an 800 number or a postage-paid reply card) to cancel the order for a full and prompt refund.

Door-to-door sales businesses and businesses that sell goods away from a regular business location (such as presentations at people's homes or at conventions), must give buyers 3 business days to change their minds and cancel their order. This is called the Cooling Off Rule.

Telephone and fax marketers must comply with the FTC's Telemarketing and Consumer Fraud & Abuse Prevention Act, the Tele-marketing Sales Rule, and the FCC's Telephone Consumer Protection Act. Unsolicited fax marketing is prohibited unless you have an established business relationship.

Textiles, fabric, wool, furs and clothing must be labeled according to a variety of FTC rules. Generally, a label must state (1) the composition of the fabric—the fiber content, (2) the country of origin, (3) the names or registered identification numbers of the manufacturer and the business marketing the fabric, and (4) instructions for care and cleaning.

All packages and labels on goods must conform to the Federal Fair Packaging and Labeling Act. Basically, a label must identify the product, list the manufacturer, packer, or distributor, and show the net quantity, both inch/pound and metric. The Act specifies how the label must be printed and where on the goods it must appear.

Advertising, product offers, and claims are regulated by the Federal Trade Commission Act (that's all it is called; it was the very first law the FTC passed, back in 1914, and it is still simply called "The Act"). You must have a reasonable basis for all advertising claims. You must have evidence to support your claims. Advertising may not be deceptive or misleading. Environmental benefits cannot be exaggerated. If you say its free, it must be free. There is a long list of other trickery prohibited by the Act.

Although all businesses, big and small, are subject to the various FTC rules, enforcement of the laws is directed primarily at large companies that, due to their size, can and do take advantage of many, many people. As one FTC official explained to me, "We're too busy keeping track of large businesses to worry about a mom- and-pop grocery store in Kansas City which may be violating one of our laws. We've found that small businesses, though they may not adhere to the letter of the law—most of them don't even *know* about a lot of these laws—tend to be much more honest with their customers. We rarely get a complaint about a small business."

Whether you think you can or whether you think you can't, you're right.　　　　—Henry Ford

INSURANCE

If you bought all the different kinds of business insurance available to you, you'd be broke before you made your first sale. So you must determine what insurance, if any, is required by law (usually worker's compensation for employees, and vehicle coverage), what insurance is extremely important (such as liability coverage if a customer is injured, and basic coverage for buildings and expensive assets), and what insurance you can do without. Some of the types of insurance include:

Basic Fire Insurance. Covers fire and lightning losses to your equipment and inventory and to your premises. Fire premiums vary widely and are based upon the location of your property and the degree of fire protection in your community, the type of construction of the building, the nature of your business and the nature of neighboring businesses. If you move into a building next to a woodworking or dry cleaning shop, your fire premiums will be high even if your business is a low fire risk. A sprinkler system in your building will sharply reduce your premium.

Extended Coverage. Protects against storms, most explosions, smoke damage, riot, and damage caused by aircraft or vehicles.

Liability Insurance. Pays for claims brought against your business because of bodily injury. A customer, or possibly a delivery person, slips and falls, breaks a leg and slaps you with a $50,000 lawsuit; it's not uncommon. Premiums for merchants usually are based upon the square footage in the store. The bigger the store, the higher the premium. For manufacturers and contractors, premiums increase as payroll increases.

Liability insurance does not cover you, the owner, nor any of your employees, though it would normally cover an outside contractor. It does not cover injuries caused by vehicles or by defective products.

Fire Legal Liability. Covers fire damage to your landlord's building—the portion you occupy only. The rest of the building would be covered by Property Damage Liability. Even if the landlord has fire insurance on the building, you may still be liable if your business caused the fire.

Property Damage Liability. Provides coverage for damage to property of others. There are two different types of property damage liability. The first type is damage to property that is not under your control or in your custody. A fire starts in your small office. The damage is minimal but smoke and water destroyed $30,000 worth of Persian rugs in the business next door. Property damage liability covers this situation.

The second type of property damage liability is damage to others' property that is under your control or in your custody, such as property leased or rented to you, and—especially important for repair businesses—property that belongs to your customers. Insurance for this second type of property liability usually must be written as a special, separate policy.

Products Liability. Covers products designed, manufactured or sold by the insured once the product leaves the business' hands. It covers the business in case the user of the product sues for injury or property damage. The courts generally hold manufacturers strictly liable for any injury caused by their product, sometimes even when the product has not been used correctly.

Even retail stores can sometimes be liable for products they sell, though not usually. If the products are in their original packages, and if the retailer provides no assembly or advice, the risk is greatly reduced. Some manufacturers will indemnify retailers against product liability claims (sometimes called a "vendors endorsement").

Malpractice. Also known as "errors and omissions" and "professional liability". Protects you from lawsuits and losses from professional, ah, "mistakes". This insurance is often expensive and hard to find. Sometimes available from professional societies or associations.

Bonds. "Surety" bonds guarantee the performance of a job. If you do not complete a job, for any reason, your surety company must do so. Surety bonds are most often used in the construction industry and are always required on public construction projects. Surety bonds are difficult to obtain unless you have $30,000 or more in liquid assets such as cash and inventory.

"Fidelity" bonds are placed on employees, insuring the employer against theft or embezzlement by the bonded employees.

7-30

overhead expenses you incur during long periods of disability.

Business interruption insurance may seem to be something of a luxury. But if you have a fire or some other disaster, it might be months before you are back on your feet, even with fire insurance and extended coverage. Most small businesses are not prepared to handle such a calamity, and many never reopen.

For tax purposes, some business interruption premiums are deductible, and some are not. The proceeds from an insurance claim may or may not be taxable to you, depending on what the insurance is actually covering. Your insurance agent should have complete tax information.

Workers' Compensation Insurance. Provides disability and death benefits to employees injured or killed on the job, regardless of who is at fault. Most (but not all) states require employers to carry workers' comp insurance for all employees, even if they are occasional or part-time. You, the employer, must pay for your employees' workers compensation insurance.

Although in some states an employer may not be required by law to purchase workers' comp insurance, the employer is still legally liable for any injuries an employee incurs on the job.

You are not required to carry workers' comp for outside or independent contractors. However, if an outside contractor is injured while working for you, you may possibly be liable for the injury. Workers' comp or regular liability insurance may cover this situation. If your outside contractor hires employees, it is a good idea to verify that the contractor has purchased workers' compensation insurance for his employees. Whenever people are involved with your business, no matter how indirectly, find out what liability exposure you may have.

Some states allow businesses to self-insure rather than purchase a workers' comp policy; but for most small businesses, the required bonds or cash reserves are prohibitively expensive.

You, the owner of the business, may or may not be subject to workers' compensation insurance, depending on your state's laws. In many states, sole proprietors, partners in partnerships, owner/employees of small corporations, and owners (members) of Limited Liability Companies are exempt from workers' comp insurance. Some states make it an option; you decide if you

Theft Coverage. Covers burglary (theft from a closed business) and robbery (theft using force or threat of violence). The cost depends on the type of merchandise you stock, your location, and the theft protection on your premises: alarms, bars on the windows, dead bolts, etc. An investment in some security is certainly as important as buying theft insurance. Find out if your coverage includes inventory and equipment away from your business premises, such as at a trade show, or in transit to a customer. Theft coverage does not include customers who rip you off (bad checks, phony credit cards, not paying bills) though such coverage may be available.

Business Interruption. If your business closes due to fire or other insurable cause, business interruption insurance will pay you approximately what you would have earned. The premiums, especially when part of an insurance package, are low. There is similar insurance that provides coverage if you are hospitalized or disabled and have to shut down your business. You can also purchase "extra expense" insurance, which pays the extra cost of keeping a business operating (such as renting temporary quarters) after a fire or other building damage. "Overhead insurance" pays you for business want to purchase workers' compensation insurance for yourself.

By the way, if you have health insurance, check with your health insurance company to be sure there isn't a conflict over on-the-job coverage. Some health insurance policies do not cover any on-the-job injuries.

Workers' compensation premiums for your employees is fully deductible. Workers' comp for yourself is deductible only if your state *requires* you to have workers comp insurance on yourself. If the coverage is voluntary, the premiums are not deductible (except for corporations).

The minimum premium to obtain a workers' compensation policy, even for one part-time employee, can cost several hundred dollars a year. Premiums increase as your payroll increases (giving an employee a raise may increase your premium), and vary dramatically with the occupation. Workers' comp premiums for a roofer are about ten times higher than for a grocery clerk. So be sure the insurance company doesn't mistakenly put you in a high-risk, high-premium category.

You can keep your initial premium at or near the minimum, particularly for part-time and hourly employees, by giving the insurance company a low payroll estimate, since you really don't know how many hours your employees will be working. Once or twice a year, the insurance company will examine your payroll records, comparing your actual payroll to your original estimate. Your premium will be adjusted retroactively. Some insurance companies also pay dividends (refunds) after the end of the year if you have a clean record (no claims).

Some states offer workers' compensation insurance through a state-operated insurance fund or risk-sharing pool. In some states, the rates are comparable to or even lower than rates from regular insurance companies, particularly if you are hiring only one or two employees. In other states, the state fund is insurance of last resort, for companies who cannot get coverage from a regular company, and the state coverage may be more expensive. To locate the state-operated insurance fund, look in the Yellow Pages under Insurance or contact the State Department of Employment or Human Resources.

A special warning if your employees will be working at their own homes (not at the employer's home): Your workers' compensation premium will probably be triple the normal rate.

The insurance companies view this as a high risk situation because the employee is at the workplace 24 hours a day and can too-easily claim that any injury at home is work related.

Building contractors: If you hire subcontractors, some states hold you responsible for the subcontractor's workers' comp coverage if the subcontractor does not have the insurance. Ask to see a Certificate of Insurance from each subcontractor.

Vehicle Insurance. Liability coverage is mandatory in most states. The same coverage available to you on your personal auto is available on a business vehicle. The premiums, however, are usually higher for business vehicles. If you use your personal vehicle for business, check with your insurance company to make sure you have coverage that includes business use.

If your employees will be driving your vehicles, make sure their liability is included on your policy. If your employees will be driving *their own* vehicles on your company's business, you should also have what's called "non-owned" auto liability insurance, which protects you if one of your employees injures someone or damages someone's property. This non-owned coverage does not protect the employee, who should have his own insurance as well.

Personal or business property inside a vehicle, such as merchandise you are delivering, is not usually covered by vehicle insurance.

Environmental Impairment and Pollution Liability. Required by federal law for all gas stations and for businesses located at former gas station sites if the tanks are still in the ground. Other businesses that are at risk for pollution problems, such as quick lubes and even dry cleaners, sometimes purchase this insurance.

Is there more? Of course. There's Vandalism and Malicious Mischief coverage. Patent Owners insurance. Disability insurance. Key Person Life insurance. Insurance called Boiler and Machinery Coverage for breakdowns and equipment failures. Credit insurance for your accounts receivable. There's also specialized insurance (unusual kinds of coverage) for specific types of businesses and industries. Copyright insurance. Export insurance. And Health insurance, which is covered in detail in the Tax Section.

Where do you begin? Check with the state, your landlord, and your bank if you are getting a bank loan, to find out what insurance you *must* carry. Many leases specify that the tenant must carry liability insurance naming the landlord as an additional insured. Landlords often require tenants to carry plate glass insurance and sometimes fire insurance on the landlord's building.

Bank loans sometimes require you to carry life insurance naming the bank as beneficiary. The bank will also require you to insure any property purchased with the loan money.

Car and equipment leasing firms often require you to obtain liability and/or property insurance on leased equipment.

Over and above any mandatory insurance, liability coverage is unquestionably the most important to any business where customers and clients come to your door. One lawsuit by an injured customer can wipe you out: your business, and you personally. Make sure the coverage pays attorneys and legal fees as well as any claims.

Beyond liability and mandatory coverage, how much insurance you have or don't have is entirely up to you. How much can you afford? How much do you *want* to afford? How much of a risk are you willing to take, and how comfortable do you feel with that risk?

Most insurance companies offer a Business Owner's Policy ("BOP") or "all risk" insurance, combining many of the above coverages in one policy. Some insurance companies offer "industry specific" policies, offering special coverage to certain types of businesses. In fact, you might want to contact one of the trade associations for your type of business. Trade associations often offer reasonably-priced insurance packages to members. To find a trade association, ask other people who own similar businesses, or ask at a library if they have a directory of associations.

Insurance companies are competitive, offering different rates, packages and premium payment plans. Many insurance policies offer much lower premiums if you opt for large deductibles. For property and equipment coverage, find out if the insurance will reimburse your original cost, replacement cost, or current value at time of loss. These can be significantly different amounts. If you have more than one location, have your insurance agent explain the important difference between "blanket" and "scheduled" coverage.

It is a good idea to shop around. Pick an agent or broker who will devote time to your individual needs, who will at no extra cost survey your entire situation and recommend different insurance options, explaining the advantages and disadvantages of each.

Make sure you are dealing with a solvent, reliable company, one with a good reputation for settling claims. Your agent can show you the company's rating, or check with your state's insurance department.

And finally: Read the policy carefully before you pay for it, not after you've suffered a loss you *thought* was covered.

Self Insurance

In an attempt to reduce insurance costs, business owners sometimes attempt self insurance. Basically this means you are not insured at all but have set aside funds to cover possible losses such as fire or theft or a liability claim against the business. Some people call these funds a "reserve". While self insurance certainly saves on insurance premiums, the money set aside or in the reserve is not considered a business expense and is not tax deductible.

At the time you actually sustain a loss or have to pay on a claim or lawsuit, you may or may not have a tax write-off, depending on the nature of the loss. For example, stolen or destroyed furniture and equipment can be written off only to the extent they haven't already been written off or depreciated; inventory must be written off as part of cost-of-goods-sold; legal fees are probably fully deductible, but depend on the circumstances. The chapters on Inventory, Cost of Goods Sold, and specific items in the Tax section explain how to deduct different kinds of losses.

Remember, too, that it is unlikely your self insurance reserve will be large enough to cover a large loss or lawsuit. That's why people buy insurance in the first place. Also, insurance required by law must be purchased from an insurance company. Self insurance will not suffice.

It's just this sort of narrow focus that seems to be a key to a successful business person. The historians and philosophers have the grand sweeping views, but the ones who get rich are people of action who set themselves to a task and do it.
—Don Cusic, Middle Tennessee State Univ.

CHOOSING A BUSINESS NAME

Thinking up a name for your business can be a lot of fun, an opportunity to let your creativity and your imagination take charge. A business name, however, should be selected with care:

1. Choose a name that is pleasant, easy to pronounce, and easy to remember. If your customers choke or stumble on your name every time they mention it to someone, fewer people will hear about you.

2. Customers who hear your name once, or see it listed in the Yellow Pages, form an immediate impression of who you are. Think like a customer. Does your name sound like a company a customer would want to call?

3. If you want people to connect the business with you, using your own name as the company name may be the best choice.

4. Be wary of cute names and current popular expressions: they get stale over time. Also be wary of intentionally misspelled words. "Kute Kids Klothes" may seem to be a clever name for a business except for customers who spell it wrong and can't find you in the phone book.

5. Avoid a name that's similar to another business. Customers will confuse you with them.

6. Choose a name that will do a little advertising for you, that will tell people what you do. Wallpapers Plus, Strider Real Estate, say what they need to say, clearly and simply. "Acme Enterprises" tells people absolutely nothing.

7. Avoid names beginning with articles, that can result in your business being listed under "The" or "An".

8. If customers are likely to look for you in a directory, there may be an advantage to being close to the beginning of the alphabet. Customers go to the Yellow Pages and start calling with the A's, and stop when they find what they want.

9. Most important, choose a name that will not severely limit you, a name that will stand up to the passage of time. I know two jewelers who named their business "The Silver Workshop." They made high quality silver and turquoise necklaces and bracelets. Silver, however, is not as popular as it was three years ago, and The Silver Workshop is now making gold and beaded jewelry. These jewelers now find themselves with an albatross around their necks: the business name. On the one hand, the old customers recognize the name. But new customers, looking for gold jewelry, assume that The Silver Workshop makes silver jewelry, and they stay away.

This same warning applies to businesses with geographical names, such as Main Street Music. What happens when you move to State Street?

When you finally settle on a name you like, go to the county office that handles fictitious names (assumed names, DBAs) and ask to see their alphabetical list of all names registered with the county. If you live in a large urban area, you may find that your first, second *and* third choices are all already taken. You can, if you want, try to contact the person who owns the business name and find out if the business is still in existence. If it isn't, and if the owner of the name consents, an Abandonment of Fictitious Name (Assumed Name or DBA) Statement can be filed, whereby the prior owner gives up all rights to the name. You may simultaneously file a DBA or Fictitious Name Statement for the name. The Abandonment procedures are identical to the DBA/Fictitious Name Statement procedures. The former owner will probably want you to pay the cost of filing the statement of abandonment and may even want you to pay him a fee for his trouble.

You should be aware of possible trouble if you select a business name that is already being used by an out-of-county or even an out-of-state business. Corporations are usually granted exclusive statewide use of a business name, assuming they were the first in the state to choose the name. Some states also grant state-wide tradename protection to other businesses. Your state's Secretary of State maintains a list of business names claimed by corporations and other businesses licensed by the state.

Trademarks

Just because the county approved your DBA or the state approved your corporate name, doesn't mean some other company can't stop you from using it. You must also be aware of federal trademarks of business names and products.

Most large and even some very small businesses obtain trademarks from the U. S. Patent & Trademark Office. Trademark law is covered in the Appendix, but generally, a business with a federally registered trademark usually has exclusive use of that name throughout the U. S.

Locate a copy of the Federal Trademark Register (try your library) and look up your proposed business name. You can also do a trademark search via computer through an online service.

If your business name is the same as or very similar to a trademarked name, you may have problems, particularly if your goods or services are similar to those carrying the trademark and if you are selling in the same part of the country.

What happens if you start your business and find out later that some other business has prior claim to your business name? What almost always happens is that you will get a letter from some lawyer telling you that you are in violation of the law and that you must cease using that business name, or else they'll take you to court, sue you, etc. and etc. At that point you can decide if you really are in the wrong, and right or wrong, do you want to fight it in court? There are few clear-cut answers in this area of law. Often, unfortunately, it comes down to who has the most money for lawyers.

Another suggestion: check local telephone directories and national trade directories for your type of business. Trademark or no trademark, avoid a business name already in use.

Internet Names

Businesses and individuals on the Internet have what they call "domain" names or Internet addresses, their identification online. Within each World Wide Web (www) classification, one company or individual has exclusive world-wide use of a domain name. If you plan to have a Web site, a presence online, and if you want your domain name to be the same as your business name, you should check first to see if the name is already taken. Domain names are sold by Internet providers on a first come, first served basis.

Robert Haft, founder, Crown Books: We went out and did something like a Nielsen survey. We asked people which names they thought would be best for a bookstore. That narrowed it down to four or five. Then we took those four or five names and did another survey, asking people which of these bookstores they'd been in. 20% of the people said they'd been in a Crown Books store—and that was before we opened. So we said if 20% of the people think they've already been there, that's the name.

THE BUSINESS PLAN

If "ready, aim, fire!" is your motto, you will be tempted to skip this chapter. Don't. Business planning is essential to your success.

I can tell you from first hand experience, from seeing it happen too many times: Most new business failures are due to a lack of planning, a lack of foresight, a failure to think things through, thoroughly, completely. A failure to plan.

Although business plans are often created to try to raise money, most business plans are really for your own use. Business planning is a self-learning process. You need to know everything about your business, your industry, your customers, your competition. You especially need to think out how you are going to find customers or clients and how you are going to market your goods or services to your customers.

The greatest benefit of a business plan is that, by writing everything down, you are more likely to see the entire picture, and you are more likely not to forget some important steps to prepare yourself for this huge venture. Launching a business without a business plan is much like building a house without blueprints. You can certainly do it, but when you discover a mistake in the foundation after the roof is shingled, you're really going to kick yourself.

A Basic Plan

If you've read this entire section of *Small Time Operator*, followed through on all the suggestions, done your "market research," estimated your start-up expenses, tried your hand at the cash-flow guessing game (covered in the Bookkeeping section), and wrote it all down, you would have yourself a respectable business plan.

Such an informal plan will help you organize your thoughts and observations, show you problems that require more thought and analysis, and help you find all the jigsaw pieces and fit them together.

Don't create your plan in a vacuum. Talk about your plan, and your new business, with as many people as possible. The best way to avoid wishful thinking is to get feedback from potential buyers, clients, prospects. Listen to their answers. If your new business is going to be successful, other people must be excited about it, interested in hiring you or spending their money on your products. By creating a business that will give people what *they* want, a business that is structured to meet *their* needs, you have found the Secret To Success, the difference between an idea and a solid business.

It is also extremely important to understand the limits of a business plan, particularly one this early in the game. The ideas are only that, untested ideas. The numbers are guesses, your own inexperienced, optimistic guesses. Don't rely on them too heavily. Proceed with all caution, keep your eyes open, and let experience, not some written plan, be your guide.

Raising Capital

A business plan created just for yourself can be as informal as you like. But if you are trying to raise start-up capital from individuals or a bank, a more structured business plan will help you get your ideas across to prospective lenders and investors. Someone who is considering putting money into your venture will most likely want to see a written plan, one that includes:

1. Your business idea.
2. Your background, experience, contacts, etc.
3. Where you plan to locate.
4. How you'll obtain or manufacture inventory.
5. How you will find and keep customers.
6. The status of the competition.
7. How much money you will need to start, and what the money will be used for.
8. How much time and how much of your own money you plan to commit to the business.
9. How much you will pay yourself.
10. How you will repay the loan or investment.

If you are looking for a loan or for investors, you may be asked to include "pro forma" financial statements, which are projections of income, and expenses, profit or loss, cash flow, etc. These "projections" would be more honestly labeled "guesses" or even "hopes and dreams", because that's all they really are, and every banker and any savvy investor knows this. People who are considering putting money into your business are going to be much more interested in your experience, your knowledge—and how much collateral you have.

Business planning is an ongoing process. After you've been in business awhile, you may want to draw up a new plan to help you make some major decision, such as reorganizing or expanding, or trying out some new, bold idea. By then, you will know your business well, and you will be able to create a much more reliable plan.

Business plans can be and often are much more elaborate and detailed than what I've described here. Entire books are dedicated to the many considerations, formulas, options and everything else you can conceivably fit onto graphs, charts, schedules, computer screens, and densely packed pages, to create some mighty impressive plans indeed, some of which are quite valuable and some of which are utterly useless. Sometimes, too much "information" will work against you, unable to see the forest for the trees.

In conclusion, I'd like to suggest that every new business person take the time, at the very beginning when you are still just considering your business idea, to put together a business plan—in your head if you like, on paper if you prefer, maybe just late night thoughts, maybe just scribbled notes, maybe something elaborate right out of the business plan books and computer programs. The form the plan takes is not important. It's the conclusions you reach that are important.

Mary Baechler, founder and CEO of Racing Strollers, Yakima, Wa, talking to Inc. Magazine: "A good plan will help you get a loan about as much as a nice suit. There's a myth that you need a good plan before launching a business. Many of the people who will tell you to write a plan are consultants that, oh my gosh, make money helping you to write such a plan. When your numbers are good, you don't really need a formal plan. When your numbers are stinko, a business plan doesn't fool anyone. And bankers don't make loans unless there's collateral."

Before you dive into anything, do a little research, write up a business plan, figure out if you're going to pay the mortgage or lose your shirt. Got an idea that is too hot to take the time for all that? Well be prepared to fail.
—*Walter Jeffries, Flash Magazine*

Statistics are no substitute for judgment.
—*Henry Clay*

Section Two
BOOKKEEPING

The best memory is not so firm
as faded ink.
　　　—Chinese proverb

"If you take one from three hundred
and sixty-five, what remains?" asked
Humpty Dumpty.
"Three hundred and sixty-four, of
course," said Alice.
Humpty Dumpty looked doubtful. "I'd
rather see that done on paper,"
he said.
　　　—from Alice in Wonderland

Warming Up to an Unpopular Subject

Bookkeeping seems to be the one aspect of business that so many people dread. Columns upon columns of numbers, streams of adding machine tape, balancing the books (whatever that means), and "I'm a shopkeeper, not an accountant." Whenever I try to explain or defend the paperwork end of business to a new business person, I always feel I have two strikes against me before I even open my mouth. But once a person understands why a business requires a set of ledgers and how these records can be kept with a minimum of time and effort, the fear vanishes, the work *somehow* gets done, and you are left with the satisfaction of seeing the total picture and of having done it yourself. And that's a nice feeling.

Bookkeeping is an integral part of business, of *your* business. To attempt a definition, bookkeeping is a system designed to record, summarize and analyze your financial activity: your sales, purchases, credit accounts, cash, payrolls, inventory, equipment. Your "books"—your ledgers and worksheets—are the bound papers or the computer disks (or both) on which the bookkeeping activity is recorded or "posted."

Why Keep a Set of Books?

Most new business people think that they must keep books only because the government (meaning the Internal Revenue Service) requires them to. Well, it's true, the IRS does require every business to keep a set of books. (The IRS's basic bookkeeping requirement is, "You must keep records to correctly figure your taxes.") But there is a bit more to bookkeeping than taxes and tax law requirements.

The real reason you'd *want* to keep a set of books, as you will learn soon enough, is because you *need* the information to run your business. Can you ever expect to make a good decision based on incomplete information? Your books are your only source of complete information about your business. It is virtually impossible to keep all your business information in your head. You may think you know your business like the back of your hand, but you would be very surprised to see how much you don't know unless you can see the total financial picture. This is doubly true of a business operated out of your home where personal and business expenses can get intermingled and confused.

Business failures have been blamed, time and again, on a lack of accurate financial records. Bob Willis, former owner of Booknews, a defunct bookstore: "Our biggest mistake was that we didn't keep a regular set of books. Half of our records were on scraps of paper and receipts. We didn't know whether some accounts were paid or not. We thought we were making a profit, but a good set of books would have shown us the truth: we were going broke. And you know, had I realized that, I could have taken steps to change things, to head us in a better direction."

Without a complete set of books, you find yourself trying to evaluate your business by looking at isolated areas, such as cash and inventory—these being the most observable (and also the most misleading). If, for example, you price your product based solely on its cost to you plus some arbitrary markup—a common mistake with beginners—you could be selling at a loss and not even know it. This happened at Booknews: "We knew what the books were costing us, but we didn't have any real idea of what our total overhead was—rent, insurance, supplies, utilities, payroll taxes, the rest. We sold a lot of books because we sold at a discount, and I thought we were doing well. Do you know it took me four months to realize that every single book we sold, we sold at a loss."

A good bookkeeping system will provide you with information essential to the survival of your business. Only with a complete set of books will you be able to evaluate your business and make any needed changes and plans for the future.

Joe Campbell, Resistance Repair: "Everybody who runs a business should sit down and figure out what it costs them to turn the key in that door every morning. Overhead. And do it on a daily basis. I never knew until I sat down and calculated exactly what my expenses were, what it costs me to have that place down there. And it's eighty dollars a day! When you walk in there in the morning you know exactly what you gotta do before you start putting bread on the table. You gotta make eighty bucks for the man. And then you start making money for yourself."

Setting Up Your Books

Where do you begin? How much bookkeeping do you need?

If your business is a one man, one woman, or husband-and-wife operation, your records can be kept quite simple. A bank account, a set of income and expenditure ledgers and a few worksheets are about all you will need.

Do you sell on account? You will want to keep records of each credit customer. If you hire employees, you will need payroll records for each employee. Manufacturing and sales businesses may need detailed inventory records. Partnerships must keep records of each partner's contributions and withdrawals. Limited Liability Companies have more requirements. And corporations, even small ones, often need entire forests to supply the paper to run the business.

But let's take things one step at a time. *None* of the bookkeeping records need be too complicated for most people to keep themselves and to understand.

Computer or Hand Posted Ledgers?

Do you need bookkeeping software or can you use a simple set of hand-posted ledgers?

Computer prepared ledgers are basically identical to hand-posted ledgers. They're just faster, cleaner looking, free of mathematical errors, and easier to rearrange and fine-tune to fit your needs. Depending on the sophistication of your program, you can enter one payment that is posted to your checkbook and expense ledger, and also to your inventory, payroll, equipment, or other ledgers. You can post income to your bank account and income ledger, and update your record of credit customers. The software can give you daily, weekly, monthly and annual totals in any category you want, and keep track of your bank balance at the same time.

Hand posted ledgers, pencil on paper, have benefits as well. Although they take more time, and you've got to add everything by hand, they are easy to learn and to understand. The simple fact that you have to take the time to write things down helps tremendously in learning how the ledgers work, how they interrelate, and how to use them. Many bookkeeping teachers encourage, even demand, that their business students keep ledgers by hand, at least for a few months, because you're guaranteed to learn how ledgers work when you have to hand-post them yourself.

And with hand-posted ledgers you don't need a computer, you don't need to master any software, you don't have to worry about files that disappear, and bugs, and programs that crash, and employees that snoop. You won't have to turn on the computer every time you want to post a check.

About half the new businesses I see use hand-posted ledgers the first year, and some never see a need for anything else. The majority, however, eventually switch to computers.

This bookkeeping section is for all businesses, whether you use a computer or a pencil. The procedures are the same, the results are the same. In order for me to show you how to set up and keep your books, I have created a sample set of ledgers that are typical of both hand-posted and software bookkeeping systems.

The Ledger Section includes sample income, expenditure, credit, petty cash, inventory, equipment, depreciation and payroll ledgers, and year-end summaries that you can actually use. If you want a hand-posted system, you may photocopy the sample ledgers or copy them onto blank ledger sheets. If you use a computer, most bookkeeping programs let you choose your own column headings and categories. You can use my sample ledgers as prototypes, you can (after reading this Bookkeeping section) create your own categories, or you can stay with the default categories that come with your program.

Pencil or computer, bookkeeping is bookkeeping. Whether you arrive at your destination on a bicycle or in a limo, you'll still get there. This section of *Small Time Operator* will show you the route and explain the sights along the way.

Business Bank Account

As soon as you start your business, before you open your doors, go to the bank and open a separate business checking account. Keep your business finances and your personal finances separate. Nothing can be more confusing or cause you more trouble than mixing business with pleasure, financially.

Many states require you to have a DBA (fictitious name or assumed name statement) before you can open a bank account in your business name. Talk to your banker ahead of time and find out all the requirements. Some banks have larger service charges and require larger minimum deposits for business accounts.

There are three Important Rules to follow:

Rule One: Pay all your business bills by check. Your expenses are more easily recorded and better documented when paid by check. Some payments, of course, will have to be in cash, but keep them to a minimum. A chapter at the end of this section explains how to set up a petty cash fund for your cash payments.

Rule Two: Deposit all your income, checks and cash, into the business bank account. You will have a complete record of your earnings.

Rule Three: When you take money out of the business account for non-business or personal use, it is known as "withdrawal" or "personal draw." When you want to spend some of your hard-earned money on yourself—to meet the car payment, buy groceries, see a movie—withdraw the money from the business account by writing a check payable to yourself or payable to "cash." Then cash the check or deposit the money in your personal account. Try not to use the business account to pay personal, non-business expenses. It is too confusing (and doubles the time spent on bookkeeping) when business and personal expenses are paid from the same account.

A Few Bank Account Rules-of-Thumb:

1. Balance your bank account every month. It is too easy to make an adding error. You certainly don't want to bounce a check on your most important supplier because you thought you were down to the last ten dollars when you were really down to the last dime. Never balanced a bank account? There is a chapter in the Appendix explaining how to do it.

2. Keep your bank statements and canceled checks at least three years. They are the best documentation you have if you ever need to support your records. Three years is the normal statute of limitations set by the Internal Revenue Service for income tax audits.

3. Never write a check payable to "cash" unless it is a personal draw. Checks written to cash leave you no record of how the money was spent.

4. Expenses that are partly personal and partly business, such as automobile expenses, or rent and utilities on your home when you use part of your home for business, or your credit card bill if it includes business and non-business purchases, are partly deductible—the business portion. These expenses can be handled in one of two ways: (1) Pay these bills from your personal checking account, then post the business portion to your business ledgers (explained in the Expenditure section); or (2) Pay the bills from your business checking account; post the business portion to its proper column in the expenditure ledger, and post the non-business portion to the "Non-Deductible" column (also explained in the Expenditure section).

Joe Campbell, Resistance Repair: "My problem was that I would look in our checking account, our one and only checking account, and I'd say, Great Caesar's Ghost, there's a thousand dollars in there. Let's go buy the new tires we need for the car. And then I'd say the kids can stand to have a new pair of shoes, and I go buy them a pair of shoes. And I see we still have $700 in the bank; we're in good shape. Then all the parts bills come in, and I owe $800 worth of parts bills. And then I have to put creditors off. Having that parts money in a separate account tells you exactly where you are. And to me it's a tremendous feeling of security. It works like a charm. Plus it's emergency cash if you have to go in and get it."

Bookkeeping Simplified:
An Introduction to the Single Entry System

The ledgers in *Small Time Operator* and the ledgers in many software systems are simple "single entry" ledgers. For any transaction, only one entry is made, either to income or to expenditure. Single entry bookkeeping keeps the paperwork to a minimum while still providing you with the basic information you need to manage your business and prepare tax returns.

There are two disadvantages to this simple bookkeeping system. Single entry bookkeeping will provide a record of your income and expenditures but (if you are using hand-posted ledgers) will not provide a complete record of inventory on hand, equipment, outstanding loans or other assets and liabilities. The other drawback to single entry bookkeeping is the lack of a built-in double check of arithmetical accuracy. These disadvantages are partly offset by the additional asset records that the equipment and inventory ledgers provide, and by the Total columns in the ledgers that provide a partial math double check.

The alternative to single entry bookkeeping, the well known and elaborate system called "double entry" bookkeeping, compares to our single entry system as a fancy stereo compares to a portable cassette player. Double entry is a complete bookkeeping system that provides cross checks and automatic balancing of the books, that minimizes errors, and that transforms business bookkeeping from a part-time nuisance into a full-time occupation. In double entry bookkeeping, every transaction requires two separate entries, a "debit" and a "credit." These terms originated in double entry bookkeeping, along with the expression "balancing the books": total debits must equal total credits for the books to be "in balance."

Double entry bookkeeping is a science. It is *the* perfected bookkeeping system, and it requires a full semester in college to master. Simplicity is our goal. I find that most small businesses are better off without the refinements (and the headaches) of a double entry system.

Some bookkeeping software is programmed for full double-entry accounting; but many software systems combine the simplicity of a single-entry system with the additional entries and the math checks lacking in hand-posted ledgers.

Cash Accounting Vs. Accrual

In addition to single entry vs. double entry, you must also choose between two accounting methods: "cash" or "accrual."

"Cash method" (also called "cash basis") does not mean all your transactions are in cash. It refers to how you *record* your sales and purchases, and how you post your ledgers.

Under the cash method of accounting, income is recorded when the cash is received, and expenses are recorded when paid. (In accounting terminology, the word "cash" refers to checks and money orders as well as currency).

Credit sales for which you haven't yet been paid, and credit purchases you haven't yet paid for, do not show on cash-method ledgers. This can present an inaccurate and misleading picture of your income and expense.

Accrual accounting, by comparison, records all income and expenses whether paid or not. Credit and cash transactions are recorded when made.

Every sales and manufacturing business and any service business that stocks and sells parts is required by the IRS to use the accrual method for its inventory. These businesses can choose a full accrual system, or if it's easier for you, a hybrid system that uses the accrual system for inventory and the cash method for everything else. Small businesses with no inventory can use cash or accrual, your choice. Once a method is selected, it cannot be changed without written permission from the IRS.

For most small businesses, accrual accounting becomes a factor only at year-end. A sale made in December, for which you aren't paid until January of the new year, must be recorded on December's ledgers and becomes taxable income for the old year. When the cash is received in January, it is not part of the new year's income.

If you were instead using the cash method, the sale and the taxable income would be recorded in January when the money came in. You wouldn't pay taxes on it until a full year later!

Accruing income at year-end can be tricky if you have a contract for a large job that is partially complete at December 31. For tax purposes, the completed part of the contract must be reported as December's income, the balance as next year's income. This will probably require some estimating and guess-work on your part.

Accrued expenses at year-end, those you've incurred but not paid by December 31, become tax deductions for the year just ended, not the year paid. There is, however, a very important exception for inventory. Inventory cannot be written off until sold, regardless of when you bought it. This is covered in the Tax section, under "Cost of Goods Sold," and you should understand it thoroughly. You cannot run out at December 31, buy a truckload of merchandise, and expect to write it off immediately.

Another exception to the accrual rules are

property taxes, which cannot be deducted until paid under both cash and accrual accounting.

If you don't buy on credit or extend credit to your customers (other than credit card sales, which are handled as cash sales for bookkeeping purposes; explained later in this chapter), then all transactions are cash transactions, and the ledgers, whether you call them cash or accrual, are exactly the same. Life is simplified.

But part of the goal of *Small Time Operator* is to help simplify your life—your bookkeeping life anyway—whichever method you use. The income and expenditure ledgers can be kept by either the cash or the accrual method. And to make things easy for inexperienced bookkeepers, the posting instructions in this section are exactly the same for both methods, until year end. The year-end instructions explain how to adjust your ledgers so they are, at your choice, either cash or accrual.

This simplified system will work fine as long as you don't need precise figures at the end of each month. Since you only make your adjustments at year-end, at any time during the year the figures may be off slightly.

Corporations: Regular corporations with annual sales of $5 million or more must use accrual accounting. "Personal service corporations" operated by doctors, lawyers, engineers, architects, veterinarians, physical therapists and similar professionals, should use accrual accounting to avoid special IRS restrictions.

Defining Income

For bookkeeping and taxes, you must distinguish between "business" income and "non-business" income. Business income is what you earn from selling a product or providing a service. Only your business income is included on your income ledgers. Non-business income must be reported and taxes paid on it, but it is kept separate from your business income.

Rental income is considered business income only if you are in the rental business. All other rental income is "non-business income".

Interest income depends on its source. Interest received on loans is not business income unless you are in the business of lending money. Interest received on accounts receivable (money your customers owe you) is business income, to be included here. Interest from a bank account is non-business income, even though the business earned it, and should be reported separately.

The differentiation between business and non-business income is not just academic, not just accounting talk. Although business and non-business income are both subject to income tax, business income is also subject to self-employment tax (covered in the Tax section). Non-business income escapes self-employment tax.

"Gross income" is your total business income before any expenses. "Net income" is the income after expenses have been deducted. The income discussed here is the gross income.

Any of your own money put into the business, any money others invest in your business, and any loans received are not income to your business. You pay no taxes on this money. Do not include these amounts as part of your income.

Recording Income

Income is recorded in two steps. Step One: at the time you make a sale, record the sale on an invoice (hand written or computer generated), a cash receipt, or cash register tape. Step Two will be to summarize the sales in your income ledger.

Some software automatically combines Steps One and Two. But it is still best understood as a two-step procedure. I can't overemphasize how important it is that you understand your bookkeeping completely, which means understanding what your software is doing.

Let's first examine Step One. How you record each sale depends primarily on your volume of sales. A consultant or cabinetmaker, for example, may have only a few sales each month. For this kind of low volume activity, a special invoice can easily be prepared for each sale. Businesses with more sales often use pre-printed or computer generated receipts or invoices. A retail store with many sales will probably need a cash register.

Low Volume of Sales

If your business is of the type having only a few sales each month, you can easily prepare a special invoice for each sale.

The invoice should include: Your name or business name, address and telephone; date of sale; customer's name and address; description of sale; amount, showing any sales tax separately; a space to indicate when paid.

```
                Pinball Alley
           Box 640, Laytonville CA 95454
          We buy old Pinballs—Any Condition
                  707/984-6746

                              June 14
    INVOICE to:
    B. Bear, Laytonville

    Repair Gottlieb King Pin, 4 hours    $80.00
    2 flipper coils                       16.00
    set of rubber bands                   10.00
    bulbs                                  8.50
    sales tax on parts                     2.50
    Total                               $117.00
```

If you offer return privileges or discounts for prompt payment, these should be spelled out on your invoice. If you offer credit terms, federal law requires you to disclose, in detail, your credit terms and finance charges (see "Credit Sales").

Give the original invoice to your customer and keep a duplicate copy for your records.

Depending on your inclination and your finances, your invoices can be prepared on specially printed and custom-designed forms, or you can type the information on plain paper, or you can use your computer to produce the invoices.

Medium Volume of Sales

Most everyone is familiar with the small cash receipt books and invoice books many businesses use to record individual sales. The books contain 50 or 100 pre-numbered forms, in duplicate, one for the customer, one for you. Such books, available in any office supply store, are ideal for small businesses with more than just a few occasional sales. You can order the books with your business name custom-printed at the top, or you can purchase a rubber stamp and mark each receipt individually.

```
Sold By_____ Date _____19__

Name_____

Address _____
     REG. NO.    |   AMT. REC'D   | ACCT. FWD.
        1        |                |
        2        |                |
        3        |                |
```

Note: Don't confuse this book of cash receipts with other books labeled "Cash Receipts" that are in fact ledgers for recording income totals.

Throughout *Small Time Operator*, the terms sales slips, sales receipts, cash receipts, bills, and invoices are used interchangeably. They all refer to individual sales records. The term "statement", however, means something else to most businesses. A statement (or statement of account) is a summary of invoices and payments over a period of time. Some businesses issue statements, some don't. Most businesses don't pay from statements, so if your bill says "statement" instead of "invoice", it may not get paid.

The procedure for using cash receipts or invoices is simple. If the receipts are not pre-numbered, number them. Use a separate receipt for each sale. Make a duplicate copy of each receipt. Write the date, amount, and description of the sale. Show any sales tax separately. If this is a credit sale, write CREDIT SALE on the receipt.

Give the original receipt or invoice to your customer. Leave the duplicate in your receipt book. The duplicate copies will be summarized and posted to your income ledger.

If you void any invoice, do not throw it out. Mark it "VOID" and keep it in your receipt book. Although you should not include the voided receipt in your summary total, keep a record of it here, just so you'll know what happened to it.

Instead of a book of cash receipts, you can purchase individual two-part or three-part invoice forms from an office supply store or printer, with your name imprinted on them. These forms are used in the same way as the cash receipts.

Many computer accounting, spreadsheet and word processing programs can easily design and print invoices. The simplest programs, however, cannot prepare invoices in automatic numerical sequence. You may have to key in the invoice numbers by hand.

Large Volume of Sales

Businesses with many sales each day, convenience stores, auto parts stores, hardware stores and the like, will need a good cash register to keep track of sales. You can spend a small fortune on a new state-of-the-art cash register, or you may be able to find a good used one. Keep an eye out for businesses that are going out of business. They are often selling *everything*.

INCOME LEDGER Month of _June_

1	2	3	4	5	6	7
DATE	SALES PERIOD	TAXABLE SALES	SALES TAX	NON-TAXABLE SALES Freight	W/Sale	TOTAL SALES
1		173 24	10 39			183 63
2		217 36	13 04	7 00		237 40
3						
4						
5	3rd – 5th	577 82	34 67	18 00		630 49
6		118 71	7 12			125 83
7	closed					
8		266 94	16 02	14 19	275 00	572 15
9						

Your Name

Your Business ID

		Income Ledger	**Month of:**				June
1	2	3	4	5	6	7	8
	Sales	Taxable	Sales	Non-Taxable Sales			Total
Date	Period	Sales	Tax	Freight	Wholesale	Other	Sales
1		$173.24	$10.39				$183.63
2		$217.36	$13.04	$7.00			$237.40
3							
4							
5	3rd - 5th	$577.82	$34.67	$18.00			$630.49
6		$118.71	$7.12				$125.83
7	closed						
8		$266.94	$16.02	$14.19	$275.00		$572.15
9							

Two samples of the same income ledger. The computer version adds all the totals automatically and gives subtotals (daily, weekly, monthly, annually) anytime you want.

Recording Income, Step Two: The Income Ledger

The income ledger is a summary record of your sales invoices, cash receipts or cash register tapes. It is one of the most important business records you have. It tells you—daily, weekly if you want, monthly, and at year end—how much income you've earned and how much sales tax you've collected. It helps you manage your business by showing you the days and the months that are slow or busy so that you can better plan your expenditures, advertising, sales, even vacations. It is a guide to preparing cash flow information (cash flow and financial management are discussed at the end of this section). The income ledger also saves you time preparing your sales tax reports and income tax returns.

The sample income ledger can be used as is or adapted to your individual needs and your state's sales tax requirements.

Use a separate ledger page for each month. Each page has seven columns:

1. *Date.* You may post daily or periodically. How often you post the income ledger depends on you and the volume of sales you have.

2. *Sales period.* If you are posting daily, use the line corresponding with the date. If you are not posting daily, note the sales period here, such as "June 3rd-5th." This is explained below. This

column can also be used for any special notations you may want to make.

3. *Taxable sales*, excluding sales tax. If you do not have to collect sales tax, use this column for total sales and ignore the rest of the columns.

4. *Sales tax collected.*

5 and 6. *Non-taxable sales*. Some states require non-taxable sales to be broken down into categories, such as labor, freight, wholesale, etc.

7. *Total sales amount*, including sales tax. This column serves as a double check on your totals: the sum of the amounts in Columns 3, 4, 5 and 6 should equal the amount in Column 7.

You will be summarizing your individual sales (from Step One of Recording Income) and posting the summary totals to the income ledger.

Daily Posting

If you have a moderate or heavy volume of sales, you probably should post the income ledger daily. Add up your sales slips for the day and post your totals to the proper columns in the ledger. Compute separate totals for taxable sales (post to Column Three), sales tax (Column Four), non-taxable sales (Columns Five and Six), and total (Column Seven). No need to make any entries under Sales Period (Column Two). After you have posted the ledger, add the daily totals in Columns Three, Four, Five and Six together. They should equal the total in Column Seven, which is the grand total for the day. If you get a different amount, you will have to locate your adding error. The procedure is a lot simpler in the doing than in the explaining. You really should have no trouble getting the hang of it.

Posting Every Few Days or Once a Week

If you have only a few sales each day, you may wish to post the ledger every few days or once a week. Total all your sales for the period, keeping separate totals for taxable sales, sales tax, and non-taxable sales. Enter the totals on the line corresponding with the last day of your sales period. For example, if the sales you are combining are for June 3 through June 5, post your totals on the June 5 line. Under Sales Period (Column Two), note the period: "June 3rd-5th."

Don't feel that you must stick to one method of posting once you have started. If daily posting becomes too tedious, try posting every three days

or five days. If you post your income ledger every few days, and a very busy time comes along, switch over to daily posting for the busy period.

The posting only becomes a nightmare if the paperwork is allowed to accumulate. All of a sudden there's a three week backlog, all the receipts are mixed up, some billings are missing and, Oh, how I hate bookkeeping! It doesn't have to happen that way if you keep your ledger up to date.

How to Post Sales Returns

Sales returns, both cash and credit, should be handled as if they were negative sales:

1. Prepare a separate credit/return slip for each return, and mark it clearly "RETURN" or "REFUND" or "CREDIT MEMO."

2. Write down all the information that was on the original invoice, including the sales tax.

3. Include the return slip (credit memo, etc.) with your *current* batch of sales receipts.

4. When you add up the current receipts to post to the income ledger, subtract the amounts on the return slips from the total.

End of Month Procedure

No matter how frequently or infrequently you do your posting, run a monthly total at month-end, even though it may not be a full five or seven days since your last regular posting. Never let a posting period cross months. As with your daily or period totals, your monthly totals in Columns 3, 4, 5 and 6 should be checked against the total in Column 7.

Year-end Procedure

Record the twelve monthly totals on the year-end summary page. Cross-check your yearly totals in Columns 3, 4, 5 and 6 to Column 7 and correct any errors.

If you are keeping books on the accrual method (see the chapter Cash Accounting Vs. Accrual), that's all there is to it. No year-end adjustments are needed. You're done until next year.

When your business is still small, you think of it like a personal checkbook. Money comes in, money goes out, and if there's any left, we go out to dinner. —Business owner John Seiffer

If you are using the cash method, you must adjust your year-end total by backing off (subtracting) any credit sales that are still unpaid at year end. These are your year-end "accounts receivable". Since you haven't been paid yet for these sales, they shouldn't appear on cash ledgers. (If this doesn't make complete sense to you, go back and re-read "Cash Accounting Vs. Accrual"). Keep these unpaid sales in a separate folder. When they are paid in the new year, record them along with current new year's income.

If these cash method adjustments turn into a headache for you, or you find them too confusing, you can simplify things by not posting *any* credit sales until you receive payment. In this way your income ledger is perpetually on the cash basis, and no year-end adjustment is needed.

Altering The Ledgers

Feel free to alter the income ledger to suit your needs. Many businesses post taxable sales and sales tax (Columns 3 & 4) as one combined figure in one column, and then back off the sales tax from the monthly totals. Some businesses want a separate column for each product or group of products they sell, or for different services they provide. You may not need the non-taxable sales information (Columns 5 & 6) or you may want to re-title them. And for some businesses, the Total column may be all you want and need, period.

Filing Your Sales Receipts

Keep your sales receipts (and all other business records) at least three years. These are the source documents that support your tax returns. If your invoices are not already bound, batch and bind them monthly (staples, rubber bands, manilla envelopes) before filing them away.

Installment Sales

Installment sales, where you receive periodic payments on account, should be handled in one of two ways. If you are on the cash basis, you post your income ledger as the payments come in. If you are on the accrual basis, you post the entire amount of the sale to your income ledger when you make the sale, even though you have not yet received the money.

Under both above methods, you should also set up a record to keep track of each sale: the *full amount* of the sale, the terms agreed upon, the payments, and the balance owed. This record is kept in addition to your income ledger; installment sales are posted to both. This installment record is similar to the Credit Ledger described in this section, except that each installment sale should have its own separate page, and not lumped together with other credit sales.

Return (Bounced) Checks

If a customer's check bounces, your bank will return the check to you with an explanation. "Insufficient funds" means that there is not enough money in the customer's account to pay the check. Often, this is not an intentionally written bad check. Get in touch with your customer and find out when you can redeposit the check (better yet, ask the customer to come back and give you cash). If the check bounces a second time, the bank will not accept it a third time. Your bank will impose a service charge on you if your customer's check bounces, two charges if it bounces twice.

"Account closed" means just that. This is a bad sign. Honest people don't usually write checks on closed accounts. If the check came back from the bank marked "Stop Payment," the customer deliberately stopped payment. Stop payments are usually used when checks are lost or stolen, but sometimes a customer gets mad or changes his mind after the sale, and stops payment in order to be sure he'll get his money back. In either case, try to contact your customer, find out what happened, and get payment. "Return to maker" is a general term; usually it means the same as "insufficient funds."

One possible way to collect on a bounced check is to "put it in for collection," a procedure that is very effective when you are dealing with well-meaning customers who are always down to their last penny. You give the bounced check back to your bank and request that it be held for collection. Your bank then sends the check back to your customer's bank, which will hold the check for up to a month. If any funds are deposited to the customer's account during this holding period, any checks held for collection will be paid first. Some banks charge for this service.

If all attempts at collection prove futile, file the bounced check in a folder marked "Bad

Debts." Bad debts will be a year-end expenditure entry, explained in the expenditure ledger instructions. Make no entry in your income ledger.

Credit Sales

There is no doubt that offering credit to your customers will increase sales. "Buy Now Pay Later" has virtually replaced "In God We Trust" as America's slogan. Many, many people have come to expect, even demand, that they be allowed to buy on credit. Shoppers may not go out of their way to find a store that offers quality merchandise at low prices, but they will always be on the lookout for a store that will sell to them on credit. And they are often willing to pay higher prices for the privilege: we all know people who buy gasoline only at a station that takes their credit card, even though the gas is 5¢ cheaper at the cash-only station across the street.

There are two ways to extend credit: directly; or via credit cards such as MasterCard and VISA. This chapter is about *direct* credit, credit you extend directly to your customers. Credit cards are covered in a following chapter.

Almost all wholesale businesses extend direct credit to their business customers. Many retail stores and self-employed individuals extend direct credit to regular customers and clients.

Direct credit involves more work and bookkeeping on your part and a much larger expenditure of energy. You must decide who you will and will not extend credit to and how flexible or inflexible your credit policy will be. It is a good idea to have a formal, written credit policy that applies to all customers, although you will find,

time and again, that each customer is different and may require special handling. Any customer seeking credit should be made aware of your policy, which should clearly state (1) maximum credit allowed, (2) payment timetable, and (3) any finance charges or late charges.

Adding finance charges, late charges or interest to late payments may or may not be a good idea for your business. Customers who are always short of cash tend to give priority to bills that add finance charges. But many customers resent the implied threat, particularly when it comes from a small business where the customer knows you personally. There is something inherently unfriendly about late payment penalties.

There's an old saying, you can catch more bees with honey than with vinegar (or something like that). Rather than threatening a penalty, offer an incentive for prompt or early payment: a small discount, or free shipping, or a "special" gift. Not only will you get a better response, you will generate more goodwill with your customers. *And* you can skip the next chapter.

Federal Laws—Finance Charges

If you impose finance charges, you must abide the Federal Truth in Lending Act, Fair Credit Billing Act and Equal Credit Opportunity Act.

The Truth in Lending Act requires that all customers be told the full details of the finance charges. Before the first transaction is made on any open-end credit account (an account with no specified last payment date), the creditor (you, the merchant) must disclose in writing (1) the conditions under which a finance charge may be imposed, (2) method of determining the balance upon which a finance charge may be imposed, (3) the method of determining the amount of the finance charge, (4) the minimum periodic payment required, and (5) your customer's legal rights regarding possible errors or questions.

The Fair Credit Billing Act requires you to make prompt correction of a billing mistake. Equal Credit Opportunity prohibits discrimination against an applicant for credit on the basis of age, sex, marital status, race, religion, etc.

These acts specify what information must be presented to the customer, right down to the exact wording and size of the print, and when the information must be made available.

In addition to the above laws, you may also have to abide by the Consumer Credit Protection Act, Fair Credit Reporting Act, and Fair Debt Collection Practices Act. You can get information about all of these wonderful laws from the Federal Trade Commission, Washington, D.C. 20580.

None of the above federal laws regulate what interest you may charge your customers. Most states have usury laws that specify maximum interest, how it is to be calculated, and probably a hundred other details. Contact your state's Department of Consumer Affairs.

Credit Ledger

If you don't have a large number of credit sales, you can easily set up a credit ledger to keep track of unpaid accounts (accounts receivable). The credit ledger must be kept in addition to the income ledger. Credit sales must be posted to both. You can use the sample credit ledger page as a prototype. The ledger has six columns:

Column One: Date of sale.
Column Two: Customer's name.
Column Three: Invoice number.
Column Four: Total amount of sale (including sales tax).
Column Five: Date paid.
Column Six: Memo (for any notes you want).

Each credit sale should be recorded on a separate line on the credit ledger. Post Columns One through Four from the invoice, either when you make the sale or when you post to your income ledger. (Be sure to write the words "CREDIT SALE" on the sales receipt when you make the sale.) Post Column Five when you get paid. At any time, you can glance down your credit ledger and, by looking at Column Five, tell who still owes you money. Now, collecting that money—that's another story.

Remember, credit sales must be posted to your income ledger as well as to any credit ledger. The income ledger is your only complete record of income from all sales.

An Alternative Credit Record

An alternative to the credit ledger is to make extra copies of credit sales invoices and use them in lieu of a ledger. Order your invoices in three-part, rather than two-part forms, and use the third copy as your record of credit sales. File the third copy of all credit sale invoices in a folder marked "Unpaid." When you receive payment, pull the copy from the "Unpaid" folder and then either file it in a "Paid" folder or throw it away. Once paid, this "third copy" is an extra. There is no reason to keep it unless you want a record of paid-up customers. This method eliminates the

CREDIT LEDGER					
1	2	3	4	5	6
SALE DATE	CUSTOMER	INV. NO.	TOTAL SALE AMOUNT	DATE PAID	MEMO
1-18	Brenneman	113	53 12	2-10	
1-23	J. Ross	128	17 92		notice sent 3-1
1-24	Rygh	134	8 82	2-28	
2-12	Miley	186	10 71		

need for a credit ledger, but it involves more pieces of paper (which can be easily lost) and more expensive forms.

If you only have a two-part sales invoice (one for the customer, one for you) you should *not* put your one remaining copy in a credit file. It should stay batched with the rest of the sales receipts. If you start shuffling receipts around, some here, some there, and lose numerical control, you are just asking for trouble. The result of such haphazard bookkeeping is usually an incomplete set of records and insupportable ledgers.

Businesses that regularly make a large number of credit sales will probably need a more elaborate credit system. Stores with regular credit customers often keep a separate card on each customer with a complete record of sales and payments. Such cards can be informal or can be part of a complicated system of billings and monthly statements. For you not-so-small-time operators who need to keep close track of credit sales, there are several commercially designed systems available. Most computer bookkeeping systems also include some type of credit ledger.

You and Your Credit Customers

The hardest part of direct credit is trying to collect past-due accounts from slow or non-paying customers. I can think of no single aspect of business that is more upsetting than trying to deal with people who can't or won't pay their bills. You begin to resent the customers and they begin to resent you. Bad and sometimes bitter feelings build up. You must decide for yourself where you draw the line, where you decide that the money is no longer worth the aggravation.

In fact, extending too much credit can actually destroy a business. I know a small grocery store, owned by a nice and eager-to-please couple, that offered credit to everyone in the neighborhood.

Quite a few customers ran up large bills they couldn't pay, until the shopkeepers finally cut off their credit. The customers, unable or unwilling to face the store owners, not only didn't pay their bills, they stopped coming in the store completely. They bought their groceries elsewhere. The poor couple not only never collected on the old sales, they lost out on new sales as well. The couple went broke and the store folded. A few months later, a brand new but much wiser owner reopened the store. And, lo and behold, all the old deadbeat customers came back to shop! It wasn't the new owner's responsibility to collect the old owner's debts, this was a new business. The new owner extended limited credit to reliable customers and never let the accounts get too high or too far behind. She had the rare talent of being able to look a negligent customer right in the eye, and say, friendly yet firmly, "Pay up." And they did. And she prospered.

Posting Uncollectible Accounts

At year-end, you should review all unpaid credit sales and determine which are uncollectible. If you keep a credit ledger, write "Uncollectible" and the year in Column Six next to those accounts that are uncollectible. Add up the uncollectible accounts for the year, and record the amount in your Bad Debts folder (see the previous discussion of Return Checks). If you keep the third-part sales receipts instead of a credit ledger, pull out the uncollectible receipts from the unpaid file and mark each "Uncollectible." Add up the sales from all the uncollectible receipts. Staple the uncollectible receipts together, write the total on the front (or attach the adding machine tape), and file in your Bad Debts folder. Bad debts are a business expense computed at year-end. The procedures are explained below in The Expenditure Ledger chapters.

Only include in your list of uncollectible accounts those that you are certain are uncollectible. If you are unsure, let it ride until next year. You can write off a bad debt in any future year that it becomes definitely uncollectible.

Business is easy. You buy low and sell high. Those accountants, marketing experts, engineers and all the rest are just confusing the issues.
—R. Farmer, Indiana University

Credit Cards

Accepting credit cards such as MasterCard and VISA will eliminate most of the headaches of direct credit selling. You will not need credit ledgers, and you will never have to hound people to pay up. The banks handle all the paperwork. The fee may vary depending on your dollar volume and number of transactions a month. It usually runs 3% to 6% of the sale amount. Sometimes there is a one-time sign up fee and a fee for the imprinter, the machine that imprints the credit-card slips.

Most banks handle VISA and MasterCard sales. The sales are usually processed through your regular checking account.

You cannot apply directly to VISA or MasterCard to become a credit-card merchant. You must go through a bank, and banks are very choosy about who they will set up as credit-card merchants. Visible public operations, such as retail stores, seem to have little trouble getting credit-card merchant status. But new mail order and home businesses are often turned down. Too many fraudulent mail-order scams and shaky here-today-gone-tomorrow entrepreneurs have cost the banks too much money. If, however, you have been in business a few years or if you have a good relationship with a bank, you are more likely to be approved. Keep in mind that the banks themselves, not the credit card company, decide who gets merchant status. So if one bank turns you down, try another (and *another*).

Some businesses that are turned down by banks try to get credit-card status through third-party service bureaus, sometimes called processing centers or independent sales organizations (ISOs). Too many of these operations, however, are excessively expensive or downright fraudulent. Be very cautious of these people, especially if they want money up-front to "process" or "evaluate" your application. Find out what bank they represent and check with VISA and Master Card to find out if the ISO is properly registered. You might also join a trade or business association that offers a credit card service.

When you make a VISA or MasterCard sale, you deposit the credit tag in your bank account, just like depositing cash. The bank does the rest. They process the tags and credit your account for the amount deposited (the total amount on the credit card tags). Once a month, the bank sends a statement of activity for the month and charges your account a monthly fee—the bank's percentage of all transactions for the month.

Instead of all this paperwork, you can purchase or rent an "electronic draft capture" terminal that hooks up to your regular telephone line (no special wiring needed) and processes all credit card transactions electronically, including depositing the money in your bank account. The terminal will automatically reject any invalid card, which means you will no longer have to spend time making telephone calls for approvals. Many banks offer a lower service charge to businesses that use electronic terminals because they eliminate so much expensive paperwork.

You usually will not be responsible for unpaid credit card accounts or for stolen or invalid cards if you follow the procedures required by your bank, such as checking signatures and expiration dates, and call for required approvals. But be warned that following all the rules does not guarantee payment. If your customer refuses to pay your bill for any plausible reason, claiming that the merchandise was never received, or it was damaged, or it was returned, or never even ordered, the bank will side with the customer every time. If the dispute is not resolved to the customer's satisfaction, the bank will chargeback your account, and there is little or nothing you'll be able to do about it.

American Express credit cards are handled by mail directly by American Express, or through the same electronic terminal used for VISA and MasterCard (although the payment process is different). American Express tends to be very cooperative, even with very-small-time operators.

Debit (ATM or POS) Cards

In addition to credit cards, many retail stores accept debit cards, also known as ATM (automatic teller machine) or POS (point-of-sale) cards. This is an electronic cash transfer from your customer's bank account to yours. Merchants love debit cards because they usually have no transaction fees, and customers cannot later refuse to pay the bill as they can with credit cards.

Businesses that use an electronic terminal to process credit cards already have the necessary equipment. You need to add a PIN (personal identification number). Before a debit card can be processed, customers must enter their secret

PIN. So this payment option is best suited to businesses that deal face-to-face with customers.

Another type of card gaining acceptance is the cash card. Similar to a debit card, but without the secret PIN, cash cards are purchased for any dollar amount the customer wants on the card, and are used until the card's cash is gone. Unlike debit and credit cards, cash cards are not registered to an individual. They are just like cash, liquid and anonymous. Some banks charge merchants processing fees for cash cards.

Lara Stonebraker, Cunningham's Coffee, a retail coffee store: "We thought about having accounts for people who were in the neighborhood and then decided that was just a can of worms. We just didn't want to mess with it. It would take a lot of book work, keeping track of these accounts and what they owe and all. But we do have both MasterCard and VISA. We have to have both because people just don't carry the cash around any more. We have a $10 minimum. With the 3% they take out, it doesn't pay us to do it for smaller amounts. I think people are much more willing to spend money if they can charge it because they kind of feel they won't be billed for a long time."

Nick Mein, owner of Wallpapers Plus, a neighborhood retail store: "I don't think the credit cards are worth it. We must have had $600 of credit sales at the very most. And they take 3%, which is a lot for a mini-merchant like me. 3% does mount up. Besides, everybody has a checking account, right? I'd rather take checks than MasterCard. In my business it's easy for me to take checks because the kind of people who buy our stuff are usually fairly responsible. We've never had a bounced check."

The Expenditure Ledger

The expenditure ledger is your record of all payments: business expenses, payroll, loan repayments, personal draws (money you pay to yourself), and any other cash outlays.

The most important function of the expenditure ledger is to separate different types of expenditures. The columns in the ledger represent categories, such as inventory, supplies, rent, etc. Each expenditure must be posted to its appropriate column. For this reason, you cannot summarize a number of transactions on one line as you can with sales in the income ledger.

There are literally hundreds of different categories of expenditure on which small businesses spend their money. The Tax section of this book lists over 100 of the more typical items. But you certainly don't want to post a ledger with 100 columns, or even with 50 or 25 columns. Visions of green eyeshades, tall stool and columns and columns of numbers. Not necessary. The secret is to use only the categories you need and want.

Some categories of expenditures must have their own column because they are required to be shown separately on your income tax return. Other categories should also be listed separately because they are used repeatedly or in large dollar amounts. You will want to know where your big dollars went and so will the IRS. Occasional or small expenses can often be combined under a single title. And, of course, there is good old "miscellaneous" for the fifty bucks you loaned your brother-in-law that you know you'll never see again. (That's not really a legitimate business expense, but you get the idea.)

The sample expenditure ledger in the Ledger Section has 11 categories, specific enough to give you a good idea of how your money was spent and provide adequate information for preparing your income taxes, yet general enough to make the ledgers useful to a large variety of small businesses with little or no alteration. Although these ledger categories have worked for many businesses, they may or may not fit your particular business. Feel free to retitle columns, to add or delete columns. If you are working with a bookkeeping program, the software should include a selection of categories that are probably similar to mine, that can be kept or changed as you like.

Here is a recommended system of posting:

Payments in currency: Record the expenditure in your ledger when you make the payment. Do not put it off even a few hours; it's too easy to forget. Mark your receipts "posted" (so you'll know later on that, yes, you did post them to your ledger) and keep them in a file or envelope.

Payments by check: When you write a check, record the information in your checkbook: check number, date, amount, paid to, and a brief description of what the payment is for. Try to get an invoice or receipt for every bill you pay. Keep one copy as a record of your payment. Return or destroy duplicate copies so you won't mistakenly pay an invoice twice. Write the check number on each receipt or invoice before filing it. If there is ever a question about the bill, the check number will tell you that, yes, the bill was paid and here's the cancelled check to prove it.

If you are keeping hand-posted ledgers, you must then re-copy the information from your checkbook into the expenditure ledger. How often you sit down and copy the information depends again on you, your time schedule and the volume of checks you write. Whatever schedule you choose, stick to it. Don't get behind in the paperwork. If you are using a computer, most bookkeeping programs combine the check writing and the ledger so no recopying is necessary.

Credit card purchases: When you write a check for payment, post the business purchases to their correct columns. Post the non-business purchases to the Non-Deductible column.

Checkbook and Ledger Combined?

Probably some of you are already asking why have both a checkbook and an expenditure ledger. The expenditure ledger provides you with important information that your checkbook does not show, such as expenditures paid by currency and money order and unpaid expenses at year-end. The ledger format also makes it easy to summarize and review your important categories of expenditure. Your checkbook cannot readily show you how much you spent on inventory or parts last month, or on office supplies; it doesn't even show the total combined expenditures.

Your checkbook, on the other hand, shows your running bank balance and has space for ticking off the canceled checks, for recording void checks and adding errors, and for posting deposits.

Many computer bookkeeping systems do combine the checkbook and ledger functions. You can also buy hand-posted bookkeeping systems (often called "one-write" systems), or you can easily design your own system, that combines the expenditure ledger and checkbook. A lot of small businesses use and like them. I personally find them a bit unwieldy and just a little too complicated for people with no bookkeeping experience. The system I describe here takes more time and pencil pushing, but it is easy for a beginner to understand. Once you have mastered bookkeeping and feel comfortable with your ledgers, which

will take a few months, you will be in a better position to experiment with different methods.

Posting the Expenditure Ledger

The sample expenditure ledger in the Ledger Section is typical of many hand-posted and software systems. I suggest you try to use it as is for starters, and then modify it as you learn your way around your business and the bookkeeping.

The first column is for the date. The second column is for the check number. If you pay by currency, write "cash" in this column; if you pay by money order, write "M.O." The third column shows to whom the money was paid. This column can also be used to make any notes. The fourth column shows the total amount of the payment. This column will provide a double check of your monthly and year-end totals. Post all payments to this "Total" column and to one or more of the following detail expenditure columns:

Column One—Inventory. If you make or sell a product, this will be your most important column. Record in Column One all the goods you purchase for resale or for manufacturing, including any delivery charges. Also include all the related materials that go into or are consumed in the process of preparing your product for sale such as a jeweler's solder or a dressmaker's thread. Include packaging materials if they are an integral part of your product. If your packaging costs are only occasional or incidental, record them in Column Two. Do not include in Column One office supplies, tools, equipment or any material purchased for reasons other than resale.

Column Two—Supplies, Postage, Etc. These are expenses incidental to your work. Office supplies, paper, pencils, coffee, small tools that will not last more than a year. Do not include the supplies that become part of your product or are consumed in making your product; such expenses belong in Column One. Draws for Petty Cash should also be posted to Column Two. Petty cash is explained later in this chapter.

Column Three—Outside Contractors. Use this column for "non-employees" (see Hiring Help in the Growing Up section), independent contractors, consultants, and other individuals who are not official employees on your payroll. You can

				1	2	3	4	5	6	7	8	9	10	11
DATE	CHECK NO.	PAYEE	TOTAL	INVEN-TORY	SUPPLIES, POSTAGE, ETC.	OUTSIDE CONTRACTORS	EMPLOYEE PAYROLL	ADVERTISING	RENT	UTILITIES	TAXES & LICENSES		MISC.	NON-DEDUCT.

EXPENDITURE LEDGER

also use this column for professional services such as a bookkeeper and tax accountant.

Column Four—Employee Payroll. You must record employee payroll both here in Column Four and in a separate payroll ledger (discussed in the "Hiring Help" chapter). The separate payroll ledger must show the full detail of the payment: gross pay, amounts withheld, and net pay. Column Four, however, should show only the net pay, the actual amount of the payroll check (the employee's take-home pay).

Payroll taxes that you withhold from your employees are also recorded in Column Four, but only at the time you pay them to the government. Withheld taxes include federal income, Social Security, Medicare, state income and possibly state disability. You should not confuse these withheld payroll taxes with payroll taxes that you, the employer, are required to pay, such as employer's portion of Social Security and Medicare, and federal and state unemployment taxes. Employer-paid payroll taxes are posted to Column Eight—Taxes and Licenses. This is a confusing area because the employees' and employer's taxes are reported to the government on the same form and paid with the same check.

Payments to yourself should not be recorded here unless you have incorporated and are an owner-employee of your corporation. As a sole proprietor, a partner in a partnership, or an owner of a Limited Liability Company, your own "wage" is not an expense of your business, and should be posted to Column 11—Non Deductible.

Column Five—Advertising. You can include promotion expenses, such as brochures and business gifts, in this column or give them a separate column.

Column Six—Rent. Rent on business property is fully deductible except for some lease-purchase contracts. If you own the building your business occupies, you must depreciate the building (covered in the Tax section).

Home-based businesses: Rent on an office, workshop, studio or other business space in the home is deductible only if it meets strict IRS requirements, covered in the Home Business Section. If you do qualify, you then determine what percentage of your home is used for business. The percentage must be based on the amount of space devoted to business. For example, if one room out of five, or 20% of your home, is used for business, 20% of your rent expense can be charged to your business. You can pay your home rent from your personal checking account or from your business checking account; but only the business portion is posted as a business expense in Column Six. The personal portion is not deductible (either post to Column Eleven or do not post at all).

Column Seven—Utilities. Power, water, garbage, heating oil or propane, etc. Your telephone expenses can be included in this column or given their own column.

Home-based businesses: The business portion of your utilities is the same percentage as the business portion of your home (see Column Six above). If you are not eligible for a home office deduction, you also cannot deduct home utilities. Home business owners should also read "Telephones and Tax Deductions" in the Home Business Section. If part of your home business phone is not deductible, only include the deductible portion here.

Column Eight—Taxes and Licenses. Record any tax payment or license fee here except withheld payroll taxes (see instructions under Column Four). Be sure to note in the "Paid To" column what the payment is for; you will need this information for your income tax return.

Regarding sales tax: the only sales tax that should be posted to Column #8 is the amount you remit to the state, collected from your sales. Any sales tax you pay when purchasing supplies, tools or anything else should be included as part of the price of the goods purchased. For example, if your business cards cost $40.00 plus $2.40 sales tax, you should enter $42.40 in Column #2. Nothing should be entered in Column #8.

Column Nine—is blank. I cannot possibly foresee all your needs, so here is one extra untitled column to use or not to use as you see fit.

Column Ten—Miscellaneous. The ol' catch-all. For unusual expenditures and expenditures that do not recur enough to justify their own column. For example, this column might include: Payments for insurance. Dues and organization fees. Out-of-town travel. Education expenses. Minor repairs. Entertainment. Interest (repayment of a loan principal should be posted to Column Eleven—Non-Deductible). A more detailed list of items to post to Column Ten can be found in the Tax section.

Any expense that you are posting to Column Ten that starts to recur regularly should be moved to its own column. Use Column Nine or another column you are not using. Feel free to change the heading of any column in the ledger to suit your needs.

Column Eleven—Non-Deductible. Use this column for:

1. Personal draws—money you pay yourself.

2. Furniture, tools, equipment, machinery, buildings and other fixed (depreciable) assets. These expenses *are* deductible, but may have to be depreciated over a period of years. Some people post these asset to the Miscellaneous column; some set up a separate column just for fixed assets. But whatever column you use, these purchases should also be recorded on the Depreciation Worksheet/Equipment Ledger in the Ledger Section. Depreciation and the depreciation worksheet are explained in the Tax section.

3. Repayment of business loans—principal only. A loan is not income when received and is not an expense when paid. Any interest paid on a business loan *is* a valid expense and should be

posted to Column Ten.

4. Fines or penalties for breaking the law, including traffic tickets. These may be "valid" business expenses, but they are not deductible for income taxes. Contractual or other fines or penalties (if you did not violate state or federal law) are deductible.

5. Accounts Payable. This relates to year-end adjustments to bring your ledgers up to full accrual. Explained at the end of this chapter.

6. If you write a check on your business account for personal, non-business expenses, or if you write a check for something that is part personal and part business, the non-business portion is not deductible and should be posted here. The business portion is fully deductible (unless it is one of the exceptions covered here or in the Tax section of the book) and should be posted to its appropriate column.

Uncashed Checks

If a check you write is never cashed, lost in the mail, or stop payment issued, make a negative (bracketed) entry in your expenditure ledger, reducing the expense. Under "Payee" make a note of what you are doing. Also go back to the original entry and note there what happened and the date you posted the negative entry.

Recording Vehicle Expenses

There are two ways to record car and truck expenses. You may keep track of actual expenses, or you can take a Standard Mileage Allowance (also called the Standard Mileage Rate). The Vehicle Expenses chapter in the Tax section explains both methods. If you decide to take the Standard Mileage Allowance, you do not have to make any entries in your expenditure ledger until year-end. If you plan to keep track of actual expenses, you should record all vehicle expenses as they are incurred. Use Column Nine in your expenditure ledger to record these expenses. Note that the cost of the vehicle and any major repairs should not be included in Column Nine. These costs may have to be depreciated along with other fixed assets (see Column Eleven above and the Depreciation chapter in the Tax section). If you use the Standard Mileage Allowance, however, you do not depreciate your vehicle.

Monthly Totals

As with the income ledger, total all the columns of your expenditure ledger each month. Cross-check the monthly totals to the Total column, and correct any errors. Do not, however, start a new expenditure ledger page for each new month. If a month ends and only half a page is used, double-underline your total, skip two lines and start the next month on the same page.

Year-End Procedures

You must make several year-end ledger entries. None are difficult. The Year-End Expenditure Summary in the ledger section has been designed to help you post the year-end entries.

Step One: Post the monthly totals in their proper columns to the summary sheet.

Step Two: This step is only for people using accrual accounting. People using the cash method of accounting can skip to Step Three. People who are unsure what I am talking about should re-read the chapter Cash Accounting Vs. Accrual.

This step is the adjustment to bring your books up to full accrual. You will recall that under accrual accounting, all expenses are recorded whether paid or not. Throughout the year, for ease in posting, only the paid expenses have been recorded. So now you must post any unpaid bills to your ledger. List the bills individually, one to a line, and post to the appropriate columns. As you record each unpaid bill, clearly mark it "ACCOUNTS PAYABLE." Any other unpaid expense for the year just ended, such as payroll taxes, should also be recorded on this year-end summary, one to a line, even if you have not received a bill.

Step Three: Add up the Total column and Columns #1 through #11. Cross-check your totals: the sum of the totals in Columns #1 through #11 should equal the total in the Total column.

Step Four: For accrual accounting, total the return (bounced) checks and the uncollectible credit accounts in your Bad Debts folder (discussed earlier in this section) and post in the Total column. If, however, you are using the cash method, include the bounced checks but do not include any unpaid credit sales.

Step Five: If you use the Standard Mileage Allowance for vehicle expenses (covered in the Tax section), calculate vehicle expense on this summary sheet and post to the Total column.

Step Six: If you take depreciation, record the depreciation expense from the depreciation worksheets (discussed in the Tax section) in the Total column. If your accountant figures your depreciation for you, just skip this step.

Your work is done.

Accounts Payable

Accounts payable, or "payables", are unpaid bills and unpaid accounts that you owe, and expenses you've incurred but haven't yet been billed for.

This Accounts Payable chapter is for accrual method businesses only. Cash method businesses can skip to the next chapter.

The accounts payable that you posted to the Year-End Expenditure Summary require special handling when paid next year. These expenses are deductible the year they were incurred, which is the year just ended. They may not be deducted again next year, even though they will be paid next year. When the bills are paid (you will recognize them because you marked them "ACCOUNTS PAYABLE" when you posted them to the summary) they must be posted to Column Eleven—Non-Deductible.

Altering the Ledgers and Designing Your Own

After a year's experience with these ledgers, learning which categories of expense you need and don't need, you can easily design your own hand or computer ledgers. Do you need the Outside Contractor column, or the Payroll column, or the Advertising column? Instead, maybe you want a separate column for equipment purchases, or for freight charges, or travel, or some other category important to your business. Many small businesses set up their expenditure ledger to exactly match the categories on the income tax forms. For my own business, I try to use as few columns as possible to minimize my book work; and yet I've met business owners who felt they had to have 16 columns to keep their expenditures straight.

You can make inexpensive hand-posted ledgers using accounting ledger paper (also called accountants' work sheets), available in any office supply store. The ledger paper usually comes in 50-sheet pads and with anywhere from two to 25 columns, and is designed to go in three-ring binders.

Ledgers get a lot of use and abuse. The loose leaf ledgers do not hold up well, the pages tear out easily and the ledgers are often awkward to work with. If you can afford a higher quality ledger, purchase a heavy duty cam-lock post binder and heavy duty ledger sheets. And, of course, all varieties of commercial ledgers and prepackaged bookkeeping systems are available.

Petty Cash

A petty cash fund provides a systematic method for paying and recording out-of-pocket cash payments and payments too small to be made by check. ("Cash" in petty cash refers to currency, *not* to checks; which is just the opposite of my earlier definition. Nobody's perfect.)

I suggest, for starters, that you do not have a petty cash fund. It's more bookkeeping, more paperwork, more procedures to remember. Pay the nickel-and-dime expenditures out of what cash is on hand, and record them directly and immediately in your expenditure ledger. Any respectable accountant would roll over in his subsidiary ledgers, so to speak, if he heard me say this, because the absence of a petty cash fund can result in poor cash control, increasing the possibility of incomplete records and "misappropriation" (that means theft) of funds. But if yours is a one person business or if you alone have access to the money, the importance of cash control is outweighed, I feel, by the need for a simple set of books.

If a petty cash fund is what you want or need, I have devised a relatively simple system for handling petty cash. It is a compromise between no system at all and a bookkeeper's dream, and it requires you to follow three rules. 1. Keep no more than $50 in the fund (or $20, or whatever seems a reasonable amount to you). 2. Make payments out of the fund only for miscellaneous supplies and postage, expenses that normally would be posted to Column 2 in the expenditure ledger. 3. Use the fund only when there is no practical way to write a check instead.

If you promise to follow those ground rules here is the procedure:

1. Write a check payable to "Petty Cash" for $50 (or $20). Cash the check at your bank and put the money, a piece of accounting worksheet paper and a pencil in a separate cash box or cigar box, whatever is handy and relatively safe.

2. Record the check as an expenditure in your ledger, posting it to Column 11, Non-Deductible.

3. Every time you make a payment from the petty cash fund, record the date, payee and amount on your accounting worksheet, which has just become your petty cash ledger. Get receipts for the payments if possible and put them in the box with the cash.

4. When the fund starts to get low, total the payments recorded on the worksheet, and add up the remaining cash in the box. The worksheet total and the remaining cash should equal the

Petty Cash Ledger

1	2	3	4
Date	Payee	Amount	Balance
3/1	(Beginning balance)		$50.00
3/12	Stamps	$12.50	$37.50
3/16	C.O.D. charge	$12.75	$24.75
3/17	Office Supplies	$6.99	$17.76
3/20	donation to Boy Scouts	$4.00	$13.76
3/31	coffee for the machine	$5.29	$8.47

amount that was originally in the fund ($50 or $20). If you are out of balance, you either made an adding error, recorded a payment wrong, failed to record a payment, or else you've been robbed. If you can't find an error, adjust the worksheet total so that your petty cash fund is back in balance. Staple all the petty cash receipts to the worksheet and file it away.

5. Write a check payable to "Petty Cash" equal in amount to the total (or the corrected total if there was an error) from the worksheet. Cash the check and put the money in your petty cash box with a new worksheet. Sharpen the pencil.

6. Record the check in the expenditure ledger in Column Two—Supplies, Postage, Etc. Thereafter, whenever your petty cash fund gets low, and also at year-end, repeat steps #4, 5 and 6.

Calculators and Adding Machines

A pocket calculator is an excellent business tool. It can be carried around with you and it will give you instant answers. If you are often computing package deals or bulk prices, figuring discounts, sales tax, etc., a good pocket calculator will be indispensable to you.

But when it comes to posting ledgers, adding columns of figures, balancing bank accounts or any typical business activity involving the addition or subtraction of more than just a few numbers, the pocket calculator leaves much to be desired. Most of the calculators are very small, and their keyboards are tiny. It is easy, *too easy*, to make an adding mistake. Punch a 6, and your finger strays onto the 5. Try this: get out your calculator and add a column of 25 numbers. Note your answer, and then add the numbers a second time. Got two different answers, didn't you? Happens to me all the time. Now, which amount is correct? Here lies another problem inherent in the little calculators. There is no way to check your figures, no tape to look at.

An adding machine tape is indispensable for checking your totals, locating errors and keeping a record of your calculations. A tape will also help you when you are interrupted in the middle of a column of numbers, and what *was* the last number you entered?

Here are some guidelines when shopping for a ten-key adding machine:

1. Buy a machine with a large, easy to operate keyboard, one well-spaced to accommodate your hand, allowing maximum speed and minimum error. If the machine includes a digital display, try to find one with an LED display (real lights, usually green) instead of an LCD or liquid crystal display (the silvery and often dim-looking numbers that are difficult to read in bright light).

2. Adding machines vary in the number of digits they can handle. Select one with at least an eight-digit capacity.

3. Your machine should be able to print negative (minus) numbers and balances in red so they will stand out easily.

Financial Management: Using Your Ledgers

Your books are more than just a record of your business activity and an aid to preparing income tax forms. They are valuable tools to help you manage your business successfully.

Profit-and-Loss Analysis

Without a schedule of profit and loss, it is difficult for the owner of even the smallest business to determine whether or not the business is making a profit. Your cash balances and the day-to-day cash income and outgo, as important as they are, are not a good indication of profit or loss. Cash flow can, in fact, give you a totally misleading picture of how your business is doing.

Simple profit and loss statements (also called income or break-even point statements), prepared monthly from your ledgers, can tell you a great deal about your business. A profit and loss statement is, basically, a schedule showing your income and your expenses and the difference between the two. Here is a procedure for preparing a very simple profit and loss statement:

Income. The income on the statement is the monthly income total from your income ledger (Columns #3, #5 and #6). You should exclude sales tax, loan income and any money you put into the business from your own personal funds.

Expenses. Expenses should be separated into two groups: inventory (Column #1 in the expenditure ledger) and all other expenses (Columns #2 through #10). Do not include Column #11.

If you have inventory, you must estimate the cost of the inventory on hand at the end of the month. If it is only an insignificant amount, you can ignore it. The inventory on hand at the beginning of the month *plus* the current month's

Profit & Loss Statement

Bear Soft Pretzel Company

January through September

	Month of September		Year-to-Date	
Income from ledger		$2,095		$13,724
Beginning inventory	$900		$310	
Purchases	$1,230		$6,710	
	$2,130		$7,020	
Estimated inventory				
30-Sep-1992	($1,000)		($1,000)	
Cost-of-goods-sold		$1,130		$6,020
Gross Profit		**$965**		**$7,704**
Other expenses				
Rent	$50		$450	
Supplies	$13		$74	
Other			$27	
Total Other Expenses		$63		$551
Net Profit		**$902**		**$7,153**

purchases from Column One, *less* your estimate of inventory on hand at the end of the month gives you your actual current inventory expense. This expense is called "cost-of-goods- sold" and is covered in greater depth in the Tax section.

"All other expenses" are your operating expenses and include everything in Columns Two through Ten except sales tax paid (recorded in Column Eight—Taxes and Licenses). Be sure not to include any expenditures from Column Eleven—Non-Deductible.

Your income *less* the cost-of-goods-sold (inventory expense) gives you what is known as "gross profit." Gross profit *less* all the other expenses gives you your "net" profit or loss. By showing both a gross and a net profit or loss, you can tell more easily how your expenses relate to income. If you are losing money, you can readily determine if it is the cost of the inventory (cost-of-goods-sold) or the other expenses that are responsible for the loss. A service business that has no inventory does not have to compute cost-of-goods-sold or gross profit. For such a business, income less "all other expenses" equals net profit or loss.

A statement prepared in the above manner will give you profit and loss information for the month just ended. Some business owners like to see a second column in their profit and loss statements that shows the year-to-date cumulative activity. The year-to-date column is prepared in almost the same way as the monthly column. Year-to-date income is the sum of all the monthly income totals in Columns #3, 5 and 6 from January 1 to date, including the month just ended.

Cost-of-goods-sold is slightly different. It is the inventory on hand at January 1st, plus the sum of all the monthly totals in expenditure ledger Column One, less the same ending inventory that you estimated for the monthly column. "All other expenses" is the sum of all the monthly totals in Columns Two through Ten (again excluding sales tax payments in Column Eight).

Your profit and loss statement should look

something like the Bear Soft Pretzel Co. illustration. This type of profit and loss statement is only approximate. It does not include unpaid expenses or expenses computed at year-end such as depreciation, and it should not be used for preparing income tax forms.

CASH FLOW

One of the most damaging things that can happen to a business is a cash shortage. Here you are with a successful business, tons of customers, and no cash. Whoa! How did that happen? I know of profitable businesses actually forced to shut down for a lack of immediate cash.

To help avoid a sudden cash squeeze, many businesses prepare monthly "cash flow projec-

tions." Cash flow projections are estimates of cash that will be coming in and cash that must be spent during the upcoming month. These projections show approximately how much cash will be on hand during the month and alert you to possible cash shortages.

During the first few months your business is in operation, cash projections will be difficult for you to make. You cannot yet estimate how much income will be coming in nor will you be familiar enough with your regular expense requirements. But the first few months are a critical time for any business. You should make some attempt to estimate and be prepared for cash needs. Here is a way to project your first month's cash flow:

First determine how much cash you will need to get your business off to a good start.

Estimated Cash Flow Projection

Month of June

	Cash In	Cash Out	Balance
Cash on hand June 1........			$800
June 1 rent payment........		$250	
June 1 utilities..........		20	$530
Receipts first week........	$500		
Inventory purchase 1st week		$500	
Supplies first week........		30	$500
Receipts second week.......	$500		
Payroll second week........		$200	$800
Receipts third week........	$500		
Supplies third week........		$50	$1,250
Receipts fourth week.......	$500		
Payroll fourth week........		$200	
Inventory purch. 4th week..		500	
Personal draw.............		400	$650
Cash on hand June 30.......			$650

If yours is a sales or manufacturing business or a service business that stocks parts, estimate how much additional inventory you will need during the first month of business.

Next, add expenses that must be paid during the first month, such as supplies and payroll, and those that must be paid by the first of the next month, such as rent and utilities. Be sure to include your own wage or draw. Then add another 20% for unanticipated expenses.

The sum of the above items should give you an estimate of your first month's expenses. Now, how much income do you anticipate during the first month of operation? Obviously, this can only be a guess, but be conservative. And once you've arrived at a good guess, knock it down by 25%. All new business owners are over-optimistic.

Comparing the "guess-timated" income to the projected expenses will give you some idea of your cash needs. It is a very rough idea, admittedly; but it is better than no idea at all. Once you have a few months' actual experience behind you, cash flow projections will become easier and more accurate. A good procedure is to estimate income and expenditures week by week, showing the cash on hand at the end of each week.

The main purpose of a cash flow statement is to warn you *in advance* when cash might get dangerously low. If you know of a big cash outlay coming up next month, such as a loan payment or a tax payment, or a predictable seasonal drop in sales, the cash flow statement will show you whether your regular income will provide enough cash to meet expenses.

If the statement predicts a cash shortage, you can plan in advance to avoid the problem. Postpone a payment that is not immediately necessary, or plan a sale to generate more income, or seek a short-term loan. Banks are usually willing to loan short-term funds (usually thirty days or sixty days) to profitable businesses. What's more, the fact that you have actually prepared a cash flow statement indicates to a banker that you are knowledgeable about your business and, therefore, a better risk than someone who has no financial knowledge at all.

You can count all the grains of sand on the beach, and still find you're on the wrong beach.
—*Business owner Geoffrey D. Batrouney*

INVENTORY CONTROL

Any business that sells or manufactures goods and any service business that stocks parts must have some sort of inventory control, some way of knowing what has been ordered, what is on hand, and when it's time to reorder. For a very small business or one selling only a small variety of items, the inventory purchase records in your expenditure ledger (Column One) and your day-to-day observations of the stock on hand will probably provide you with all the information you need to maintain adequate inventory control. A periodic count, or "inventory," is the easiest and quickest way to determine what is still on hand and what must be reordered. (In business jargon, "inventory" is both a noun and a verb).

Larger businesses and those selling a large selection of merchandise will need more formal procedures for controlling inventory. Such businesses should maintain a record of all stock ordered, received and sold. "Perpetual inventory" records, as they are called, can be kept on index cards, one card for each type of item in stock, or in inventory ledgers, with a ledger page for each different item. Both the cards and the ledgers have the same format. An up-to-date and accurate inventory record can tell you at a glance your balance on hand, what is still on order, and how long it takes to receive an order.

How to Keep an Inventory Record

When you place your order, record the quantity and the date of the order in the Ordered column. When you receive the order, line out the entry in the Ordered column and enter the information in the Received column. Posting the date received will give you an idea how long it takes your suppliers to send you an ordered item. If you receive only part of your order, record the undelivered back-ordered quantity and the original order date in the Ordered column.

On the sample inventory record, 50 silver buckles were ordered on January 31. A partial shipment of 35 arrived February 13. The back-ordered 15 buckles finally arrived on March 1. The number of items sold should be recorded when the sale is made or at the end of the day, summarized from the day's sales slips.

At least once a year and preferably every six months the perpetual records should be "proven"

INVENTORY RECORD

Item *#3 Silver Buckle*   Supplier *L. J. Silver Co.*

DATE ORDERED	QUANTITY ORDERED	DATE REC'D.	QUANTITY REC'D.	QUANTITY SOLD	BALANCE ON-HAND
1-31	50				0
		2-13	35		35
				13	22
				4	18
		3-1	15		33
				10	23
3-12	50				23

(verified) by taking a physical count. If there is a discrepancy, the records should be adjusted to agree with the count. If the difference is substantial, you know something is wrong. Either you have not been updating the records correctly, or your inventory is being stolen.

Inventory control, like cash flow, is a management tool only. It is meant to help you run your business. The methods I have described for inventory control are only suggestions. Feel free to alter or ignore them. Any system or non-system that works for you is probably a good one.

Computer Inventory Control Programs

Businesses with large or varied inventories have found computer inventory programs extremely useful; some say essential. Computer inventory records should look similar to the hand-posted ledgers shown here, and they should provide you with *exactly* the information you need. Shop around for a program that meets your needs. Computer inventory records should be verified by taking physical counts on a regular basis, just like hand-posted records; a computer record is just as likely to be incorrect.

Joe Campbell, Resistance Repair: "Here's one example of not running a service business like a regular business. For years I've had parts around, and I'd use one of them and I'd say, 'I think these things cost about 50¢, so I'll charge 65¢ for them.' But it wasn't at all consistent. I had absolutely no idea how much I was spending for parts. If you get back only what you paid for it, you've lost money. Because it's taken time to order it, write the check for it, put it into stock, keep track of it and pay taxes on it.

"Now, I've got a little plastic box for every part that I stock. Inside that box is the part and a card telling me where I got it, what the number is, what I paid for it. We use a uniform markup: 100%. We're selling things that cost us 30¢. If we sell them for 40% more, for 42¢, that hasn't even paid for hassling the things.

"Every week when we tally up the income, we break it down into parts and labor. And we get separate totals. We have a separate checking account and we take 60% of the parts income total and deposit it into the parts account.

"This way, we'll be able to replace the part and have 10% left over. It gives a little bit of wiggle room. Plus we know exactly how much money we've got to buy parts with. It's very simple, it's very efficient, and it works."

Section Three
GROWING UP

Most people would succeed in small things
if they were not troubled with great
ambitions.

—Longfellow

Growing Up

"LEARN the many different methods and little known techniques used today by experienced businessmen in building small companies into Powerful Places in Industry." —*from the cover of another book on starting a business.*

Well, maybe John D. Rockefeller did start with a two-pump filling station and some spectacular ambitions. After all, bigger and better has been a trademark of this big country of ours for as long as most of us can remember. For years we have associated big business, big industry, big government with prosperity, happiness and the good life.

But today it seems that America's "powerful places in industry" are just too powerful, and they are choking, not helping, our economy. In the last few years we have witnessed huge corporations laying off thousands of employees without warning; other corporations doubling and tripling their prices, and their profits, with us apparently powerless to stop them; big city governments unable to pay their bills, on the verge of financial collapse. Bigger is no longer synonymous with better, and big business no longer seems to be able or willing to provide us a good way of life.

Small Time Operator is not going to be much help to those Rockefellers among you with dreams of building your business into "powerful places in industry." I feel that small business can offer you personal satisfaction and a good livelihood. But "small" does not have to mean that you are forever the one person business, unable to grow. Nothing in this world is intrinsically good or bad. Business growth can be a positive and pleasant experience for everyone concerned. Business growth, however, can also be mistimed and miscalculated, turning against you and doing you in.

Very often a business expands because a situation presents itself that the owner "just can't pass up": the adjacent store-front becomes vacant, and the landlord offers to knock out the separating partition and rent both stores to you; a competitor is failing and offers to sell his business to you, cheap. Or it may be that your customers have been encouraging expansion, suggesting that you offer some related product or service. And as frequent a reason for expansion as any, you're out to catch a bigger fish; success in your present business is tempting you on to bigger and better success (bigger and better?).

You should put in some real thinking time before making a decision about expanding.

1. Just as your present business was slow going at first, maybe even losing money, the expanded business will take time to get on its own feet. You will probably be making less money for a while, possibly even losing money for a year or two. Are you prepared for a repeat of the early, lean days?

2. Expansion is going to require more capital. It means investing your savings or borrowing.

3. If you plan to acquire a second business location, be prepared for a major increase in the amount and type of work you will have to do. Someone will have to be hired to run one of the stores for you, and suddenly you will find yourself not only buyer, seller, bookkeeper, market analyst and the rest, but manager also. Some real skills are required to manage a multi-store operation, not the least of which is being able to deal with employees: hiring, training, delegating authority and responsibility, and sometimes firing.

4. The paperwork—bookkeeping, payrolls, forms—will just about double. How well do you handle it now?

5. Your own leisure time away from business will be reduced, possibly eliminated.

He is well paid that is well satisfied.
  —Shakespeare from Merchant of Venice

A re-warning about financial commitments: in the eyes of the law, you and your unincorporated business are one and the same. Any liabilities of your business are also personal ones.

Hugo said, "Caution is the eldest child of wisdom." Think this decision through. Don't let any outside factors lure you into a move that you aren't ready for. Whether you choose to stay small or take a chance on expansion, be totally satisfied that you have made the right decision.

This Growing Up section covers hiring help, partnerships, corporations, and Limited Liability Companies (LLCs).

Hiring Help—How to Save Time and Money By Not Becoming an Employer

Hiring employees will just about double the amount of your paperwork. As an employer, you must keep separate payroll records for each employee; withhold federal income, Social Security and Medicare taxes; withhold state income and possibly other state taxes; prepare quarterly and year-end payroll tax returns; pay employer's portion of Social Security and Medicare taxes and unemployment taxes; purchase workers' compensation insurance; and prepare year-end earnings statements for each employee. It's been estimated that the employer's taxes, worker's compensation insurance and paperwork will cost you an additional 30% of your payroll. In other words, if you pay a wage of $7.00 per hour, it's really costing you about $9.00.

Businesses hiring employees are also more closely regulated than one-person businesses. The IRS and the states demand prompt payroll tax returns and require strict adherence to employment laws. If you are late filing your payroll tax return, if you don't pay the employment taxes when due, the IRS is likely to move very quickly. Whenever you hear about the IRS padlocking a business and impounding the bank account, it's usually because of unpaid payroll taxes. And the penalties are severe.

I'm comfortable taking one step at a time, getting it right, then moving on. I don't like thinking big. You'll never get hurt by taking a small step, making sure the ground is firm, then taking the next step. I got big by thinking small.
—Restaurant-chain owner Richard Melman

Independent (Outside) Contractors

Some small businesses can sometimes get outside help without hiring employees. These businesses often hire independent contractors, also called outside contractors: "Outside" refers to being from outside your business. It has nothing to do with working out of doors.

Independent (or outside) contractors are in business for themselves, people who sell their services to you. When you hire an independent contractor, you pay the contractor his or her fee in full. You do not withhold taxes, pay employment taxes or file payroll tax returns.

Who is an independent contractor? The IRS says, "Generally, people in business for themselves are not employees. [Individuals] in an independent trade in which they offer their services to the public are usually not employees."

A key determining point, as far as the IRS is concerned: Does the person perform service for more than one business? A person working solely for you is usually your employee. A person providing services to several businesses is probably an independent contractor. Independent contractors usually have DBAs, business licenses, business cards, a business bank account, printed invoice forms, their own office, their own tools and equipment, a set of ledgers, and similar indications of being self-employed. Independent contractors are basically small business owners, just like the businesses hiring them.

Who is an employee?

The IRS is more likely to consider a person your employee and not an independent contractor if the individual: (1) Uses your tools, materials and equipment instead of his or her own; (2) Receives on-the-job training; (3) Does the work on your premises; (4) Must follow hours that you set; (5) Works specifically according to your instructions; (6) Hires or supervises your workers; (7) Receives health insurance, sick pay, vacation pay, or similar employee benefits.

The IRS has 20 factors they use to determine employee vs. contractor. The factors I covered above, however, are the most important ones.

Here are two hypothetical examples to help illustrate employees vs. non-employees:

Example 1: The Clever Leather Company (that's you) needs help making belts. You want someone to cut the leather into two inch wide strips so you can devote your talent to the design work. You hire your buddy for $8.00 an hour, sit him down in your shop, and tell him to cut out 250 two-inch wide belts, each three feet long.

The Clever Leather Company has just become a bona-fide employer. When you pay your friend, you must withhold income, Social Security and Medicare taxes, send the withheld taxes to the government, pay employer Social Security, Medicare and unemployment taxes, keep payroll ledgers, prepare year-end earnings statements. Ugh.

Example 2: The More Clever Than Ever Leather Company (that's me) needs help making belts. I want someone to cut the leather into two-inch wide strips so I can devote my talent to the design work. I call up the Leather Cutting Company (that's *my* buddy) and order up 250 of his standard 2" wide, 3' long belts. The Leather Cutting Company produces the belts on its own work schedule and delivers the completed order to me.

The More Clever Than Ever Leather Company just conducted business with an independent contractor. More Clever Than Ever Leather wrote a check for the full amount billed and recorded it in the expenditure ledger.

Seriously, it is important that you carefully determine the legal status of your hired help. A person who falls within the definition of an employee is an employee no matter what you call him. Says the IRS: "If an employer-employee relationship exists, it does not matter what it is called. The employee may be called a partner, agent or independent contractor. It also does not matter how payments are measured or paid, what they are called, or whether the employee works full or part-time."

If you are still unsure how to classify your worker, you can request a formal "Determination of Employee Work Status" from the IRS on form #SS-8. Not many businesses file this request because the IRS nearly always rules that workers are employees.

Contracting With Your Contractor

When hiring someone you plan to pay as an independent contractor, it is also important that the person fully understands what you are doing: that he or she is not your employee, that he considers himself in business for himself, that he knows he is responsible for his own taxes and insurance and Social Security, and that he will not be eligible for unemployment insurance when the job is finished. I suggest a signed contract with the contractor, clearly defining the work and the legal relationship.

Many small businesses have gotten into expensive trouble with the federal and state government because former "independent contractors" (who really should have been paid as employees) complained to the IRS when they were turned down for unemployment insurance or fined for not paying their own Social Security.

There is another and much more serious problem if you hire people and treat them as independent contractors when the law says they should be employees. If one of these people gets injured on the job and is not covered by workers' compensation insurance, you could find yourself with medical bills and a large lawsuit.

"If we don't have it you're out of luck."
    —sign on a tiny general store in the middle of nowhere, Branscomb, California

"If it's in stock, we have it."
    —sign in farm supply store, Ukiah, California

PAYER'S name, street address, city, state, and ZIP code

MONKEYWRENCH MOTORS
7831 Claremont Avenue
Berkeley CA 94705

1 Rents $

2 Royalties $

3 Prizes, awards, etc. $

OMB No. 1545-0115

Miscellaneous Income

| PAYER'S Federal identification number | RECIPIENT'S identification number | **4** Federal income tax withheld | **5** Fishing boat proceeds |
| 123-45-6789 | 987-65-4321 | $ | $ |

Copy A

For Internal Revenue Service Center

RECIPIENT'S name

Crystal Rose

6 Medical and health care payments $

7 Nonemployee compensation $ 5,650

File with Form 1096.

Street address (including apt. no.)

485 Buena Vista

8 Substitute payments in lieu of dividends or interest $

9 Payer made direct sales of $5,000 or more of consumer products to a buyer (recipient) for resale ▶ ☐

For Paperwork Reduction Act Notice and instructions for completing this form, see **Instructions for Forms 1099, 1098, 5498, and W-2G.**

City, state, and ZIP code

San Francisco CA 94117

10 Crop insurance proceeds $

11 State income tax withheld $

Account number (optional)

2nd TIN Not. ☐

12 State/Payer's state number
CA--same

Form **1099-MISC**

Cat. No. 14425J

Department of the Treasury - Internal Revenue Service

File a 1099-MISC for every outside contractor who received $600 or more during the year and for outside sales people who purchased $5,000 or more in goods from you.

Form **1096**

Department of the Treasury
Internal Revenue Service

Annual Summary and Transmittal of U.S. Information Returns

OMB No. 1545-0108

ATTACH IRS LABEL HERE

FILER'S name
Monkeywrench Motors

Street address (including room or suite number)
7831 Claremont Avenue

City, state, and ZIP code
Berkeley CA 94705

Name of person to contact if the IRS needs more information
Samuel Thesham
Telephone number
(510) 555-1212

For Official Use Only

If you are not using a preprinted label, enter in box 1 or 2 below the identification number you used as the filer on the information returns being transmitted. Do not fill in both boxes 1 and 2.

| **1** Employer identification number | **2** Social security number 123-45-6789 | **3** Total number of forms 1 | **4** Federal income tax withheld $ | **5** Total amount reported with this Form 1096 $ 5,650.00 |

Check only one box below to indicate the type of form being transmitted.

If this is your FINAL return, check here . . . ▶ ☐

| W-2G 32 | 1098 81 | 1099-A 80 | 1099-B 79 | 1099-DIV 91 | 1099-G 86 | 1099-INT 92 | 1099-MISC 95 | 1099-OID 96 | 1099-PATR 97 | 1099-R 98 | 1099-S 75 | 5498 28 |
| ☐ | ☐ | ☐ | ☐ | ☐ | ☐ | ☐ | ☒ | ☐ | ☐ | ☐ | ☐ | ☐ |

Please return this entire page to the Internal Revenue Service. Photocopies are NOT acceptable.

Under penalties of perjury, I declare that I have examined this return and accompanying documents, and, to the best of my knowledge and belief, they are true, correct, and complete.

Signature ▶ *Samuel Thesham*   Title ▶ owner   Date ▶ 2/28

A 1096 Form must accompany the 1099 Form sent to the IRS.

IRS Forms For Independent Contractors

For each contractor you paid $600 or more during the year, you must file a federal form #1099-MISC, report of Miscellaneous Income. The form shows the contractor's name, address, Social Security number and amount paid. You must include your name, address, phone number and ID number as well. One copy of the 1099 goes to the IRS and another to the contractor.

In addition, if your outside contractors are independent sales agents, you must report, on

Form 1099-MISC, each sales agent who purchased $5,000 or more in goods from you.

The 1099-MISC forms must be given to your contractors no later than January 31 of the new year. The IRS copies of the 1099 forms must be accompanied by a Form 1096, Annual Summary and Transmittal of U.S. Information Returns. The 1096 and 1099's must be sent to the IRS by the last day in February (although you can get a 30-day extension to file your 1096 with the IRS by filing Form 8809). Don't you love all these numbers?

The Internal Revenue Service provides a form W-9 for your independent contractor to fill out, showing his or her name, address and Social security number (or Employer Identification Number if the contractor uses one). By signing the W-9 form, the independent contractor certifies to you that he or she is giving you correct information. You keep the form in your files; it does not get sent to the IRS. This W-9 form is optional. The independent contractor is not required to fill out the form, but he is required to give you his Social Security or Employer ID number. If the contractor refuses, you will probably be required to withhold taxes from his pay.

Incorporated Independent Contractor

Some independent contractors incorporate themselves. When you hire an incorporated independent contractor, you are contracting with a corporation and not an individual. The incorporated contractor is an employee of his or her own company, which means more paperwork and corporate forms and tax returns for the contractor, but makes it much easier and safer for you. You don't have to concern yourself with the contractor vs. employee rules, and you don't have to file 1099 or 1096 forms.

It is getting more and more common to find independent contractors who have set up their own one-person corporations, just so that companies, particularly larger corporations with worried lawyers and penny-pinching accountants, will hire them without having to put them on the payroll and deal with payroll taxes and fringe benefits or any worry of lawsuits over discrimination and fun stuff like that.

"Under the Table" Payments

A final word, about paying a worker "under the table". The term means that the worker is not on the payroll as an employee, the payment is usually in cash, and no record is made of the payment. This is usually done to avoid payroll taxes and the expense of workers' comp insurance, which is illegal and can get you in more trouble than it's worth.

If the worker is supposed to be an employee, not only can you get in the same trouble as the independent contractor problems mentioned above, you have no defense whatsoever when you get caught. At least when you are mislabeling employees as independent contractors, you can argue the issue and possibly minimize penalties.

If your "under the table" worker doesn't file taxes, that's fraud, and you could well be implicated. Again, an injury on the job could be disastrous. On top of all this misery, since you don't record the payment, you lose the expense deduction and pay more income taxes. Have I said enough?

One thing I hate is staff meetings. And, you know, you read all these things about motivating people. I hate doing that. Why do I want to spend my time motivating people? I want to make some deals, make some money, and have a good time.
—Small business owner Sam Leandro.

We prefer the no-frills motivation style for our employees. If they want to do it, they do it. If they don't, I get somebody else, simple as that.
—Kevin Gallagher, partner, Quicksilver Messenger Service.

Legislators have done their level best to create a legal environment that tempts us, when hiring, to focus on everything but finding the best person for the job.
—George Gendron, editor, Inc. magazine

Special Situations

Subcontractors. Are subcontractors employees or outside contractors? This is a touchy area, and some states have special employment regulations just for subcontractors. For IRS purposes, the general rules regarding employees versus outside contractors apply to subcontractors. A subcontractor who is actually in business for himself, offering services to several building contractors, is most likely an outside contractor. Some states, however, require contractors to purchase workers' compensation insurance for subcontractors if the subcontractors do not have the insurance themselves, even if the subcontractor is legally an outside contractor. Some states require subcontractors to be licensed.

Statutory Employees. One strange exception to the above rules applies to certain people the IRS calls "statutory employees": full-time life insurance sales people; commission truck drivers who deliver laundry, food, or beverages other than milk; home workers such as maids and cooks; and traveling sales people working full-time for one employer and selling to other businesses (not to consumers).

Statutory employees are subject to regular employee Social Security and Medicare taxes, but otherwise are treated as outside contractors. They file Schedule C like a sole proprietor and are entitled to regular business deductions. If you are a statutory employee, or someone employing a statutory employee, you should get more details from the IRS or an accountant. (No, I don't know who made up these laws, or why.)

Statutory Non-Employees. The IRS has another special rule, applying only to travelling salespeople selling consumer goods (not selling to businesses), to real estate agents, and to some newspaper vendors. The IRS permits these salespeople, called "statutory non-employees", to be classified as outside contractors, but only if there is a written agreement stating that they are independent contractors and responsible for their own taxes. The regular employee-versus-contractor tests do not apply.

Out-of-State Residents. If you hire an outside contractor who resides in another state, who comes into your state to work for you, you may be required to withhold state taxes on the contractor. This is not an IRS law. It is a state law, only for some states, and only for state taxes. Check with your state's income tax or employment offices.

Steps to Becoming an Employer

To meet the legal requirements of becoming an employer, you will have to deal with the federal government and the state government, and you will probably have to obtain workers' compensation insurance. These are one-time-only procedures, but they require quite a bit of paperwork. If possible, start these procedures a month before you plan to hire your first employee.

Federal Requirements

1. Contact the IRS and tell them you are about to become an employer. Request Form SS-4, Application for Employer Identification Number. Ask for a free copy of Publication #15, Circular E–Employer's Tax Guide. Circular E has detailed instructions for complying with federal requirements and includes federal withholding tables.

2. Ask the IRS for several copies of Form W-4, Employees Withholding Allowance Certificate. Each new employee must fill out a W-4 showing marital status and the number of exemptions claimed. You keep the W-4's in your files (except for employees claiming 11 or more exemptions; or employees claiming to be exempt from withholding whose wages are expected to exceed $200 a week. These W-4's must be sent to the IRS).

3. All employers must comply with Occupational Safety & Health Administration (OSHA) regulations. If you have more than ten employees, OSHA requires you to keep routine job safety records (some retail businesses with low injury rates are exempt from this requirement). Write OSHA, U.S. Department of Labor, Washington D.C. 20210 for complete information.

Owner of a small factory in New Orleans offered a $25 bonus to employees for money saving ideas. First winner paid was the man who suggested the bonus be cut to $10.

—Reported in the San Francisco Chronicle

4. Almost all employers are subject to the Fair Labor Standards Act. This act sets a minimum wage for employees, and sets overtime pay (more than 40 hours per week) at not less than 1½ times the regular rate of pay. Child labor laws, equal pay for men and women, comp time, and a host of other regulations are included in the FLSA. It does not require vacation, holiday or sick pay or fringe benefits. It does not place any limit on number of hours people work. Specifically exempt from the Act are most executives, administrators, professionals, outside sales people, and some amusement park employees, seamen, farm workers, and some computer-related work. Also exempt are unincorporated family businesses that employ only family members. For more details, write the Department of Labor, Washington D.C. 20210.

5. The Americans With Disabilities Act prohibits job discrimination against certain disabled people, and requires employers with 15 or more employees to provide reasonable accommodations for disabled employees.

State Requirements

1. Contact your state department of employment and ask for their forms and instructions. Most states assign employers a state Employer's ID Number, in addition to your Federal EIN.

2. Every state that has an income tax on wages requires employers to withhold state income tax. The states usually publish their own employer's tax guides including state withholding tables. Request a copy of these tables. Some states have other required withholding from employee wages.

3. Most states have employer-paid state unemployment insurance, in addition to federal unemployment insurance (discussed below). The state will require you to submit an application and receive an insurance rating. The rates vary from state to state and within states from occupation to occupation. The unemployment insurance rate for your business will initially be based on the prevailing rate in your particular occupation. For future years, your own business experience, that is, how many of your former employees receive unemployment insurance, will determine your rate. A "favorable" record will mean lower rates.

4. Most states require employers to have Worker's Compensation Insurance. See the Insurance chapter in the Getting Started section. Some states have laws similar to the federal Fair Labor Standards Act. And some states set their own minimum wage, higher than the federal minimum.

An entrepreneur is someone who takes a prospective employee out into the country, to a hill overlooking a great estate, points to the mansion, the swimming pool, the stables, the tennis courts, and says, "If you come with me and work your butt off, someday all this will be mine."

—Harvey Mackay, "Swim With The Sharks"

Federal Procedures and Taxes for Employers

Outlined here are the basic federal procedures most employers must follow. These laws have changed very little in recent years, but you should get and read the IRS's "Circular E, Employer's Tax Guide" to verify all the rules. Unlike income taxes, there is no "grey" or questionable area where payroll taxes are involved. There is only one way to do it—their way.

These payroll taxes apply regardless of how you pay your employees. You cannot avoid the taxes by paying in goods and services instead of cash, by bartering or trading, or paying the money to a third party.

1. The IRS requires that you withhold income tax from each employee's paycheck. The amount is calculated from the tables in "Circular E".

2. The Federal Insurance Contributions Act (FICA) requires employers to withhold Social Security tax (also known as OASDI—old age, survivors, and disability insurance) and Medicare tax (also known as Hospitalization). Social Security tax is 6.2% on each employee's earnings, up to an earnings maximum of $65,400. The Medicare tax, levied in addition to the Social Security tax, is 1.45% on each employee's earnings, regardless of how much they make; there is no maximum earnings for the Medicare tax. So, the total tax on employees making $65,400 or less is 7.65%. (1997 figures—they go up every year).

3. You are liable for an employer's portion of Social Security and Medicare taxes in addition to the taxes withheld from your employees. This is money you, the employer, pay out of your own pocket on behalf of your employees. The employer's tax is exactly the same as the employee's tax: 6.2% Social Security tax on each employee's earnings up to $65,400; and 1.45% Medicare tax on each employee's earnings, with no maximum. So, the total employer's tax on employees making $65,400 or less is also 7.65%. Do not confuse this employer's tax with the self-employment tax discussed in the Tax section of the book. They are different taxes.

Minimum work for minimum pay.
—Minimum wage earner Tim Hanna.

4. Federal Payroll Tax Returns (Form #941) are due quarterly on April 30 for January, February and March; July 31 for April, May and June; October 31 for July, August and September; and January 31 for October, November and December. Taxes reported on Form 941 are taxes withheld from your employees (federal income, Social Security and Medicare), and the employer's portion of employee Social Security and Medicare. Do *not* include self-employment tax.

As long as the total payroll taxes due in any one quarter are less than $500, the entire amount can be remitted with the return. If, however, at the end of any month in the quarter, total taxes due (combined employee and employer portions) are $500 or more, you must deposit the full amount by the 15th day of the next month. Deposits are reported on yet another form, #8109, "Federal Tax Deposit (FTD) Coupon", and paid to an authorized commercial bank or to a Federal Reserve bank. You can obtain the names of authorized banks at any local bank. Deposits can also be made electronically.

The deposit information is confusing enough to warrant an illustration. (Maybe it's confusing enough to go back and read the chapter, "How Not To Become An Employer.") In January, let's say you withheld from your employees $140 in income tax and $80 in social security and Medicare taxes. Your tax liability at the end of January is the $220 withheld plus $80 (your employer portion) for a total of $300. Since this amount is under $500 there is no need to file anything at that time. Okay so far?

Now in February, let's say the same taxes recur: $220 withholding and $80 employer's portion, or $300. Your total tax liability is now $600 for the two months. Since you are now over the $500 limit, you must deposit the full $600 with an authorized bank by March 15. Taxes for March, the last month of the quarter, are due when you file the quarterly return on April 30, assuming that March's taxes are less than $500. If your payroll jumped in March, and March's taxes alone are $500 or more, a deposit of the full amount must be made by April 15. A different and more complicated set of deposit rules apply if your total annual payroll taxes exceed $50,000.

5. Ask the IRS to send you several copies of form W-2, "Wage and Tax Statement." The W-2 is a five-part form that you must prepare for

each employee, annually at year-end. You must mail or give out the W-2 forms by January 31. Three copies of the W-2 are given to the employee, one copy you retain, and one copy is sent to the Social Security Administration (the SSA).

The Social Security Administration copies of the W-2's should be batched and sent with form W-3, "Transmittal of Income and Tax Statements," no later than February 28. W-3's are available from the IRS. You can get a 30-day extension to file your W-3 by filing Form 8809.

6. As an employer, you are subject to Federal Unemployment tax (F.U.T.A.) if during the year you, (a) paid wages of $1,500 or more in any calendar quarter, or (b) had one or more employees for some portion of at least one day during each of twenty different calendar weeks (better re-read that slowly).

Unemployment tax is imposed on you, the employer. It is not deducted from your employee's wages. An annual return must be filed on Form #940, or for many small businesses, the simpler

A W-2 must be sent to each employee by January 1 of the new year.

A W-3 accompanies the W-2 forms sent to the Social Security Administration.

Form #940-EZ, Employer's Federal Unemployment Tax Return, on or before January 31 of next year. The rate is 6.2% of the first $7,000 of wages paid to each employee during the year. You may receive credit of up to 5.4% for state unemployment taxes you pay, so your net federal tax could be as low as 0.8%.

7. The Immigration & Naturalization Service (INS) Reform & Control Act makes it a crime to "knowingly hire any alien not authorized to work in the U.S.". All new employees must have "proof of employment eligibility" such as a Social Security card, military registration card, or immigrant "green card" (which is actually pink or salmon colored). Employers must record this information for each new employee on an Employment Eligibility Verification Form #I-9, available from INS offices, and retain the forms in your files. For more information, see the INS Publication #M274, "Handbook For Employers."

Restaurant and nightclub owners: Employees must report their tips to you, if they are more than $20 a week. You must withhold income and payroll taxes, and also pay employer's payroll taxes on the tips, just as you do on wages. Restaurant owners may claim a special tax credit equal to the employer's portion of FICA taxes paid on tips, to the extent tips and wages exceed the minimum wage. If you have more than 10 employees, you must report income and tips-related information on Form #8027.

Agricultural employers come under different federal laws, particularly regarding Social Security and Medicare taxes, minimum wage and overtime pay. See IRS Publication #51, "Agricultural Employer's Tax Guide."

Family Employees

If you plan to hire your husband or wife, you should read the chapter "Husband and Wife Partnerships" in the Appendix. It will explain all of your options and the tax consequences of each. Generally, putting your spouse on the payroll will neither increase nor decrease your combined income or payroll taxes.

You may have a significant tax savings if you hire your children to help out in the business. If you stay within certain limits, you can pay each of your children up to $4,000 a year (1996 max-

imum), and write it off as a business expense. The kids pay no federal income taxes and do not have to file an income tax return. Neither the kids or the parents pay any Social Security, Medicare or federal unemployment taxes. The children are usually exempt from the minimum wage and child labor requirements of the Fair Labor Standards Act.

Here are the rules:

1. Your business must be a sole proprietorship, or a husband-and-wife partnership.

2. The child must perform legitimate work to justify the salary earned. The work must be business related: You can't hire your 17 year old to baby sit your 3 year old and then take a business deduction.

3. The child must be under the age of eighteen.

4. The child must have absolutely no "unearned" income such as interest.

5. Child can earn no more than $4,000 a year.

If your child is 18 or older, or has any unearned income, or earns more than $4,000 a year, you still may be able to hire your child and save on income and payroll taxes. But the rules start changing, with a lot of variables. The IRS's "Circular E, Employer's Tax Guide" includes a chart that explains what federal payroll taxes are required for children on the payroll.

You should also check your state's employment laws before you hire your children. Many states have laws similar to the IRS, and impose no state income or payroll taxes, nor require worker's compensation insurance on your children. Check your state employer's guide. Do not rely on verbal information from state agencies. People who work at state employment departments are often unaware of child employment laws.

Children who hire their parents get no special tax breaks. The parents are considered regular employees, subject to all regular employment and income taxes.

Payroll Ledgers

Every employer must keep a payroll ledger in addition to the expenditure ledger. The payroll ledger must show all the details of every paycheck for every employee. Payroll ledgers can be purchased ready to use or you can easily design your own. The Ledger section includes a sample payroll ledger that you can use as a prototype.

Payroll ledgers should be permanent. Keep

PAYROLL LEDGER

Name _____ Social Security _____

Address _____ Pay Rate _____

_____

1	2	3	4	5	6	7	8	9	10	11	12	13
PAYCHECK DATE	CHECK NO.	PAY PERIOD	HOURS REG	O/T	GROSS	F.I.T.	SOCIAL SECURITY	MEDI-CARE	STATE INCOME	OTHER WITHHOLDING		NET PAY

them as long as you own the business, longer if possible. Long-gone employees can come back to haunt you years later, usually when there's some problem with Social Security retirement.

Use a separate ledger page for each employee. Head the page with the employee's name, address and Social Security number. Write down the employee's hourly or monthly rate of pay at the top of the page. If the rate changes during the year, show the new rate as well as the old and the date of change.

The payroll ledger should have a column for each of the following:

1. Date of paycheck.
2. Check number.
3. Payroll period.
4. Number of regular hours worked.
5. Number of overtime hours worked.
6. Gross pay.
7. Federal income tax withheld.
8. Social Security taxes withheld.
9. Medicare taxes withheld.
10. State income taxes withheld.

11-12. Columns for any other withholding: state requirements, retirement, health insurance, etc.

13. Net "take-home" pay.

Remember that the net pay must also be posted to your expenditure ledger in Column 4.

Mike Madsen, Mike Madsen Leather: "When you're first getting started you don't always hire the best people. You don't know what you are looking for. You might hire somebody who is sympathetic to you or flatters you or somebody who is good looking. But they might not fit the job that you have. You've got to think in terms of what the job is, and hire the people for the job, and not hire friends. I'd say it's better always to make friends of those people that work for you, but never to hire friends."

Nick Mein, Wallpapers Plus: "A person's gotta be happy if he or she is going to work for you. The women working for me were terribly unhappy. This one woman who worked for me, who I really liked, was a great saleswoman. She'd been going to a Freudian shrink, and she switched to a Jungian psychologist. He said, 'Work's bad for you.' So she called up and said, 'I won't be in.' A lot of jobs depended on her charm; she brought a lot of people in the store. And she just gave up on it. That's irritating. No 'stick-to-it-ivity' my father calls it; no perseverance.

"It's very difficult to be nice to your employees because they're going to take advantage of you. They're going to start coming in late. All the people who worked for me are perfect examples. I'd say, 'Get in at 9:30, do what ordering needs to be done, and open the doors at ten. I want you to be ready to sell at ten.' And they do that for a while, but then they say, 'I want to get in a little later because there's no ordering to do, there's no backlog.' I say okay. And then eventually, they're coming in at eleven. Because they felt nobody was coming in the shop until 11 or 11:30. If you're not on it everyday, you get screwed. You have to be on it all the time. And then, they leave early.

"If you have somebody working for you you've got to make it absolutely plain that they're being paid for the specified hours. I find that really hard to do, keep people to that, because I'm a little bit like that myself. On a really slow day, I'd say, 'Go ahead, go home early.' Then it always happens: next day some woman would call and say, 'I came by your shop at 5:20 and you weren't there.' That's bad service."

PARTNERSHIPS

Partnerships offer opportunities often not available to the one-person business: more capital, more skills and ideas, the extra energy generated when two or more people are working together. Partnerships are the traditional meeting ground of the "idea" person and the "money" person. Having a partner can relieve the sole proprietor pressures of having to do everything yourself. And, at last, you can take a little vacation without having to shut down the business.

Most partnerships are planned as a long-term relationship, to last the life of the business (hopefully). But many partnerships are temporary arrangements, often on a project-by-project basis. When the project is completed, the partnership dissolves, and you move on to the next venture.

Partnerships have drawbacks as well. The independence and sole decision making that only the sole proprietor has must now be shared. There is more paperwork. Inter-personal relations with your partners may require both time and tact. Most important, the legal consequences of having one or more partners can be serious.

General Vs. Limited Partnerships

There are two kinds of partnerships. The kind covered in this chapter, the typical business partnership, is called a "general" partnership.

There is also something called a "limited" partnership, which is not a partnership in the usual sense. A limited partnership is an investment financing arrangement, with one general partner who owns and operates the business, with full legal and financial responsibility, much like a sole proprietor; and one or more limited partners, who are investors only. The limited partners have no involvement in the management or operations of the business, and usually have no personal liability beyond their investment. Limited partnerships are covered under "Equity Financing" in the Getting Started section of the book. This chapter is for general partnerships only.

There is also a third kind of partnership, a Limited Liability Partnership, or LLP (not to be confused with a limited partnership), used almost exclusively by legal and accounting firms. LLPs are covered in the Limited Liability Company chapter.

Legal Aspects of General Partnerships

A partnership is legally inseparable from the owners, the partners. Individual partners can be held personally responsible for debts and legal obligations of the partnership. Most important: all partners can be held personally, individually liable for the acts of any partner acting on partnership business. If your partner, representing the business, goes out and gets a bank loan, you can be personally responsible to repay the debt, even if you didn't sign the papers yourself, even if you didn't know about the loan. If your partner gets into legal trouble while on partnership business, you may also be in legal trouble.

The only way out of this unlimited liability is to incorporate or set up a Limited Liability Company (LLC). Both are covered in this Section.

Like sole proprietors, partners cannot be employees of their partnerships. Partners can draw a "wage" (called a "guaranteed payment"), or they can merely share in the profits of the partnership, or some combination of the two. Profits and guaranteed payments are taxable to the individual partners. Partners are subject to Self-Employment tax (covered in the Tax section).

A partnership must have a federal identification number, obtained by filing Form SS-4, Employer's Federal Identification Number. If the partnership will have no employees, be sure line 12 on the form, asking about employees, is marked "Not Applicable" (N/A). This will alert the IRS not to send you payroll forms.

Partnerships file a partnership income tax return, on form 1065, although the partnership itself pays no taxes. Each partner pays income tax on his or her share of the profits, on Schedule E of the regular 1040 tax return. Each partner is taxed on his or her full share of the profit whether distributed to the partners or not.

Partnerships must get the same licenses and permits as any other business. In some states, partnerships must be officially registered with the county clerk (in addition to getting a Fictitious Name Statement or DBA) or a state office.

Death or withdrawal of one partner or the addition of a new partner legally terminates a partnership. The business need not be liquidated, however. A new partnership agreement can be made. The original agreement can include provisions for continuation of a partnership.

Partnership Agreements

A partnership agreement is an "understanding" between partners as to how the business will be conducted. Many partnership agreements are nothing more than a handshake and a "Let's do it". Often such agreements turn out to be more of a *mis*understanding than anything else. A written partnership agreement is not required by law; but if you don't have one, you are asking for nothing but trouble. What's more, without a written agreement, state law, not the partners, will dictate how the partnership is run.

Most states adhere to a law called the Uniform Partnership Act. The UPA says that if you don't have a written agreement, each partner shares equally in the profits (regardless of the time or money contributed) and has equal voice in the management of the partnership. A partnership with a written agreement will not be bound by UPA rules; you get to make up your own rules.

Partnership agreements are not binding on outside ("third") parties. A lender or a creditor can go after any and all partners, no matter what the partnership agreement says.

A written partnership agreement should be signed by all the partners and should specify:

1. A simple, written statement of business goals is the first and most important step in any partnership agreement. Long range goals should be included as well. For example, one partner may want a business that will provide a good livelihood for many years; while the other partner may be dreaming of building up the business and when it becomes successful and established, selling it for a big profit. These two partners obviously have a serious conflict of interest. If partners do not agree on the basics, the partnership is doomed from the start.

2. How much each partner is to contribute, in cash, property and time, and when the contributions are to be made.

3. How each partner will share in the profits and losses. The easiest and most common arrangement is an equal division of profits between partners. You may wish, however, to provide for an unequal division of profits to compensate for differences in time or money contributed or for differences in ability and experience.

A partner can also draw a wage to reflect actual time spent running the business. The wage is known as a "guaranteed payment to partner." It is not a regular employee wage for tax purposes. There is no withholding, employee Social Security or unemployment insurance. It is part of the partner's total partnership income. Paying a wage is common when one partner works day-to-day at the business and the other doesn't, or when partners do not put in equal time. After the wage is paid, any remaining profit (or loss) for the year is then divided between the partners according to your agreement. Specify in the agreement who gets a wage and the amount.

4. Who will have authority to sign checks?

5. Procedures for withdrawing funds and paying profits: how much and when. This will prevent partners from arbitrarily withdrawing money from the partnership. No federal law requiring partners to make equal or simultaneous withdrawals.

6. Provisions for continuing the business if one partner dies or wants out. Without such a provision, a partner can legally quit or retire any time the partner wants, and demand to be paid fair value for his or her share of the partnership. Your biggest problem is determining how much money the departing partner (or estate) should receive and over what period of time. For example, the business may be worth a lot of money because it is established and successful or because it owns a lot of inventory and equipment, but there may be little cash on hand to pay the departing partner. Some insurance companies offer "key person" life insurance for partnerships to buy out a deceased or seriously ill partner.

Your agreement should state how a partner's share of the business is to be valued. Is it based on the value of the business assets; that is, what you actually have invested in the business? Or is it based on what the going business is worth on the open market, what an eager new owner might pay for it? And who will be the lucky person to determine this "worth?"

There are tax consequences to a partner buyout that vary depending on how the agreement is worded. The tax interests of the remaining and outgoing partners are often diametrically opposed. These tax aspects can be substantial if the business is worth a lot of money; they will require professional help.

The agreement might include a "non-competing clause" so that a departing partner cannot engage in a similar business (for a reasonable period of time and in a limited geographical area) and take some of the partnership's customers with him. This is a tricky area of law that might be difficult to enforce. It may require legal help.

6. You may also want a clause specifying the financial and legal powers of each partner. Such a clause is not binding on outside parties, such as a lender. It will not relieve any partner of partnership obligations entered into by other partners. It only reduces the possibility of misunderstanding among the partners.

7. Can any of the partners have a separate outside business? You would not want a partner to compete with the partnership, possibly siphoning off partnership business.

8. If the partnership dissolves or if one or more partners leave, who will own the right to the business name?

Most of the professional advice I have heard suggests that you hire a lawyer to draw up any partnership agreement. Certainly a knowledgeable lawyer—not all lawyers are familiar with partnership problems—will draft up an iron-clad agreement that leaves nothing to doubt. But you will pay a high fee for this service. I feel it is not necessary to see a lawyer if the agreement is a simple one (such as 50-50, equal sharing, equal contributions) and if you know your partner well enough to be confident you aren't being used.

All the people we talk to or survey seem to want a partner, until they actually have one.
                                    —Inc. Magazine

You and Your Partners

My friend Rory said, "Having a partner is just like having a wife, only more so." Well, Rory is a long-time loner, but his words are basically true. Partnerships are more than business. They are often complex inter-personal relationships. And like marriages, partnerships can bring out the best and the worst in people. By acquiring a partner you are adding a whole new dimension to your business venture, one you should be fully prepared to deal with.

Anyone who has lost a friend after an argument can quickly realize the possible problems and complications of having a business partner. It is not uncommon for partners to have a disagreement, a difference of opinion, or worse. You may feel that your partner is not working as hard as he should (and he may be feeling the same about you!). When trouble arises between partners, the logical step is to try to work it out: sit down with your partner, get the problems "out front", and hopefully get them solved. Much more easily said than done. Like divorces, partnership dissolutions are more common than ever and often just as problematical. The alternatives—dividing up the assets and going out of business, or one partner buying out the other—can be difficult even with a good written agreement, can require lawyers and almost always cause the business to suffer.

Marriage counselors can sometimes save a marriage. But it's a little out of my field, and there is little advice I can give you retrospectively. Knowing that such things happen should warn you to take every precaution prior to going into a partnership to reduce the possibility of problems later on. The best advice I can offer is to pick your partners *very* carefully. This may seem basic, just common sense; but a poor choice of partners is the root cause of many partnership failures. How well do you know your partner? Are you old friends? Have you worked together before? What business experience does your partner have? What is his or her "track record?"

Partnership Bookkeeping

The basic bookkeeping for a partnership is the same as for a sole proprietorship. You will be able to use the ledgers and worksheets in the ledger section with no alteration. In addition to the income and expenditure ledgers, partnerships must keep a separate "partners' capital ledger" which provides a complete record, by partner, of all contributions and withdrawals and of each partner's share of profit or loss.

The partners' capital ledger has two columns for each partner. One column shows *activity* in the partner's account—contributions, withdrawals and the partner's share of profit or loss. The second column is the *balance* of the partner's capital remaining with the partnership.

Contributions and withdrawals should be recorded when they occur. Contributions are shown as positive amounts and increase the partner's balance. Withdrawals are shown as negative, bracketed amounts and decrease the partner's balance. A partner's "guaranteed payment" (wage) is shown as a withdrawal.

Each partner's share of the partnership profit or loss is posted to the partners' capital ledger once a year at year-end. A profit is posted to the Activity column as a positive amount; a loss is shown as a negative amount. Profits and losses increase and decrease a partner's balance accordingly. The Total Balance column is the sum of all the individual partners' Balance columns.

The sample partners' capital ledger above shows activity for 1996 and part of 1997 for a new partnership, Wesley's Farm Fresh Eggs, owned by two partners.

Entry 1: The partnership began on January 1, 1996. Each partner contributed $2,000 to the business. Each partner's balance is $2,000, and the total balance is $4,000.

Entry 2: On March 31, Huck (Partner A) contributed another $800, and Pippi (Partner B) contributed another $400.

Entry 3: The partnership made a $7,000 profit in 1995. At December 31, 1996, the partners' shares of the profit were posted to their individual accounts.

Entry 4: On February 5, 1997, Huck withdrew $400 from the business.

Entry 5: On May 1, 1997, Pippi withdrew $350 from the business.

With each entry, the partners' individual balances and the total balance were adjusted.

		Wesley's Farm Fresh Eggs					
		Partners' Capital Ledger					
		Huck (Partner A)		Pippi (Partner B)		Total	
Entry		Activity	Balance	Activity	Balance	Balance	
1	Contribution 1-1	$2,000.00	$2,000.00	$2,000.00	$2,000.00	$4,000.00	
2	Contribution 3-31	$800.00	$2,800.00	$400.00	$2,400.00	$5,200.00	
3	Income for Year	$4,000.00	$6,800.00	$3,000.00	$5,400.00	$12,200.00	
4	Withdrawal 2-5	($400.00)	$6,400.00		$5,400.00	$11,800.00	
5	Withdrawal 5-1		$6,400.00	($350.00)	$5,050.00	$11,450.00	

A partnership income tax return must sometimes include a balance sheet (explained in the Appendix) and schedule of partners' capital. The Appendix also includes a chapter on husband and wife partnerships. For more tax information about partnerships, ask the IRS for a free copy of Publ. 541, "Tax Information on Partnerships."

Partnership Post-Mortem

Lara Stonebraker, former partner in Aromatica, a retail coffee store: "It's been my experience that partnerships rarely work, especially if there is an odd number of partners. Because it's always going to be two against one in all decision making, and there's always going to be an odd man out. Unless you have such well matched personalities that everybody is always good friends, it creates incredible hassles. That was the most anxiety-ridden period of my life. There were three of us and I happened to be the odd one.

"And then one of the partners turned out to be a religious fanatic, just impossible to deal with. She'd bring her bible to the store and talk to the customers about it, and there was no way to stop it. Finally she decided she had to go to this retreat in the mountains to prepare for the holocaust, so she sold her partnership. I blotted out a lot of that whole experience."

———————————

Key Dickason, former partner in Xanadu, a computer service: "I was in a partnership once, and my partner and I disagreed, not on the running of the business, but on the way we handled employees. We bought a computer service which had two employees. One of the conditions of the sale was that we continue the old employees on and honor their vacations. But when one of the employees got married and gave us notice she was quitting, my partner said, `No one quits on me,' and he refused to pay her vacation. So I wrote a check for her vacation money.

"The keypuncher working for us got a fully-paid scholarship from the university. In May, she told us she'd be leaving in August. My partner fired her on the spot. That was 15 years ago and I've never had another keypuncher who even approached her. He just arbitrarily fired her. Because I disagreed on that, it eventually led to the dissolution of the partnership.

"I also discovered that he was putting his personal debts into the business. I finally went to a CPA. He looked at the books and advised me to see an attorney.' So I went to see my attorney, and he told me that if I got out of the business, I would be liable for all the debts, and the business would be defunct. So I just signed all the assets and everything over to my partner. The only way I could try and get my money out of it, which was gone, was to sue for dissolution of the partnership. Then once you go into litigation, according to my attorney, everything's tied up.

"The partnership agreement doesn't mean a thing unless both parties want to honor it. Jack and I disagreed on a philosophical—a better word is ethical—aspect of employee relationships. To Jack, an employee was somebody you used and discarded. To me an employee was somebody you had an obligation and a commitment to. If you have this basic disagreement, no partnership agreement will handle it. Do you put in there, `You agree to treat employees fairly?' Well, that doesn't mean anything. 'Cause to Jack, Jack was treating them fairly.

"The biggest mistake in the world is to start a partnership if there is disagreement in the beginning when you're laying the groundwork for the business. If you enter into basic disagreement on ethics, management, or whatever the objective of the business is, you shouldn't go into business together. Putting your doubts about the situation into a partnership agreement doesn't accomplish anything unless you're prepared to fight, which isn't what it's all about."

———————————

Jan Lowe, former partner in Midnight Sewing Machine, a retail dress shop: "I went into business with my sister who is a dear person, and who taught me everything I know. I didn't sew a stitch in my life before we bought this dress shop, and she handed me a pattern and scissors and said, `I'm going to lunch now. If you have any problems, let me know.' So I started off real cold there, which is no way to do it. I'd run into problems when people would want something intricate done or they'd want something altered, and I wouldn't know how to handle it. I wasn't really prepared to do what I did for a living.

"One of our basic problems was non-communication. My partner would borrow money from someone and I didn't know about it, which I thought was a cheap shot. You've got to be in constant communication. If somebody's going to lunch, they've got to tell you. We didn't have anything in writing between us. How things were going to be run was not made clear and that I think was another downfall. That should be made clear right from the start—exactly what do you want to see happen, how is it going to happen, who's going to make what work, who is best at handling what; and stick to it. I think you should be willing to bend when that system does not work. Face it immediately and try something else. To hang onto a system that doesn't work can get you into lots of trouble."

...And a Partnership That Works

"Kipple is a made-up word that means, um, kipple, the dumb stuff that you gather around you that you can't live without." Pat Ellington is a partner in Kipple, a small antique store: "We function pretty well as a four-way partnership. Miriam and I are old friends, friends for fifteen years or more. Her downstairs neighbor is the third partner, and a friend of hers is the fourth. Everybody's really working part time. But this way we can operate a full time business.

"When we first came into this, I was the only one with any kind of business skill. Neither Miriam or Pam ever held an office or business job of any type. Ann has been a housewife all her life.

"We've had personality troubles, but not serious ones, because we squashed them right away. The inter-personal stuff can be worked out if everybody agrees it's going to happen, that there's no blame attached to differences of opinion or feelings. We all agreed when we set out that everybody was going to make mistakes, some of them are going to cost us money, but no blame should be attached to anybody, and we would not throw it up to each other. When Ann joined us, Miriam made a lot of noises, 'She did this wrong, she never should have bought that ...' Pam and I would say, 'Miriam, you made your mistakes too, back off.' And she slowly but surely got over that. She felt, being the one partner with the most money in at that point, like the business was hers. None of this was conscious. People don't consciously set out to be that way about things, it's sort of inbred. We all have moments of 'mine' mentalities: 'That's mine. She's threatening it.'

"Miriam is a crackerjack saleswoman. She can sell anybody anything. But she couldn't keep a set of books to save her soul. She can't balance a checkbook. But she can sell. That's a real asset. She doesn't have to keep books if she can do that. Pam's got a good eye when it comes to buying. She's good at that. And Ann, who's much better organized than the other two when it comes to shows and things like that, she's the one who sits down and makes out a list: we're gonna need lights, display material, we need this, we need that. Pam says, 'Well, we need so much inventory; where's the rest of it?' These are skills.

"And I'm the bookkeeper. And between the four of us we can really operate."

YOU, INCORPORATED: A Corporation Primer

The corporation is truly a misunderstood animal. People, even business people, have more misconceptions about corporations than about any other form of business. Some small-time operations will benefit by incorporating, but many will not. In order for you to make an intelligent choice between "You" and "You, Incorporated," you will need a basic understanding of what a corporation is and what can and cannot be accomplished by incorporating.

"In Twenty-Five Words or Less"

A corporation is...just another business. The basic day-to-day operations, the management, the bookkeeping, are virtually no different from the operations of an unincorporated business. A corporation can be as tiny as the tiniest unincorporated business. It can be loose and easy and very personal. Just as there are grey-suits-and-elevators corporations, there are blue-jeans-and-pure-funk corporations.

A corporation is just another business...but the rules of the game are different. Owners of corporations are the stockholders (also called shareholders). They own shares of stock, pieces of paper. Your corporation may have one or more stockholders (one or more owners) with one or more shares of stock, depending on your needs and your state's laws (discussed later).

Corporate Myth Number One: You're going to lower you taxes by incorporating. Not so. The fact is, most small businesses will not save tax money by incorporating. Corporate profits are taxed *twice*: once as corporate income and again when distributed to the shareholders (owners) as dividends. In contrast, the profits from your sole proprietorship, partnership or Limited Liability Company (LLC) are taxable only to the owners; the business itself pays no federal income tax. So even though corporate tax rates are sometimes lower than individual tax rates, the effective corporate tax rate because of the double taxation is always higher. Small corporations do have ways to reduce the combined corporation and shareholder taxes (discussed later), but none will result in taxes lower than those paid by an unincorporated business. (Actually there is *one* situation where incorporating will save you tax money. See "Retained Earnings", below).

Most states impose income taxes on corporations. Some states call their income tax an "excise" tax, not to be confused with federal excise taxes described in the Tax section.

Many states also impose an additional tax on corporations called a "franchise tax". The franchise tax may be a flat annual fee; or may be a percent of income (like a second income tax); or may be based on the value of stock or assets. In some states the franchise tax is really a minimum income tax: you pay your income tax or the franchise tax, whichever is greater.

Limited Liability

Rules regarding liability are also different for corporations. These liability rules, which offer protection to the owners (the stockholders) of corporations from creditors and from some lawsuits, are the most convincing reason for you to consider incorporating your business.

A corporation is recognized by law as a "legal entity," which means that the business is legally separate from its owners. If your corporation does not pay its debts, the creditors usually cannot get their money from your personal, non-business assets. Sole proprietors and partners, by comparison, are personally liable for all business debts and obligations. (Limited Liability Companies, LLCs, covered later in this section, have the same limited liability as corporations.)

If you don't make mistakes, you aren't really trying.
                              —*Coleman Hawkins*

The main reason for corporate limited liability is to protect you from creditors—suppliers and others you owe money to in the normal course of business—should the business go broke. Many people think they should incorporate to protect themselves from lawsuits, but this rarely works. In some cases you will not be personally liable for lawsuits brought against your corporation. But if you are sued by an angry customer, or someone who was injured or suffered a loss, you will be personally dragged into the lawsuit, corporation or no corporation. Do not be fooled by this common misconception about liability protection.

A corporation will not shield you from personal liability that you normally should be responsible for, such as not having car insurance, or acting with gross negligence, or if your company breaks the law. Limited liability will not protect you if you fail to deposit taxes withheld from employees' wages. As to financial commitments, any bank lending money to a small corporation will require the stockholders or officers to co-sign as personal guarantors of the loan.

Partnerships often incorporate to protect individual partners from possible losses and lawsuits resulting from the actions of other partners. If you plan to incorporate primarily with the intention of limiting your legal liability, I suggest you find out first, before you invest the time and money in incorporation, exactly how limited the liability really is for your particular venture. Talk to a good lawyer or accountant.

People who own more than one business sometimes incorporate each business separately so if one business fails, it won't drag the other business down with it.

Professionals such as doctors and lawyers cannot hide behind a corporation to protect themselves from malpractice suits. A corporation, however, will shield you from a malpractice suit brought against one of your partners. This is a major reason that doctors, lawyers, architects and similar professionals set up corporations. Some states have a separate Professional Corporation category, with different requirements than regular corporations.

Finally, many people (including many accountants) believe that small corporations are less likely to be audited by the IRS than unincorporated businesses. I sure wouldn't use this as an excuse to incorporate, but for some people it may well be the icing on the cake.

Change of Ownership

Incorporating a business eliminates much of the legal and tax complications of a change in ownership. New shareholders can be added easily (within certain legal limits, discussed later). Selling a business, passing a family-owned business from generation to generation, giving or selling your employees an ownership interest, and taking on investors in the company are all much easier with a corporation than with an unincorporated business.

Sale of stock or death of a shareholder will not end the business. The same corporation can continue in business with new shareholders. By comparison, a sole proprietorship ceases to exist when the owner sells or gives away the business, takes on a partner, or dies. A partnership ceases to exist when one partner quits or dies. A sole proprietorship or a partnership can be sold or otherwise acquired by new owners. But the result, legally, is a new business requiring new records, new valuation of assets and liabilities, new business licenses, etc.

Owner-Employees

A corporation is the only form of business that can hire its owners as employees. You are in the unique position of being your own boss and your own employee. Hiring yourself as an owner-employee is one way to reduce corporate income taxes. Every employee's wage, including that of an owner-employee, is a deductible expense of the business. The wage is taxable to the owner-employee as personal income. But unlike regular corporate profits, which are taxable to the corporation and again to the owners, wages paid to owner-employees are not subject to the double taxation. In many small corporations, the owner-employee's salary and year-end bonus eat up all the corporate profits, bringing corporate income taxes to zero. (For tax purposes, year-end bonuses are considered part of regular salaries. As long as salary and bonus combined are not "unreasonable", the IRS allows this tax maneuver).

Many fringe benefits, particularly medical expenses, are 100% tax deductible for the corporation, and are not taxable to the employees at all. This is a much larger tax deduction than that available to sole proprietors, partners in partnerships, owners of Limited Liability Companies (LLC's), and owners of S corporation(who come under differenr rules than owners of regular C corporations; see below). If your health insurance costs are high, this alone may be an excellent reason to consider incorporation.

Retired people collecting Social Security can lose part of their Social Security income if any outside income, such as earnings from a small business, gets above a certain level. By setting up a corporation, you may be able to pay yourself a low enough salary so it stays under the social security limits. This arrangement cannot be accomplished with a sole proprietorship, a partnership or an LLC because all of the profits of an unincorporated business are considered personal income whether you take a salary or not. This is an area you should discuss with an accountant.

If you do become an owner-employee of your own corporation, you should be aware of IRS limitations on employee business expenses. Your corporation can take tax deductions for any allowable business expenses, as long as the corporation itself spends the money. If you, as an employee, spend the money, your tax deductions are greatly reduced, even though you may be the sole owner of the business and even though the expenses may be totally legitimate. It is important that you learn the IRS rules, because it's easy to avoid this trap.

Retained Earnings

The remaining significant difference between incorporated and unincorporated business is the corporation's legal ability to retain up to $250,000 ($150,000 for some businesses) of undistributed profits within the company, and not pay the profits out to the owners. Though the corporation must pay income tax on these "retained earnings," as they are called, the owners do not have to pay the "double" or second tax because the profits have not been paid out to them. Retained earnings can be reinvested in the business, distributed to the shareholders at a later date or retained indefinitely by the company. An unincorporated business can also retain the profits in the business, but the owners must pay income tax on the profits whether distributed to them or not.

This is the one situation where incorporating might reduce your taxes. If the corporate tax rate is lower than your personal tax rate (which depends not only on how much profit you earn, but also on marital status, and how many dependents and personal deductions you claim) any retained earnings—profits you choose not to take out of the business this year—will be taxed at the lower corporate rate. If you reinvest those retained earnings in the business in a future year, you're fine. But if you ever withdraw the retained earnings, they become taxable dividends, and you are penalized with the double taxation.

S Corporations

The type of corporation described above is commonly called a "regular" or "C" corporation. (Don't confuse a C corporation with a Schedule C tax return. The two C's are not related. Schedule C is for sole proprietors, not corporations.)

There is another form of corporation different from the C corporation. It is a hybrid between a C corporation and a partnership or sole proprietorship, with some of the advantages of both.

The S corporation (so called because it is covered in Subchapter S of the Internal Revenue Code) has the same basic structure as a C corporation and offers the same limited liability protection to the stockholders. The S corporation, however, pays no federal income tax. Like a partnership, sole proprietorship and Limited Liability Company, the S corporation is what the IRS calls a "pass through entity": profits "pass through" to the owner or owners who pay taxes on the business profit at their regular individual rates.

Unlike an unincorporated business, however,

"It's a jungle up here, Martha!"

owner-employees of S corporations are treated similarly to owner-employees of regular C corporations. If you work for your S corporation, you must be on the payroll as a regular employee with regular payroll deductions. Any S corporation profits in excess of your salary are also taxable directly to you, as dividends. Unlike a C corporation, S corporation dividends are taxable to you the year earned, whether you actually receive the money or not. This might be a problem if the business earned a profit but doesn't have the cash to distribute to shareholders to pay their income taxes.

S corporation dividends, unlike your salary, are not subject to employment taxes. Since you decide how much of a salary you earn, you obviously also get to decide how much of the corporation's annual profit is subject to payroll taxes, and how much escapes payroll taxes as "dividends". But look out: if the IRS thinks that your salary is too low and your dividends too high, they may declare that the dividends were a salary in disguise, and hit you for back taxes and penalties. This may require an accountant's help.

As an employee of your own S corporation, you may be eligible for some tax-deductible fringe benefits, but not fully-deductible medical coverage. Owners of S corporations come under the same health insurance rules as partners, sole proprietors and LLC's. Employee-owners of regular C corporations, you will recall, are eligible for 100% tax-deductible medical coverage.

There are three significant tax advantages to an S corporation. The first and most obvious is the elimination of the double taxation. Second, where corporate tax rates are higher than individual rates, as is the case in some tax brackets, S corporations allow you to have the corporate structure without the higher tax rates.

The third advantage is due to some complex tax laws that allow current business losses to be carried back to prior years to offset prior years' taxes, bringing immediate tax refunds. Any business, corporation or otherwise, can avail itself of operating loss carryback laws (explained in more detail in the Tax section). But if a corporation is brand new and sustains a loss, there are no prior years to carry the loss back to. In the case of an S corporation, the loss passes through to the stockholders, and they can carry the loss back to their personal prior years' returns even though the business did not exist then. Losses that cannot be carried back can be carried forward to offset future years' earnings, but obviously you must wait a full year or more, instead of getting immediate refunds from a carry-back.

An S corporation can have up to 75 shareholders (stockholders). A husband and wife are counted as one stockholder. All shareholders must be U.S. citizens. All shareholders sign and file IRS Form #2553. There are limitations on who may be a stockholder, how profits are to be distributed, how and when the election to become an S corporation must be made, what kind of stock can be issued.

For more information, see IRS Publication #589, "Tax Information on S Corporations."

For state income taxes, most states recognize the S corporation, but a few states do not. Some states impose franchise, income or other corporate taxes on S corporations.

People who like the pass-through tax benefits of an S corporation, but who cannot or do not want to meet the requirements, might consider setting up instead as a Limited Liability Company. LLCs are very similar to S corporations (covered at the end of this section).

Steps to Incorporating a Business

The states, not the federal government, license corporations. The laws vary from state to state, as do the fees. Your state may have filing fees, organization fees, charter fees, license fees, qualification fees, annual report fees—which can run from minimal amounts in some states to thousands of dollars in others. Unless you are willing and able to study all the corporation laws, and file all the necessary forms yourself, add another $200 to $600 for a lawyer's assistance.

Start by contacting the Secretary of State, Office of Corporate Commissioner, or whatever state office registers corporations. Ask for their instructions, forms and fee schedules.

Generally, the first and most important step in the required incorporation procedures is the preparation of a "certificate" or "articles" of incorporation (sometimes called a "corporate charter" or "articles of association"). In some but not all states, the state itself can give you a printed form for the Articles of Incorporation. All you do is fill in the blanks, much like a deed or a mortgage. The Articles usually must include:

1. The proposed name of the corporation. The state can reject your proposed name if it is too similar to another corporation's name or if it is deceptive so as to mislead the public. Some states prohibit certain words in a corporation's name, typically words that might make the company sound like it is a government agency.

2. The purposes for which the corporation is formed. In some states, the wording of this section can be critical and, if improperly worded, can limit the type of business you can conduct.

3. Names and addresses of incorporators.

4. Location of the principal office of the corporation. Most small corporations obtain their charter from the state in which they are located.

Much has been written about the benefits of incorporating in a state other than your own, particularly Delaware, where the corporate statutes are lenient and the filing fees minimal. Most states, however, require in-state corporations, particularly small corporations where the majority of stockholders are state residents, to abide by state laws, pay in-state incorporation fees, and pay resident corporate income and franchise taxes, regardless of where the business is officially incorporated. In most cases, small corporations should incorporate in their home states.

5. The names of the future shareholders (called, depending on the state you live in, incorporators, subscribers or promoters) and the number of shares each subscribes to. This is known as a "limited stock offering". Corporate stock is issued either as a "limited offering" or as a "public offering". Most small (closely held) corporations make a limited offering, with each shareholder individually named in the articles of incorporation. After the initial issuance of stock, you need permission from the state to sell new shares or to sell old shares to new stockholders.

A corporation that is "going public"—making a public offering—can sell stock to anyone. States charge much higher fees to charter public corporations. Public corporations must register with the Federal Securities and Exchange Commission (the SEC) and hire CPA's to prepare annual audited financial statements.

When a certified public accounting firm audits your financial statements, they make a thorough examination of your ledgers, checking accuracy, examining supporting documents, following the "paper trail," doing their best to prove that your figures are correct. Then they issue an opinion, that your financial statements are accurate and prepared in accordance with "generally accepted accounting principles." This, as you can imagine, is a rather expensive undertaking. All public corporations are required by law to hire CPA's and publish audited financial statements. Most private corporations (those with "limited offerings") are not required to have their statements audited; and, of course, most don't.

6. The type and maximum amount of stock to be issued. Stock is classed as "common" or "preferred." Holders of preferred stock have prior or "preferred" claim on corporate assets over common stockholders. Preferred stockholders are often just investors with no interest in the corporation other than making money on their money. Stock must have either a "par value" (a stated value per share) or "no-par value" (value is not stated). You will probably avoid complications by issuing no-par stock. You must specify the number of shares authorized, often an arbitrary figure. Not all authorized shares have to be issued. As you can tell, there is a lot of legal double-talk here, but the correct wording can make the difference between a complicated and an easy incorporation.

7. Capital required at time of incorporation. This is another important decision and requires a knowledge of corporate "equity", which is comprised of "stated capital" and "paid-in surplus."

"Stated capital" is, basically, an amount of money that belongs to the corporation and cannot be paid out to stockholders until the corporation is liquidated. All corporations must have some stated capital. Some states specify the dollar minimum. Some states require the corporation to bank the stated capital in cash. This is protection for your creditors, to prevent the stockholders from raiding the company's assets and make it unable to pay its debts. Corporations try to keep stated capital as small as possible.

"Paid-in surplus" is money in excess of stated capital and generally not restricted.

In addition to filing the articles or certificate of incorporation, your state may require you to officially "reserve" your corporate name before you file your articles, file a separate form naming the elected officers, and request formal permission to issue stock.

If a lot of this sounds like a duplication of information already included in the articles of incorporation, you're right—it is. But the states still require separate forms (and additional fees).

Corporations must also have bylaws. Bylaws describe, in much greater detail than the articles, how to corporation is to be run: the rights and responsibilities of shareholders, directors and officers, the fiscal year, when meeting are to be held, how bylaws can be amended, and other issues important to the owners and to the operation of the business.

Acting Like A Corporation

In most states, one person can incorporate a business. But be it a one person corporation or a huge conglomerate, if you are going to incorporate you must play the corporate game entirely.

Your corporation must have at least one stockholder. The stockholders elect the directors: you must have at least one director. Directors make policy and oversee the operation. The directors appoint officers: you must have officers (though one person can hold all the positions) who run the business. Officers, in turn hire employees, who do the work. In a small corporation, one person often wears all four hats: stockholder, director, officer and employee.

Stockholders and directors must either hold meetings and keep written minutes of the meetings, or (if your state permits) take action by unanimous written consent.

It is important for even a one-person corporation to play by all the rules and to follow all the formalities. Most states require that you always identify your business as a corporation, using whatever terminology the state requires, such as Inc. or Corp. Make it clear to people you do business with, and anybody loaning money to the business, that you are an officer of a corporation, and not acting as an individual. In correspondence, writing checks, and signing contracts, sign your name "Julia Smith, President, Company Name Incorporated (or Inc., or Corp.)" rather than just Julia Smith. Do not sign "DBA" (doing business as) after your name, as this also implies that you are acting as an individual.

If you don't act like a corporation— issuing

stock, holding meetings, maintaining minimum capitalization requirements, keeping separate records, filing annual reports, and making sure all correspondence, contracts, checks, etc. indicate that this is a corporation—a court might rule that creditors can ignore the limited liability rules and go after your personal assets, like they can if your business is not incorporated. This is called "piercing the corporate veil (or shield)". This is something you do not want to happen.

A corporations can also lose its limited liability protection if it is undercapitalized, if the owners constantly drain the business of cash so it has ongoing problems paying its bills. Also be warned that if a corporation fails to file state tax returns or pay state taxes owed, your state may be able to suspend or revoke your corporate charter.

Joe's Janitorial, Inc.

We had a "credit manager", a "warehouse manager", the whole bit. I'd put people on hold, wait, and pick up again.
—John Egard, First Team Sports Co.

Incorporating an Existing Business

A business can incorporate when it first opens its doors or any time afterward. You can start you business as a sole proprietorship or a partnership, both of which cost much less to start and involve a lot less paperwork than a corporation; and incorporate the business later, after you know the business is going to be successful, and you can afford the additional cost, and you can see a real reason to incorporate.

LIMITED LIABILITY COMPANY (LLC)

The Limited Liability Company is a new form of business similar to a corporation. LLCs are being used more and more as alternatives to S corporations, general partnerships and limited partnerships. LLCs offer many of the benefits, yet few of the drawbacks of these more familiar forms of business.

The Limited Liability Company is similar to an S corporation, with limited liability for the owners (who are usually referred to as "members") and pass-through profits taxable to the owners but not to the business.

But there are important differences. Most states require two or more people to set up an LLC. One person can usually set up a corporation. A husband and wife count as two people, so they could set up an LLC in most states.

Many states put a limited life on LLCs, often a maximum of thirty years. Corporations can continue in business indefinitely. Some states restrict transferability of ownership of LLCs. One of the major reasons people incorporate is to get that ease of ownership transferability.

LLCs offer more generous loss deductions than S corporations, allow more classes of ownership (such as voting and non-voting), have more freedom in deciding how profits and losses are to be divided, and are not limited to the S corporation's maximum of 75 shareholders nor to the S corporation requirement that shareholders be U.S. citizens

Depending on your state's laws, LLCs possibly are not bound by sometimes-troublesome corporate rules such as minimum capitalization. In most states, LLCs do not have to hold director or shareholder meetings, don't have to keep minutes, and don't issue corporate stock certificates. Some states require LLCs to pay franchise taxes and organization fees similar to corporations, but many states exempt LLCs from these taxes.

LLCs are also similar to general partnerships, with the important difference that owners of LLCs have limited liability just like corporate stockholders. Each member (owner) of an LLC is only personally liable for his or her own negligence and not the negligence of other members, which is a main reason many partnerships are restructuring as LLCs.

Some limited partnerships are restructuring as LLCs for the liability protection previously not available to the general partner (all limited partnerships must have at least one general partner with full, personal liability); and also because LLCs usually have fewer restrictions on ownership and fewer state regulations to follow than limited partnerships. Investors prefer LLCs over limited partnerships because they can take an active role managing an LLC, which they are prohibited from doing in a limited partnership.

LLC rules vary, sometimes quite a bit, from state to state (of course). LLCs are more attractive in some states than in others, because some states do have ownership restrictions, and some states impose corporate-type franchise taxes.

Some states do not allow some professional firms, particularly CPAs and lawyers, to set up as LLCs. There is another new business form, called a Limited Liability Partnership, or LLP, created just for these professionals. The LLP is only for those professionals not allowed to operate as LLCs. Regular general and limited partnerships can become LLCs, not LLPs.

LLCs, however, are still too new to be able to offer reliable answers to many questions you're likely to have. Reliable legal interpretations of LLC laws are not available, because there have been very few court rulings.

As people start using LLCs to circumnavigate old restrictions on general and limited partnerships and on S corporations, restrictions that were built into the rules to protect individuals from deception and fraud and negligence, and restrictions designed to close tax loopholes, new laws are likely to get passed placing some of these same restrictions on LLCs.

Setting Up An LLC

To become an LLC, you will have to register with your state's Secretary of State. An LLC may need Articles of Organization (similar to Articles of Incorporation) and an Operating Agreement (a cross between a partnership agreement and corporate by-laws).

For federal income tax purposes, the IRS treats most LLCs as partnerships, requiring a standard 1065 partnership tax return. Because LLCs are treated as partnerships, LLCs do not pay federal income taxes. The members (owners) pay income tax on their shares of the profits, whether distributed to them or not, just like partners in a general partnership.

Owners of LLCs (those active in the business) are subject to self-employment tax just like partners in a partnership. Unlike corporations, LLC owners are not employees of their business.

If any of the LLC owners are investors only, not active in the management or operation of the business, they are exempt from self-employment tax—but only if the LLC can qualify as a Limited Partnership. The Articles and Operating Agreement will require careful wording.

For state tax purposes, most states follow the federal rules and tax LLCs as partnerships. But some states tax LLCs as corporations. You definitely should find out about your state tax laws before deciding on becoming an LLC.

Members (owners) of LLCs, like owners of corporations, should make it very clear to everyone you do business with, that you are not acting as an individual but as a representative of a Limited Liability Company. Include "LLC" as part of the business name on all checks, stationery, contracts, business cards, etc. As with a corporation, members of LLCs can lose their liability protection if they fail to follow the rules.

Members of LLCs come under the same health coverage rules as sole proprietors, partners and owners of S corporations.

An existing business can convert to an LLC at any time in the future, should you find it suitable to your needs. Converting an existing corporation to an LLC may cause tax problems, but most partnerships can convert easily.

There is a brick wall out there waiting for everybody who grows too fast. It's invisible before you hit it.

—Arthur Lazere, Northgate Computers

**Section Four
TAXES**

"If the adjustments required by Section 481(a) and Regulation 1.481-1 are attributable to a change in method of accounting initiated by the taxpayer, the amount of such adjustments, to the extent such amount does not exceed the net amount which would have been required if the change had been made in the first taxable year, shall be taken into account by the taxpayer in computing taxable income in the manner provided in Section 481(b)(4)(B) and paragraph (b) of this section.

—Internal Revenue Code

Well as through this world I've rambled
I've seen lots of funny men
Some will rob you with a six-gun
And some with a fountain pen.

—"Pretty Boy Floyd" by Woody Guthrie

Deep In the Heart of Taxes

Throughout *Small Time Operator* I've made enough comments—maybe more than enough—about the intrusion of government into all our affairs. And an introduction to Taxes is an ideal setting to get into it again. But rather than criticize or defend that Wonderful American Institution known as Income Taxes, I'd just like to give you some information to help you deal with it.

This tax section of *Small Time Operator* will discuss federal income, self-employment and excise taxes; state income and gross receipts taxes; and a few other local taxes.

Because of the nature of the beast—the non-stop modifications and the complexity of the tax laws—this tax section is handled differently from the rest of the book. The tax section is like a third grade reader, simple and basic. Rather than presenting a step-by-step "all you need to know" guide to taxes (which would require at least five times the space), the tax section will provide you with a general education about taxes, including specifics of some of the basic and more important federal laws.

Even if you take your tax problems to an accountant, I think you should familiarize yourself with the information in this tax section. There is more to taxes than just filling out the tax forms every April 15. Many of the tax laws outlined in this section relate directly to every-day management of your business. The federal income tax laws affect your bookkeeping and, through a knowledge of which expenditures are and are not tax deductible, your business profit. What's more, you will be of greater help to your tax accountant, which means your tax accountant can be of greater help to you, if you have at least some familiarity with the federal income tax laws. In fact, the information here may help you think of some tax savings that your accountant may have overlooked.

The Tax Laws As They Apply to You

Many of the federal tax laws are designed solely to keep you from cheating the government out of what they think is rightfully theirs—your money. But a lot of these laws were enacted to save you money, to give you some sort of tax break. The Internal Revenue Service does make an effort, albeit a lame one, to educate people about beneficial tax laws; but basically it's up to you to dig in and find out how to save yourself tax dollars. The problem is that income tax laws tend to overwhelm most people because of their complexity and because of their sheer volume: so many different possibilities, so many "if's, and's and but's."

A lot of special effort has been put into this section of the book to help you understand the tax laws without getting trapped in the octopus tentacles of exceptions. This is accomplished by a four- step procedure:

Step 1: The basic tax rules, those that apply to most small businesses, are explained as simply as possible in plain English; no accounting doubletalk and no "if's, and's and but's."

Step 2: Following the basic rules, any special situations, exceptions or tricky catches in the law are explained. This is designed so you can skim over them rapidly and spot an area that may apply to you.

Step 3: Unusual and complex rules, most of which apply only to a minority of people, are mentioned in order to alert you to their existence but are not explained in detail.

Step 4: Free sources of complete tax information are listed so that you can more thoroughly study the subjects you need to know.

A tax is a compulsory payment for which no specific benefit is received in return.

—U.S. Treasury

93

A Warning

This Tax section does *not* provide complete information on all federal tax laws nor was it ever intended to. It is meant to be a general guideline to help you wade through the maze of rules and regulations that our government in its wisdom has seen fit to enact into law. Read the Tax section with this warning in mind, and I think you will find it helpful and informative. And remember, tax laws are in a constant state of change. Never assume that any tax law in effect last year is going to be in effect this year. It is your responsibility, and it could be to your benefit financially, to keep abreast of current tax law.

As additional help, you should get a copy of the IRS's *Tax Guide For Small Business* (Pub. #334), free from any IRS office. This Guide is surprisingly well written, revised every year, and contains about 200 pages on income, excise, and employment taxes for sole proprietors, partnerships, corporations and LLCs. If you use the IRS's *Tax Guide* in conjunction with *Small Time Operator* you shouldn't go wrong. (Hopefully.)

A warning about IRS help: Although IRS publications are usually accurate and reliable, the same cannot always be said of tax information the IRS gives out over the phone or in person. The IRS people do, on occasion, give out totally incorrect information. Tax laws are vastly complicated and even the experts make mistakes. Do not rely on verbal information unless you can verify it. Ask the IRS person for a reference in their *Tax Guide* or in one of their other publications, and look it up.

Please also keep in mind that these are federal laws, applicable to federal tax returns. For state returns, most state income tax laws are very similar or identical to these federal laws; but some states have different laws, different ways to compute depreciation, different deductions allowed or not allowed. Many of the differences are covered in this section. You should, however, study the instructions that come with your state tax forms. You might find additional state deductions that the IRS does not allow, and save some money on your state taxes. State taxes are covered more thoroughly at the end of this section.

It's an endless sequence of small details.
—*Business owner Kitson Logue*

Accounting Period: Calendar Year vs. Fiscal Year

Every business must keep books and file tax returns based on what the IRS calls a "taxable year", which is either a "calendar year" or a "fiscal year." A calendar year begins on January 1 and ends on December 31. A fiscal year is a twelve month period ending on the last day of any month other than December.

Most small businesses use a calendar year simply because it's easier. All of the federal and state tax procedures are geared to the calendar year: issuance of W-2's, 1099's and dividend and interest statements, and publication of the new tax forms and instructions.

The calendar year is also preferred by the Internal Revenue Service. They have strict and rather complex rules about who can adopt a fiscal year and when the decision must be made. The rules vary depending on how your business is legally structured.

Generally, sole proprietorships must use the same taxable year as the owner, which means the calendar year in most cases. The same rule applies to partnerships, S corporations, Limited Liability Companies (LLCs) and personal service corporations (corporations that primarily sell services performed by the owner-employees). The IRS will allow these businesses to adopt a fiscal year if there is a valid business reason for using a fiscal year. File form #8716, "Election to Have a Tax Year Other Than a Required Tax Year." Regular corporations can choose either a calendar or a fiscal year.

Why choose a fiscal year at all? Some businesses have definite yearly cycles and find that coordinating their taxable year with the business cycle better reflects actual income and expenses. Large department stores have traditionally chosen a January 31 fiscal year so they can have their January "white sales", to reduce their stock of merchandise on hand, thereby making the year-end inventory count much easier and less expensive. Corporations sometimes choose a fiscal year coinciding with the month the business first began operation, in order to avoid a short-period tax return and extra taxes the first year.

The tax laws discussed in this tax section apply to both calendar year and fiscal year taxpayers, except where otherwise noted.

Who Must File A Tax Return

Sole proprietors must file a federal income tax return if your *net* earnings from self-employment (your business *net* profit) is $400 or more. Business income minus expenses equals *net* profit. If you operate more than one business, combine the profits and losses of the different businesses to arrive at the total net profit.

Partnerships, corporations and LLCs must file a return no matter what the profit or loss is.

Which Tax Return To File

Sole Proprietors: Most sole proprietors will have to fill out a Schedule C, Profit or Loss From Business. Schedule C is part of your regular 1040 return. The profit or loss on Schedule C is combined with any other taxable income or loss on your 1040. If you have more than one business, file a separate Schedule C for each business.

Some very small service businesses may only have to fill out the much simpler Schedule C-EZ, "Net Profit From Business", which truly is "EZ": one total figure for gross income, one total figure for expenses, and your net profit. That, and a few questions about your vehicle, is it. Schedule C-EZ, however, can only be used by sole proprietors who meet all nine of the following requirements:

1. Business expenses of $2,500 or less.
2. No inventory at any time during the year.
3. Did not have a net loss.
4. Had no employees.
5. Deducted no depreciation, amortization, or first year write-off of depreciable assets.
6. Deducted no expenses for a home office.
7. Used the cash method of accounting.
8. Owned only one sole proprietorship.
9. No prior year passive activity losses (if you don't know what that means, you probably didn't have any).

Partnerships and LLCs: File Form 1065, "U.S. Partnership Return of Income". No taxes are due with this return. Each partner or LLC member gets a copy of Schedule K-1 (1065), "Partner's Share of Income, Credits, Deductions, Etc.". Partners report their individual share of the partnership or LLC income (whether distributed to them or not) on their 1040 return, using Schedule E, "Supplemental Income and Loss". (LLCs are taxed as partnerships by the IRS, so

all federal partnership tax laws apply to LLCs.)

Corporations: Regular C corporations report income and pay taxes on Form 1120 or 1120-A. S corporations file Form 1120-S, but like partnerships, pay no income taxes. Each S corporation shareholder gets a copy of Schedule K-1 (1120-S), "Shareholder's Share of Income, Credits, Deductions, Etc.". Shareholders report their individual share of the S corporation income on their 1040 return, using Schedule E, "Supplemental Income and Loss".

Filing Dates for Tax Returns

For calendar-year businesses other than corporations, the federal income tax return is due April 15. For corporations, due date is March 15.

Automatic extensions to file returns (but not to pay the taxes):

Sole proprietors, members of LLCs and partners in partnerships (not the partnership itself) can obtain an automatic four-month extension, to August 15, by filing IRS Form #4868, and paying the estimated tax due, on or before April 15. Beyond the automatic four-month extension, the IRS will sometimes allow an additional two-month extension, to October 15, but only for "very good reasons" (those are the IRS's words, and they make the decision). File Form #2688, but only after you first file Form #4868.

Corporations can obtain an automatic six-month extension, to September 15, by filing Form #7004 and paying the estimated tax due, by the March 15 due date.

Partnerships and LLCs can obtain an automatic three-month extension, to July 15, by filing Form #8736 by April 15. Since partnerships and

LLCs pay no income taxes, no taxes are due with the extension. Partners and LLC members file their own personal extensions on Form #4868.

All the above extensions (except Form #2688) must be filed by the original due date of the return and must include payment for all taxes due. If you underpay your taxes by more than 10%, the IRS will hit you with a penalty.

Fiscal year taxpayers: For businesses other than corporations, the federal income tax return is due on the fifteenth day of the fourth month following the end of the fiscal year. Corporate returns are due on the fifteenth day of the third month. The same extensions described above are available to fiscal-year businesses.

State tax returns: Many states offer extensions of time to file state returns. Some states go by the federal rules, but some are different. Check your state income tax instruction book.

Tax Calendar for Businesses

The tax calendar lists due dates for federal and state tax reports. Each date shown is the last day on which to perform the required action without penalty. If the due date for filing a return, making a tax payment, etc. falls on a Saturday, Sunday or legal holiday, the date is moved to the next regular work day.

Tax deposits that are due weekly and monthly throughout the year are listed at the end of the calendar.

To help you spot the dates applicable to your business, the first word in each description will tell who the information applies to, such as Employers, Corporations, etc. "Individuals" refers to sole proprietors, partners (not partnerships), corporate stockholders (not the corporations), and LLC members (not the LLCs).

These dates apply to calendar year taxpayers. Businesses using a fiscal year must change some of the dates (see the end of the calendar). These dates don't usually change from year to year, but they can. Verify them before relying on them.

JANUARY 1-MARCH 16

Corporations that meet certain requirements may elect, during this period, to be treated as S corporations during current and future years. Use Form 2553.

JANUARY 15

Individuals must either pay the balance due on prior year's estimated income tax or file an income tax return (Form 1040) on or before January 31 and pay the full amount of the tax due. See January 31.

Farmers and fishermen may elect to file declaration of estimated income tax (Form 1040-ES) for prior year and pay estimated tax in full, and file income tax return (Form 1040) by April 15. If declaration of estimated tax is not filed, see February 28.

JANUARY 31

Individuals should file an income tax return for prior year and pay the tax due, if the balance on their prior year's estimated tax was not paid by January 15. Use Form 1040. Farmers and fishermen, see February 28.

Employers last day for giving every employee Form W-2 showing income and social security information. Also see February 28.

Employers deposit federal unemployment tax (FUTA) at an authorized bank if the tax is more than $100. If the amount is $100 or less, you are not required to deposit it, but you must add it to the taxes for the next quarter. Then, in the next quarter, if the total undeposited tax is more than $100, deposit it by the last day of the month following the quarter. Use Form 8109.

Employers file Form 941 for income tax withheld and social security and Medicare taxes for the fourth quarter of the prior year and pay any taxes due. If timely deposits were made, see February 10.

Businesses liable for excise taxes must file quarterly excise tax return. Use Form 720.

Employers subject to federal unemployment tax file annual return for the prior year. Use Form 940. If timely deposits were made in full payment of the tax, see February 10.

All businesses: most state sales tax returns for the 4th quarter of last year are due.

Corporations that paid $10 or more in dividends or interest must prepare Form 1099 & give one copy to each recipient. See also February 28.

All businesses that paid $600 or more to an individual in commissions, fees or other compensation including payments to subcontractors must prepare Form 1099 & give one copy to each recipient. See also February 28.

All businesses that sold $5,000 or more of goods to independent sales agents must prepare Form 1099 and give one copy to each agent. See also February 28.

All businesses that paid $600 or more in interest must prepare form 1099-INT & give one copy to each recipient. See also February 28.

All businesses that paid $10 or more in royalties must prepare Form 1099-MISC & give one copy to each recipient. See also February 28.

Operators of fishing boats give each self-employed crew member a statement showing member's share for the year, using Form 1099-MISC. See also February 28.

FEBRUARY 10

Employers who made timely deposits in full payment of all income taxes withheld and social security and Medicare taxes due for the 4th quarter of the prior year file 4th quarter return. Use Form 941.

Employers subject to federal unemployment tax who made timely deposits in full payment of the tax file annual return for the prior year. Use Form 940.

FEBRUARY 28

All businesses that prepared Form 1099 (See Jan. 31) file the 1099's with transmittal Form 1096 with IRS.

Employers must file Form W-3, Transmittal of Income and Tax Statements, with the Social Security Administration if you have issued Form W-2 (See Jan. 31). Copy A of each W-2 must accompany Form W-3.

Employers whose employees receive tips must report those tips on Form 8027.

Farmers and fishermen who did not file declaration of estimated tax on January 15 should file final income tax return (Form 1040) for prior year.

MARCH 15

Corporations must file federal income tax return, Form 1120, or application for extension, Form 7004, and pay to a depositary the balance of tax still due.

S Corporations must file federal income tax Form 1120S.

Corporations must file state income tax returns for the following states: Ala., Alaska, Calif., D.C., Ill., Maine, Mass., Md., Minn., Miss., Nebr., N.H., N. Mex., N.Y., N.C., Okla., R.I., S.C., Vt., W. Va., Wis.

MARCH 31

Corporations must file state income tax returns for the following states: Conn., Del., Fla., Ohio, Tenn.

APRIL 15

Individuals must file a federal income tax return for the prior calendar year. The tax due must be paid in full with this return. Schedule C or C-EZ must be filed (Schedule F for farmers), and in addition, Schedule SE must be completed. If you desire an automatic 4-month extension, file Form 4868 accompanied by payment of your estimated unpaid income tax liability.

Individuals file a declaration of estimated income tax (including self-employment tax) for the current year and pay at least 25 percent of such tax. Use Form 1040-ES.

Partnerships and LLCs must file a return for the prior calendar year. Use Form 1065 (no tax due).

Corporations deposit first installment of this year's estimated income tax.

Individuals must file a state income tax return for all states collecting income tax except Ark., Del., Hawaii, Va., La., and Iowa.

Corporations must file state income tax returns for the following states: Ariz., Colo., Ga., Idaho, Ind., Kans., Ky., Mo., N.J., N.D., Ore., Pa., Utah, Va., La.

APRIL 20

Individuals in Hawaii file state income tax return.

Corporations in Hawaii file state income tax returns.

APRIL 30

Individuals living in Del., Va. or Iowa must file a state income tax return.

Corporations in Mich. & Iowa file state income tax returns.

All businesses: most states sales tax returns for the first quarter are due.

Employers file Form 941 for income tax withheld and social security & Medicare taxes for the 1st quarter, pay taxes due. If timely deposits were made, see May 10.

Employers deposit federal unemployment tax (FUTA) at an authorized bank if the tax is more than $100. If the amount is $100 or less, you are not required to deposit it, but you must add it to the taxes for the next quarter. Then, in the next quarter, if the total undeposited tax is more than $100, deposit it by the last day of the month following the quarter. Use Form 8109.

Businesses liable for excise taxes must file quarterly excise tax return. Use Form 720.

MAY 10

Employers who made timely deposits in full payment of income tax withheld, & social security & Medicare taxes for the 1st quarter, file 1st quarter return. Use Form 941.

MAY 15

Individuals in Ark. & La file state income tax returns.

Corporations in Ark. & Mont. file state income tax returns.

JUNE 15

Individuals must pay 2nd installment of estimated income tax.

Corporations deposit second installment of estimated income tax.

JULY 31

Employers file Form 941 for income tax withheld and social security and Medicare taxes for the 2nd quarter and pay any taxes due. If timely deposits were made, see August 10.

Businesses liable for excise taxes must file quarterly excise tax return. Use Form 720.

Employers deposit federal unemployment tax (FUTA) at an authorized bank if the tax is more than $100. If the amount is $100 or less, you are not required to deposit it, but you must add it to the taxes for the next quarter. Then, in the next quarter, if the total undeposited tax is more than $100, deposit it by the last day of the month following the quarter. Use Form 8109.

All businesses: most state sales tax returns for the 2nd quarter are due.

Employers with an employee benefit, pension, profit sharing, or stock bonus plan, file Form 5500 for the previous calendar year.

AUGUST 10

Employers who made timely deposits in full payment of all income tax withheld and social security and Medicare taxes due for the 2nd quarter, file 2nd quarter return. Use Form 941.

AUGUST 15

Individuals who received an automatic 4-month extension for filing last year's federal income tax return must now file the return. Form 1040.

AUGUST 31

Heavy-duty truck owners and operators must pay the federal use tax on highway motor vehicles used on the public highways. Use Form 2290.

SEPTEMBER 15

Individuals must pay 3rd installment of estimated income tax. Use Form 1040-ES.

Corporations deposit 3rd installment of estimated income tax.

Corporations that received an automatic 6-month extension for filing last year's federal income tax return must now file the return, on Form 1120, 1120-A or 1120-S.

OCTOBER 31

Employers file Form 941 for income tax withheld and social security and Medicare taxes for the 3rd quarter and pay any taxes due. If timely deposits were made, see November 10.

All businesses: most state sales tax returns for the 3rd quarter are due.

Businesses liable for excise taxes must file quarterly excise tax return. Use Form 720.

Employers deposit federal unemployment tax (FUTA) at an authorized bank if the tax is more than $100. If the amount is $100 or less, you are not required to deposit it, but you must add it to the taxes for the next quarter. Then, in the next quarter, if the total undeposited tax is more than $100, deposit it by the last day of the month following the quarter. Use Form 8109.

NOVEMBER

Employers should request a new Form W-4 from each employee whose withholding exemptions will be different next year.

NOVEMBER 10

Employers who made timely deposits in full payment of income tax withheld & social security & Medicare taxes due for the 3rd quarter, file 3rd quarter return. Use Form 941.

DECEMBER 15

Corporations deposit the 4th installment of estimated income tax.

WEEKLY AND MONTHLY ALL YEAR

Corporations that meet certain requirements may elect, any time during the year, to be treated as S corporations in future years. Use Form 2553. To be treated as an S corporation this year, see Jan. 1.

Employers: tax deposits of social security and Medicare (NOT self-employment) and withheld income taxes required monthly (by the 15th of the following month) whenever amount due is $500 or more; required 8 times a month whenever amounts due are $3000 or more.

Businesses liable for excise taxes are required to make monthly deposits on the last day of the month when more than $100 in excise taxes is collected. For more information, see IRS publication #510.

FISCAL YEAR TAXPAYERS

Individuals: federal tax return 1040 is due the 15th day of the 4th month after the end of your tax year.

Partnerships and LLCs: federal tax return 1065 is due the 15th day of the 4th month after the end of your tax year.

Corporations: federal income tax return 1120 or 1120-S is due the 15th day of the 3rd month after the end of your tax year.

All fiscal year businesses: many states follow the same schedule as the federal government for filing state income tax returns, but some states have different dates. Consult your own state.

Individuals: federal estimated tax payments are due on the 15th day of the 4th, 6th, & 9th months of your tax year, & on the 15th day of the first month after your tax year.

Corporations: federal estimated tax payments are due on the 15th day of the 4th, 6th, 9th & 12th months of your tax year.

Corporations electing to be S Corporations must file Form 2553 by the 15th day of the 3rd month of the tax year.

Employers maintaining an employee benefit, pension, profit sharing, or stock bonus plan, must file Form 5500 by the last day of the 7th month following the end of the taxable year.

Business Expenses

All legitimate business expenses, except those specifically disallowed by law (covered later), are deductible in computing your taxable income, as long as they meet the IRS's three basic rules:

One: The expenses must be incurred in connection with your business.

Two: The expenses must be "ordinary and necessary." "Ordinary" expenses are ones that are common or accepted in your type of business. They do not have to be recurring or habitual. A "necessary" expense, according to the IRS, is one "that is appropriate and helpful in developing and maintaining your trade or business".

Three: The amounts must be "reasonable."

Expenditures that are partly personal (non-business) and partly business can be prorated and the business portion expensed or depreciated. Sometimes your home or your automobile fall in this category. Proration of rent was explained in the bookkeeping section. Proration of automobile expenses is explained in this Tax section. Business expenses that you pay on your personal credit card are also fully deductible.

Any asset that you originally purchased and used for non-business purposes that you are now using for business or using partly for business can be depreciated as of the date you began using the asset in your business. It does not matter when you purchased the item. The depreciation chapter has complete information.

And remember, try to get receipts for everything, and keep them.

Partners in partnerships, and owners of corporations and LLCs: Try not to pay business expenses out of your personal funds. Business deductions are sometimes disallowed when claimed by owners or employees, instead of by the companies themselves. If you must pay any business expenses out of your own pocket, have the business reimburse you, so the business itself can claim the deductions.

Start-Up Expenses

Business expenses incurred before you start your business (called start-up expenses, though they are really pre-start-up expenses) come under two different tax rules.

General preliminary costs incurred before you actually pick a specific business, such as investigating different business possibilities and checking out locations, are usually not deductible at all. The IRS considers these "personal expenses," no tax write-off ever.

Once you've decided on a particular business, the start-up expenses (not including the general preliminary costs mentioned above) are deductible, but not 100% the year you incur them. You have the option to capitalize them, which means no deduction at all until you quit or sell your business; or to write them off ("amortize" them) over a 60-month period, or longer if you prefer, starting the month the business begins operation. ("Amortize" is an accounting term for writing off intangible assets over a period of years).

To figure your deduction, divide your total start-up costs by the number of months in the write-off period (at least 60, but more if you want to spread the tax deduction over a longer period). The result is the amount you can deduct each month. Use Form 4562, the part labeled Amortization, to show your calculations. To get this amortization option, you must start taking the deduction the first year you are in business. Otherwise, you lose the option and will be required to capitalize the start-up expenses.

Start-up expenses are a real sore spot for new businesses, because the expenses include any and all business expenditures incurred before you are open for business. They include organizational expenses, such as hiring an accountant or a lawyer to draft up legal documents; and even conventional pre-opening expenses such as rent, telephone, advertising, stationery, etc.

The IRS has often wrangled with taxpayers over which costs are and aren't "start-up," and at what point a new venture is actually "in business." The IRS has stated that a business hasn't actually started until it produces income. Tax Courts have disagreed and have ruled that once a business is set up and "open for business," it is officially started even if it has not made a sale yet. This is an area to discuss with an accountant. I suggest you put off as many expenses as possible until after the business is operating.

Don't let a lack of qualifications stop you from pursuing your career goals. I was never qualified for any of the positions I achieved.

—*U.S. Congressman (and singer) Sonny Bono*

One way around some of the start-up expense hassles is to start your business at home if that's feasible, just as small an operation as possible to meet IRS requirements. Once you have generated a little income, *then* spend your money on finding a new location, on stationery, furniture and equipment, and on accounting and legal advice. Since you are now officially in business, the expenses are deductible as regular business expenses, no longer subject to the start-up rules.

If you do incur start-up expenses but never actually start a business, the expenses may, in some situations, be deductible as a capital loss under the IRS's capital gains and loss rules. You will probably need an accountant's help.

If You Already Are In Business: If you are expanding a business, adding a new outlet, adding a new division, etc., it is not considered a start-up. The expenses are deductible. If you are starting a second business, if possible try to structure it as an expansion of your current business to avoid these start-up rules.

100 Typical Business Expenses

Below is a listing of over 100 typical business expenses that can be deducted on your income tax return. If you would like a much more extensive list of deductions, my book **422 Tax Deductions For Businesses and Self Employed Individuals** lists and explains many, many more than I can fit into this book. Remember, you get a raise every time you find a legitimate tax deduction! It's worth the hunting.

The expenses marked with an asterisk (*) are explained in more detail on the following pages. The number following each expense corresponds to the column number in the expenditure ledger, so you can tell at a glance in which column to post the expense. "Y/E" after an item means that the expense is recorded on the year-end summary only. Year-end procedures were explained in the bookkeeping section.

Any expense that meets the IRS's three rules (incurred in connection with your business, meets the "ordinary and necessary" test, is "reasonable"), if not specifically disallowed, should be taken whether it is on this list or not. Those expenses specifically disallowed are listed later in this section.

This listing is also a guide to filling out your income tax return. The Schedule C tax form, "Profit or Loss From Business", lists only 20 or so categories of expense. These are broad, general categories. There are many legitimate, deductible expenses not listed on the tax form.

To help you figure out your tax form, I've grouped the 100-plus expenses by tax return category. But don't feel this is cemented in stone. It is not critical which expenses go on which lines on the tax form. The IRS is not going to be upset if an expense that belongs on one line winds up on another. Even I'm not sure whether some expenses should be called "office expenses" or "supplies". If you have an expense you don't know where to put on the tax return, just pick a reasonable category and put it there.

It is a good idea to make a worksheet showing which expenses you combined for the tax return, and keep it with your copy of your return (no need to send it to the IRS). This will make things a lot easier should you ever face an audit, or if you need to check your figures later, or if you are just looking back a year later trying to figure out how to fill out the next year's tax return.

The bold categories below are from a recent Schedule C, though there's no telling if the IRS will suddenly decide to redesign the tax form, *again*, and change these.

Advertising
Advertising (5)
Business gifts (5)*

Bad Debts
Bad debts (Y/E)*

Car and truck expenses
Vehicle expenses (9 or Y/E)*
If you rent or lease a vehicle, the expense goes under "Rent or lease", not here.

Commissions and fees
Commissions (3)
Consultant fees (3)
Independent and outside contractors (3)
Fees for services (3)

Depreciation
Amortization of intangibles (Y/E)*
Depreciation (Y/E)*
Equipment (see Depreciation)
Machinery (see Depreciation)
Office furniture (see Depreciation)

SCHEDULE C (Form 1040)
Profit or Loss From Business
(Sole Proprietorship)

▶ Partnerships, joint ventures, etc., must file Form 1065.

Department of the Treasury Internal Revenue Service (R) ▶ Attach to Form 1040 or Form 1041. ▶ See Instructions for Schedule C (Form 1040). Sequence No. **09**

Name of proprietor: Samuel Thesham

Social security number (SSN): 123 45 6789

A Principal business or profession, including product or service (see page C-1): auto repair

B Enter principal business code (see page C-6) ▶ 8 9 5 3

C Business name. If no separate business name, leave blank: Monkeywrench Motors

D Employer ID number (EIN), if any

E Business address (including suite or room no.) ▶ 7831 Cavemont, Berkeley CA 94710
City, town or post office, state, and ZIP code

F Accounting method: (1) ☐ Cash (2) ☒ Accrual (3) ☐ Other (specify) ▶

G Method(s) used to value closing inventory: (1) ☒ Cost (2) ☐ Lower of cost or market (3) ☐ Other (attach explanation) (4) ☐ Does not apply (if checked, skip line H) — Yes / No

H Was there any change in determining quantities, costs, or valuations between opening and closing inventory? If "Yes," attach explanation — X (No)

I Did you "materially participate" in the operation of this business during 1994? If "No," see page C-2 for limit on losses. — X (Yes)

J If you started or acquired this business during 1994, check here ▶ ☐

Part I — Income

1	Gross receipts or sales. Caution: If this income was reported to you on Form W-2 and the "Statutory employee" box on that form was checked, see page C-2 and check here ▶ ☐	32,364
2	Returns and allowances	0
3	Subtract line 2 from line 1	32,364
4	Cost of goods sold (from line 40 on page 2)	2,008
5	Gross profit. Subtract line 4 from line 3	30,356
6	Other income, including Federal and state gasoline or fuel tax credit or refund (see page C-2)	0
7	Gross income. Add lines 5 and 6	30,356

Part II — Expenses. Enter expenses for business use of your home only on line 30.

8	Advertising	150	19	Pension and profit-sharing plans	
9	Bad debts from sales or services (see page C-3)		20	Rent or lease (see page C-4):	
10	Car and truck expenses (see page C-3)	480	20a	Vehicles, machinery, and equipment	
11	Commissions and fees	5,650	20b	Other business property	1,200
12	Depletion		21	Repairs and maintenance	
13	Depreciation and section 179 expense deduction (not included in Part III) (see page C-3)	136	22	Supplies (not included in Part III)	218
			23	Taxes and licenses	267
14	Employee benefit programs (other than on line 19)		24	Travel, meals, and entertainment:	
15	Insurance (other than health)	650	24a	Travel	
16	Interest:		24b	Meals and entertainment	
16a	Mortgage (paid to banks, etc.)		24c	Enter 50% of line 24b subject to limitations (see page C-4)	
16b	Other	637	24d	Subtract line 24c from line 24b	
17	Legal and professional services		25	Utilities	221
18	Office expense	78	26	Wages (less employment credits)	
			27	Other expenses (from line 46 on page 2)	70
28	Total expenses before expenses for business use of home. Add lines 8 through 27 in columns ▶		28		9,757
29	Tentative profit (loss). Subtract line 28 from line 7		29		20,599
30	Expenses for business use of your home. Attach Form 8829		30		
31	Net profit or (loss). Subtract line 30 from line 29.		31		20,599

- If a profit, enter on Form 1040, line 12, and ALSO on Schedule SE, line 2 (statutory employees, see page C-5). Estates and trusts, enter on Form 1041, line 3.
- If a loss, you MUST go on to line 32.

32 If you have a loss, check the box that describes your investment in this activity (see page C-5).
- If you checked 32a, enter the loss on Form 1040, line 12, and ALSO on Schedule SE, line 2 (statutory employees, see page C-5). Estates and trusts, enter on Form 1041, line 3.
- If you checked 32b, you MUST attach Form 6198.

32a ☐ All investment is at risk.
32b ☐ Some investment is not at risk.

For Paperwork Reduction Act Notice, see Form 1040 instructions. Cat. No. 11334P Schedule C (Form 1040)

Schedule C (Form 1040) Page 2

Part III — Cost of Goods Sold (see page C-5)

33	Inventory at beginning of year. If different from last year's closing inventory, attach explanation	33	$100
34	Purchases less cost of items withdrawn for personal use	34	1,958
35	Cost of labor. Do not include salary paid to yourself	35	
36	Materials and supplies	36	
37	Other costs	37	
38	Add lines 33 through 37	38	$2,058
39	Inventory at end of year	39	50
40	Cost of goods sold. Subtract line 39 from line 38. Enter the result here and on page 1, line 4	40	$2,008

Part IV — Information on Your Vehicle. Complete this part ONLY if you are claiming car or truck expenses on line 10 and are not required to file Form 4562 for this business.

41 When did you place your vehicle in service for business purposes? (month, day, year) ▶ / /

42 Of the total number of miles you drove your vehicle during 1993, enter the number of miles you used your vehicle for:
a Business _____ b Commuting _____ c Other _____

43 Do you (or your spouse) have another vehicle available for personal use? ☐ Yes ☐ No

44 Was your vehicle available for use during off-duty hours? ☐ Yes ☐ No

45a Do you have evidence to support your deduction? ☐ Yes ☐ No
b If "Yes," is the evidence written? ☐ Yes ☐ No

Part V — Other Expenses. List below business expenses not included on lines 8–26 or line 30.

New car manuals	$70

46	Total other expenses. Enter here and on page 1, line 27	46	$70

© U.S. Government Printing Office:

Software (Y/E)*
Tools (see Depreciation)

Insurance
Bonding fees (10)
Insurance (10)*
All deductible business insurance except health (unless incorporated as a C corporation), and vehicle (if taking the Standard Mileage Allowance or if included in "Car Expenses" above).

Interest
Interest on business debt (10)*

Legal and professional services
Accounting fees (3)
Auditing fees (3)
Bookkeeping services (3)
Burglar alarm service (10)
Cleaning services (3)
Collection agency fees (10)
Credit bureau fees (10)
Dues, business and professional associations (10)
Dues, union (10)

Employment agency fees (10)
Fees to organizations (10)
Janitorial services (3)
Lawyers (3)
Legal expenses (10)
Merchant's associations (10)
Night watch service (10)
Professional organizations (10)
Security service (10)
Tax preparation (business portion only)(3)

Office Expense
Account books (2)
Bank service charges (2)
Books (2)
Business cards (2)
Coffee service (2)
Computer supplies (2)
Credit card fees (2)
Ledgers (2)
Magazines (2)
Office Supplies (2)
Periodicals (2)
Postage (2)

Professional journals (2)
Publications (2)
Safe deposit box (2)
Software (useful life one year or less)(2)*
Stationery (2)
This book (2)

Rent or lease
Rent (6)
Rent or lease of a vehicle goes in this category, not under "Car and Truck Expenses".

Repairs and maintenance
Minor repairs (10)*

Supplies
This category refers to industrial supplies. Office supplies should be included with "Office Expense". If this is a significant category for you, it should have its own column in the expenditure ledger. This "Supplies" category does NOT include manufacturing supplies or supplies that are part of inventory. Such supplies must be part of the Cost of Goods Sold calculations.
Clothing, special (10)*
Shipping supplies (10) (*but see Inventory*)
Tools (small, useful life one year or less)(10)
Uniforms (10)

Taxes and licenses
Business license (8)
Employer's taxes (8)
Floor tax (8)*
Income taxes (state only)(8)*
Inventory tax (8)
Gross receipts tax (8)*
License fees (8)*
Passport fees (8)
Permit fees (8)
Property taxes (8)*
Sales tax (collected from customers)(8)*

Travel, meals and entertainment
Conventions (see Travel Away From Home)(10)*
Entertainment (10)*
Trade shows (see Travel Away From Home)(10)*
Travel away from home (10)*

Utilities
Electricity (7)
Garbage (7)
Gas (not for vehicles)(7)

Heating (7)
Telephone (7, or its own column if you want to keep separate track of telephone bills).
Water (7)

Wages
Payroll (4)
Withheld payroll taxes (4)
Employee benefits
Employee pension and profit-sharing plans

Other expenses
Some casualty losses (burglary, vandalism, fire, storm, etc.) may be deductible here. See Casualty losses* (10 or elsewhere)
Charitable contributions (corps. only)(10)*
Education expenses (10)*
Moving expenses (10)*
Research & experimentation (in some cases)(10)

Cost of goods sold
Cost of goods sold (1)*
Freight (see discussion)*
Inventory (1)*
Shipping (see discussion under Freight)(1 or 2)*

VEHICLE EXPENSES

All expenses of operating a vehicle for business are deductible *except regular commuting expenses* between your home and your usual place of business, which the IRS considers personal and not deductible. There are two ways of figuring vehicle expenses. As in so many other situations, one is difficult and one is easy.

Method One: You can keep itemized records of all your vehicle expenses. These include gasoline, oil, lubrication, maintenance, repairs, insurance, parking and tolls, garage rents, license and registration fees, interest on the purchase, even auto club dues. The purchase price of the vehicle and the cost of major repairs such as an engine overhaul may have to be depreciated over several years. See the Depreciation chapter.

Vehicle expenses must be prorated between personal use (not deductible—and remember commuting to and from the office is considered personal use), and business use (fully deductible). The most common method of proration is based on the miles driven. For example, if you drove

10,000 miles last year of which 2,500 miles was for business, 25% of all your vehicle expenses are deductible, and 25% of the cost of your vehicle can be depreciated.

Keeping itemized records of all your vehicle expenses is tedious work. The Internal Revenue Service realizes this also. In one of their rare helpful moods they have come up with...

Method Two: An optional Standard Mileage Allowance (Standard Mileage Rate). Instead of recording each fill up and every oil change, you may take a standard flat rate for every business mile driven (again, not including the commute). The 1997 rate is 31.5¢ per mile. The standard mileage allowance is in lieu of depreciation and all vehicle expenses except parking, tolls, interest, and state and local taxes, which are deductible in addition to the mileage allowance (sales tax on the vehicle is not deductible).

Sole proprietors report vehicle expenses on form #4562 if you are required to fill out that form for depreciation or first-year write-off of any assets; or on the back of Schedule C, if form #4562 isn't otherwise required.

The Fine Print: You may not use the Standard Mileage Allowance if you lease the vehicle, if you use the vehicle for hire such as a taxi, or if your business operates more than one vehicle at a time (you can use more than one vehicle for business as long as both vehicles are not being used at the same time). Business vehicles that do not qualify for the Standard Mileage Allowance may still use Method One, itemizing expenses.

Using the standard mileage rate reduces the cost basis of your vehicle (for figuring profit or loss when the vehicle is sold). You must reduce the basis by 12¢ for each business mile driven.

The method you choose the first year you use your vehicle for business determines what methods you can use in future years (for that vehicle). If you use Method One (itemizing) the first year, you must stay with that method as long as you use that vehicle. If you use the Standard Mileage Allowance the first year, you can switch back and forth if you want, itemizing some years and using the mileage allowance other years. If you do switch from the mileage allowance to itemizing, you must use straight line depreciation.

If you choose Method One, depreciation is limited if the vehicle costs over a certain amount or if the vehicle is used 50% or less for business. See the Depreciation chapter.

Leasing a Vehicle

The business portion of a vehicle lease is deductible, as long as it isn't a lease-purchase. A lease-purchase is considered a purchase for tax purposes. A lease, however, may require you to report part of your lease payments as income. No, that's not a typo! When you lease a car, you get a tax deduction *and* you may have to report additional income, even though you didn't bring in any income. It's a strange tax law that you'll need to investigate, because I'm not going to cover it here.

For more information, see IRS Publication #917, "Business Use of a Car".

INTEREST EXPENSE

Interest paid on business debts (including interest on credit-card purchases) is deductible, with a few important exceptions.

Interest on loans to purchase, improve or construct real estate must usually be capitalized; that is, added to the cost of the property.

Interest on back taxes is not deductible (except for corporations), according to the IRS. Some Tax Courts disagree. Check with your accountant.

If you borrow money to purchase part or all of an existing business, the laws can get complicated. If the business is a sole proprietorship, partnership or S corporation, part of the interest may be deductible as a current business expense, but part may have to be capitalized. Generally, the interest on the part of the loan that applies to actual business assets (equipment, inventory, etc) is deductible. The interest that applies to intangibles (goodwill, trademarks, etc.) must be capitalized. If you are purchasing a regular C corporation (not an S corporation), you are actually buying stock, and the interest comes under a different set of rules (investment income and expense) and is not deductible as a regular business expense. Obviously, this is an area where you will probably need professional help.

Corporations: If you are an employee of your own corporation, and you get a personal loan to purchase business assets, the interest is not deductible as a business expense. If the corporation itself borrows the money, the interest is deductible. As you can see, how you structure corporate finances can have a major effect on how much you pay in taxes.

ENTERTAINMENT

Only 50% of entertainment expenses are deductible on your tax return. In some cases there is a fine line as to what is entertainment (subject to the 50% limit) and what is not entertainment and therefore fully deductible. A company or holiday party where all employees are invited (as well as customers and prospective customers) is 100% deductible. A fashion show put on by a dress designer would not be considered entertainment, but a 100% deductible business expense. A party or lunch after the show, however, would be entertainment subject to the 50% limit.

Entertainment is more likely to get an IRS second look than other expenses. So don't classify an expense as entertainment unless it truly is.

For more information, see IRS Publ. #463, "Travel, Entertainment and Gift Expenses."

BUSINESS GIFTS

Tax deductions for business gifts are limited to $25 per recipient in any one year.

Samples of your merchandise, given to prospective buyers or to people who might review or publicize your products, are not considered gifts and are not subject to these gift limitations. You write off the cost of the free samples (not the retail or market value) as part of cost-of-goods-sold. See the chapter on Inventory.

Gifts to employees come under stricter rules. Gifts of nominal value, such as a turkey, a bottle of wine, a framed photo of the boss, are deductible and not taxable to the employee. But any gift of significant value, and *any* cash gift or "cash equivalent" such as a gift certificate, even for a very small amount, is considered taxable wages to the employee, reported on their W-2, subject to income and all payroll taxes. The same rules apply to any awards given to employees. Ebenezer Scrooge himself is writing these tax laws.

There is a big gap between what the IRS permits and what companies do in practice.
—Nation's Business, U.S. Chamber of Commerce

MEALS

Regular meals at work are generally not deductible. Some meals, however, are deductible.

The famous business lunch, wining and dining a current or prospective customer, is 50% deductible but only if business is specifically discussed at the meal and if the cost is not "lavish or extravagant." You must have a receipt and write on it who you took out and why. Tips are considered part of the meal and are also 50% deductible.

Meals while traveling away from home on business are 50% deductible. See the chapter "Travel Away From Home."

There are a host of exceptions to the 50% rule. Food samples made available to the general public are fully deductible. Cost of the annual company picnic or Thanksgiving turkeys you give your employees are fully deductible. Meals that are included as part of a business meeting or seminar are probably fully deductible (the IRS has not ruled on this one). Meals provided to employees on the business premises are sometimes deductible, depending on the circumstances. But taking employees out to lunch, even to discuss important business, is not deductible.

The IRS's "Tax Guide for Small Business" (Pub. 334) has more information.

DUES

Some club dues and memberships are not deductible, and others are. Dues and membership fees in clubs run for pleasure, recreation or other social purposes are not deductible. These include athletic, luncheon, hotel, airline, sporting and business clubs. The term "business club" refers to an entertainment facility, not to business groups. Dues for business groups, professional organizations, merchant and trade associations, chambers of commerce, etc. are deductible. Dues to community service organizations, such as Rotary, Lions, etc., are also deductible.

FREIGHT

"Freight" refers to all shipping and delivery charges. Freight-in is shipping to you; freight-out is shipping of goods you sell. Freight-in on inventory must be included as part of the cost of the inventory. Freight-in on expensive assets (machinery, furniture, etc.) should be added to the cost of the asset. Freight-out on goods you sell are fully deductible expenses.

BAD DEBTS

Business bad debts (customers' bounced checks and other uncollectible accounts) are fully deductible. The chapters "Return Checks" and "Uncollectible Accounts" in the Bookkeeping section, explain how to set up a bad debts folder.

Businesses using the cash method of accounting cannot take a bad debt expense for unpaid and uncollectible accounts, because the income was not recorded in the first place. Bounced checks, however, are deductible bad debts, because they were posted to the income ledgers.

A few businesses that anticipate large bad debts sometimes set aside money in a bad debt reserve fund, sort of like self-insurance. Such reserves are not really business expenses and are not tax deductible.

LOSSES: Casualty Losses/Theft Losses

Business losses from fire, storm or other casualty, or from theft, shoplifting or vandalism are fully deductible to the extent they are not covered by insurance. There is no limitation as in the case of non-business losses.

Inventory that is stolen or destroyed should not be shown as a casualty loss. The inventory loss is part of your cost-of-goods-sold (discussed in this section) and cannot be deducted a second time. Stolen or destroyed depreciable property can be deducted as a casualty loss, but only to the extent of the undepreciated balance. For example, let's say your box of tools was stolen.

You paid $200 for it two years ago and have already taken $40 depreciation on it. You may show a theft loss of only $160 ($200 less the $40). If you wrote the entire thing off the first year, you have no deductible loss.

The IRS says that business losses are not deductible if covered by insurance even if no claim is filed with the insurance company.

EDUCATION EXPENSES

Here is an opportunity to get some additional education and charge the cost to your business, *if* you are careful in selecting your courses of study. The cost of education and any related expenses are deductible only if the education maintains or improves a skill required in your business. Education expenses are *not* allowed if the education is required to meet minimum educational requirements of your present business or if the education will qualify you for a new trade or business.

A self-employed welder who takes a course in a new welding method can charge the expense to the business. A self-employed dance teacher who also takes dance lessons can deduct the cost of the lessons. On the other hand, a leather craftsperson who takes a woodworking course cannot deduct the expenses. The education must be directly related to the business you already operate. Taking a course in pottery *before* opening your pottery shop is not deductible. Any self-employed person can take a course in bookkeeping or taxes or computers and deduct the cost.

Education expenses include tuition, course fees, books, laboratory fees, and travel expenses while away from home overnight. Overnight travel is subject to special limitations. See the chapter "Travel Away From Home."

INSURANCE

Most business-related insurance premiums are deductible. Vehicle insurance is deductible if you don't take the Standard Mileage Allowance. Workers' comp insurance is deductible for your employees. Workers' comp on yourself may or may not be deductible; see the Insurance chapter in the Getting Started section. Life insurance premiums are not deductible. If you pay an insurance premium covering more than one year, you deduct only the current year's portion, even if you're on the cash accounting method. Next year's portion can be deducted next year.

Premiums for "business interruption insurance" may or may not be deductible, depending on what the insurance actually covers. See the Insurance chapter in the Getting Started section.

HEALTH INSURANCE

Sole proprietors, partners in partnerships, members of LLCs, and owners of S corporations can deduct 40% of the cost of health insurance for themselves, their spouses and dependents. The balance of the insurance premium can go on Schedule A of your 1040 return if you itemize deductions.

The 40% deduction is not allowed if you are eligible for health insurance through your own employer (if you have another job) or through your spouse's employer. The deduction may not exceed the net profit from your business.

The deduction does not apply when computing self-employment tax. You pay self-employment tax based on your net profit before the 40% health insurance deduction.

Medical Savings Account (MSA)

You can also set up what's called a Medical Savings Account (MSA). You make tax-deductible contributions to a special IRS-approved account; and you can withdraw money from the account, tax free, to pay medical bills. MSAs can be set up only if you also have a high-deductible health insurance policy. MSAs cannot be used to pay for the insurance itself. MSAs can be set up for you, your family, and your employees. Your bank or insurance company can give you full details.

Employee Health Insurance

You are not required by law to provide health insurance for employees. But if you provide health insurance for yourself, you do not get the 40% deduction unless you also provide the same health coverage to all your employees. The IRS has something called "nondiscrimination requirements", defining who is and isn't an employee for this particular law.

Providing health insurance for your employees—if you can afford it—will be a key selling point to attract and keep good workers. Health insurance is a major reason employees come, and stay. I often hear the story of some small business that finds a good employee, trains and nurtures the employee, comes to depend on the employee, just to lose the person to another company that offers health benefits.

Instead of, or in addition to, health insurance for your employees, you can pay your employees' actual medical bills. (Self-employed individuals cannot get a deduction for paying their own medical bills; they only have the 40% deduction for medical insurance). You can also set up MSAs for your employees (see above).

Health insurance for your employees and their families (spouses and dependents), and any of their medical expenses you pay out of your pocket, are 100% deductible for you and are not taxable to the employees.

Family Employees

If you employ your spouse or your children, officially on the payroll and doing legitimate work, they are eligible for the same 100% deductible health benefits offered to all your employees. In fact, if you employ your spouse, you also get 100% deductible coverage for yourself, instead of the 40%. How come? Your spouse is an employee, and employee's spouses are covered, and you are your spouse's spouse, so...you're covered, too. Keep in mind that all of your employees must be covered, not just your family, to get this tax gold mine. (S corp. owners cannot use this loophole).

You must file a 1099-MISC form with the IRS if you paid any physician or insurance company $600 or more during the year.

Corporations

In a regular C corporation (not an S corporation), you, as an employee of your corporation, are fully eligible for tax-free employee health benefits, and your corporation is allowed a full deduction for the cost. No 40% limitation. But the insurance must be available to all employees, not just yourself.

MOVING EXPENSES

You may deduct all the expenses of moving your business from one location to another. There are no mileage and other restrictions.

For home-based businesses, the business portion of the move is fully deductible, if you are allowed the home office deduction. See the chapter, "Office in the Home".

REPAIRS

Minor repairs on business property or equipment are fully deductible as a current expense.

Major repairs that add to the value or extend the useful life of an asset must usually be treated as a permanent investment and handled in the same manner as the purchase of a depreciable asset. See the Depreciation chapter.

TRAVEL

Local business travel, when not going somewhere overnight, is limited to transportation expenses only. Regular commuting expenses, home to work and back, are not deductible. Side trips to customers or to suppliers are deductible.

You are allowed deductions for food and lodging and miscellaneous expenses only if you are away from home overnight. "Home" is defined as your place of business, not where you live.

For years, the IRS has been in and out of tax court with people, arguing the definition of "home". Self-employed itinerant workers, traveling contractors, and salespeople are continually challenged by the IRS on travel deductions, the IRS claiming that the road is home, so no deductions allowed. If your business is of this nature and if travel expenses are substantial, I'd advise consulting a good tax accountant.

If you are working away from home for over one year, the IRS automatically considers the road to be home, and disallows travel expenses.

Business Trips

A business trip within the United States that is 100% business is 100% deductible. That includes round trip travel, lodging, transportation, and incidental expenses such as phone, fax, laundry, etc. Two exceptions: Meals and entertainment are only 50% deductible. Deductions for travel on luxury boats or cruise ships have some limitations (check with the IRS).

A business trip outside the United States may also be 100% deductible (with the same exceptions of meals, entertainment and luxury water

travel). But if you attend overseas conventions, seminars or meetings, a deduction is allowed only if the meeting is directly related to your business and if, in the IRS's opinion, there is a valid business reason for holding the meeting overseas. (Some countries are exempt from this restriction; check with the IRS.)

What about a trip that is part business and part vacation? You may be able to write some of it off, and you may be able to write all of it off, if you carefully follow the rules.

If the reason for your trip is primarily personal (more than half the days are for vacation), none of the traveling expenses to and from your destination are deductible. Only expenses directly related to your business can be deducted.

If your trip is primarily for business (more than half the days are for business) and it is within the United States, the cost of the round-trip travel is fully deductible even if some of the trip is for pleasure. So you *can* tack a short vacation onto a business trip, and the only costs that aren't deductible are the non-business expenses, such as the extra days' lodging and meals and entertainment. And if you have a business trip that overlaps a weekend, requiring you to be there Friday and the following Monday, lucky you: you can write off the weekend as well, as a business expense, even though all you did was sit on the beach and dance in the clubs (as long as it is less expensive to stay the weekend than to go home Friday and come back Monday morning).

If you take your husband or wife, the spouse's expenses are not deductible unless he or she is an employee or partner and has a legitimate business reason for accompanying you.

If you travel outside the U.S., more stringent rules apply. If the trip is no more than one week *or* the time spent for pleasure is less than 25 percent, the same basic rules apply as a trip within the U.S. But if the trip is more than a week, or if the vacation days are 25% or more of the trip, you must allocate travel expenses between the business and the personal portion of your trip.

When counting business versus vacation days, you'll be pleased to know that a "business day" does not require you to do business all day. The travel days count as business days. Any day you put in at least four hours of work is considered a business day. And any day your presence is required, for any amount of time, is considered a business day.

The IRS Does Not Like Business Trips

As you can tell from the generous way the law is written, it's a bit too easy to write off a business trip that is really a disguised vacation. The IRS knows this all too well, and they are forever suspicious of business travel expenses, particularly sole proprietorships where the owner is accountable to no one else: you feel like taking a business trip (and you can afford it), you take it. The IRS wants to be sure it's not a vacation in disguise. You want to be sure you can prove, if audited, that the trip wasn't a vacation. A log of daily activities and business contacts is not required by law, but it may help convince a skeptical IRS auditor that your trip to the Bahamas or to New Orleans really was for business.

One tax client of mine who owned a retail coffee shop took an expensive trip to Scandinavia and wrote it off as a business deduction. When she was audited, which didn't surprise either of us, she was able to show the IRS auditor photos she took of coffee shops she visited throughout her travels. She showed the auditor Scandinavian coffee mugs that she is now importing. She got through the audit successfully.

Keeping Track of Expenses

For meals, lodging and incidental expenses, you can keep a record of actual expenses or, at your option, you can use a standard "per diem" rate set by the IRS—so much per day. The standard rate varies from city to city. For rates and details, ask the IRS for Publication 1542, "Per Diem Rates." The IRS offers yet another option: you can figure your actual lodging and incidental expenses, and then add a "standard meal allowance" (which also varies from city to city).

For more information see IRS Publ. #463, "Travel, Entertainment, and Gift Expenses."

INVENTORY and Something Very Important Called Cost-Of-Goods-Sold

"Inventory" is merchandise—goods, products—held for sale in the normal course of business. Inventory also includes repair shop parts, "raw materials" and supplies that will go into the making of a finished product, and work in process (partly finished goods you are making).

Inventory does *not* include tools, equipment, furniture, office supplies or anything purchased for reasons other than resale.

Not all of your inventory purchases can be deducted as current year expenses. *Only the cost of those goods actually sold is deductible.* This is a very important distinction; you should understand it completely. The cost of inventory *un*sold at year-end is an asset owned by you and will not be a deductible expense until sold (or until it becomes worthless; covered later in the chapter).

Cost-of-goods-sold is your most important and usually your largest item of expense. The federal income tax form has two main categories of expense: (1) cost-of-goods-sold, and (2) all other. You will be required to show on your tax return how you calculated your cost-of-goods-sold.

Let's first use a simple example of cost-of-goods-sold. My friends John and Karen Resykle buy antiques, junk and old clothes at garage and rummage sales and then resell the merchandise at a profit at flea markets. Last year, John and Karen purchased a total of $4,200 worth of merchandise (cost to them). At year-end, they still had $300 worth of merchandise on hand and unsold (again, at their cost). John and Karen's deductible cost-of-goods-sold is $3,900 ($4,200 purchased, less $300 unsold). Note that the selling price of the inventory has no bearing on the calculation of cost-of-goods-sold.

The above example assumes that there was no inventory on hand at the beginning of the year. Let's now say there was $400 on hand (their cost) at January 1. John and Karen's cost-of-goods-sold is now $4,300:

Inventory on hand at January 1	$ 400
Add: Inventory purch. during the year	4,200
Total inventory available for sale	$4,600
Subtract: Inventory on hand at Dec. 31	(300)
Cost-of-goods-sold	$4,300

Inventory On Hand At Start of Business

If you are starting a new business and already have inventory on hand that you will be putting into the business, inventory you purchased before going into business, you can add the cost of that inventory (or the market value if less than cost) to the current year's purchases—even though you didn't buy it this year—and include it in your cost-of-goods-sold calculations. You can record this inventory in your expenditure ledger as "Inventory on hand at start of business" and post to Column One.

Taking Inventory

As you can see, at the end of the year you will need to make a list of inventory on hand. This is called "taking inventory" or "taking a physical inventory." (Business folk use the word "inventory" to refer both to the goods and to the procedure of counting the goods.) *Do not value the inventory at sale price.* The inventory should be valued at your cost.

Manufacturers and Crafts Businesses

Computing the cost of your inventory will be a difficult task, for two reasons. First, you must calculate the cost not only of your raw materials but of your finished and partially finished goods as well. This will require a lot of educated guess-work—it always does. Value your inventory at its cost to you. That cost includes materials and paid labor. It does not include your own labor (unless you are an employee of your own corporation).

The other complication in computing cost-of-goods-sold is a nasty law called Uniform Capitalization Rules. The rules apply to all manufacturers and other businesses that, to quote the IRS, "construct, build, install, manufacture, develop, improve, create, raise, or grow property." Crafts businesses come under this rule. The term "manufacture" applies to making crafts.

Under Uniform Capitalization Rules, the cost of a manufacturer's inventory must include the cost of overhead attributable to the manufacturing operation. Such manufacturing overhead becomes part of the cost of the manufactured product, just like the cost of the materials, and cannot be deducted until the product is sold.

"Overhead" in this context is very broad and refers to almost everything related to manufacturing: repairs, maintenance, utilities, rent, indirect labor and production supervisory wages, indirect materials, tools and equipment, warehousing costs, administrative costs, insurance, taxes, employee benefits, you name it.

You only have to deal with the Uniform Capitalization Rules if you have goods that you have manufactured (finished or partly finished) on

hand and unsold at the end of the year. If all your manufactured goods are sold, then all the overhead is also "sold" and can be fully deducted this year. The Uniform Capitalization Rules also do not apply to inventory that has not yet been worked on (unused parts and raw materials). This untouched inventory is valued at its cost without adding these overhead costs.

I'll try a "simple" example. Let's say that the space in your shop is divided, half for manufacturing and half for sales. Your expenses for the year included $5,000 for rent and utilities (half of which is for manufacturing, half for sales), and $10,000 for inventory. At the beginning of the year, there was no inventory. At year-end, there was $1,000 (cost) on hand. Your cost-of-goods-sold must be computed as follows:

Inventory on hand January 1	$0
Inventory purchased during year	10,000
One-half rent and utilities (manufacturing portion)	2,500
Cost of goods available for sale	$12,500
Subtract: inventory on hand Dec. 31	(1,000)
$1,000 is 10% of the inventory purchased during the year; therefore, 10% of the manufacturing portion of the overhead is also still "on hand". So you must subtract 10% of the manufacturing half of rent and utilities	(250)
Cost-of-goods-sold	$11,250

This $1,250 inventory ($1,000 goods and $250 overhead) "on hand" at year-end will become the inventory on hand January 1 of the next year, to be written off next year when it is sold. This example assumes no other overhead expenses related to the inventory, no paid salaries in the manufacturing, no inventory stored in the sales area. These costs would have to be included in computing cost-of-goods-sold.

In the above example, the entire $1,000 inventory on hand at year-end is finished goods. Had it instead been untouched parts or materials, the entire $2,500 in manufacturing overhead could have been deducted instead of only $2,250. If the $1,000 inventory included both manufactured goods and untouched inventory, well, as you probably already figured, the computations get all the more complicated (but relax, we won't go through them).

Inventory Loss of Value

In computing cost-of-goods-sold, inventory on hand at year-end is usually valued at its cost to you and not at its sales price, which normally is higher than its cost. If for any reason your year-end inventory is worth less than what you paid, the inventory should be valued at this lesser amount. "Worth" refers to its retail value, what you can sell it for. Clothes no longer in fashion, damaged or destroyed goods, goods unsalable for any reason—all such items should be reduced to their market (sales) value. If year-end inventory is totally worthless, it should be valued at zero. This inventory valuation method is known as "lower of cost or market."

You may have figured out by now that reducing the value of your inventory—"writing it off" as a loss—increases your expenses, thereby decreasing your profits and your taxes. Let's look again at our first example, John and Karen Resykle, the flea market entrepreneurs. Their purchases during the year were $4,200; cost of inventory on hand at year-end was $300. Originally, their cost-of-goods-sold was $3,900 ($4,200 less the $300 on hand). Karen finds, however, that she made some bad purchases, and the inventory on hand at year-end for which she paid $300 cannot be sold for more than $200. Year-end inventory is therefore reduced to $200, that being the lower of cost or market. The cost-of-goods-sold, instead of being $3,900, is now $4,000 ($4,200 purchased, less $200). The additional $100 cost-of-goods-sold increases deductible expenses by $100. Since John and Karen's income is unchanged, the additional expense reduces their profits by $100 and, therefore, reduces their taxes also.

Inventory Lost, Stolen or Given Away

The cost of stolen or missing inventory and the cost of samples given away are deductible as part of cost-of-goods-sold. This inventory is not on hand at year end, so it is not included in your year-end inventory count. Therefore, it automatically becomes part of your cost-of-goods-sold (even though it really wasn't sold—the term cost-of-goods-sold really should be "cost of goods sold, lost, stolen, given away, damaged, unsalable, etc."). No additional write-off is allowed.

Inventory Valuation—LIFO & FIFO

Businesses may value inventory using the first-in, first-out method (FIFO), which is calculated as though the oldest inventory is sold first and the newest inventory is on the shelves; or the last-in, first-out method (LIFO), which is calculated as though the newly purchased inventory is sold before the older inventory. The actual inventory on hand doesn't have to actually correspond to the method you choose. You can sell your inventory first-in, first-out yet account for it using the LIFO method, and vice-versa.

Most businesses use the FIFO method because it is easier to calculate and because the IRS rules are straightforward. But if you find LIFO might save you significant tax dollars, which might be the case if the newest inventory (the last-in inventory) is much more expensive that the older (first-in) inventory, I suggest you get an accountant's help. The LIFO calculations and IRS rules can get confusing.

BUSINESS ASSETS:
Equipment, Furniture, Machinery, Etc.

Business assets such as machinery, equipment, tools, furniture, fixtures, display cases, office machines such as computers, faxes and copiers, and vehicles, can (with some exceptions) be written off the year of purchase. The total write off under this rule, all assets combined, cannot exceed $18,000 in any one year (calendar year: January through December). Both new and used assets qualify as long as they were purchased for the business and not before going into business.

This rule is variously known as the Section 179 Deduction, Expensing Allowance, or Expensing Election. The assets are sometimes called capital, or fixed, or depreciable assets. The IRS calls the assets "Section 1245 Property".

This write-off rule does *not* apply to intangible assets such as patents, copyrights, trademarks, goodwill, etc.; to inventory, parts, or office supplies; or to buildings (one exception: single-purpose livestock and horticultural structures can be written off).

Government is a reality of life. Denying it is just letting your own biases influence your business judgment. —Bill McGowan, founder, MCI

Here are the requirements:

1. Married couples are allowed a maximum write-off of $18,000 between them.

2. If you have more than one unincorporated business, the $18,000 is the maximum for all combined businesses.

3. If you purchase more than $200,000 in depreciable assets in any one year, the $18,000 maximum is reduced, dollar for dollar, by the amount in excess of $200,000. So if you spend $202,000 on depreciable assets this year, the maximum you can write off is $16,000 (that's $2,000 less than the $18,000). If you spend $217,500 or more, no write-off is allowed.

4. The write-off cannot exceed the total taxable income from all businesses and salaries combined (both husband and wife if filing jointly). Any write-off disallowed because of this income limitation can be carried forward to the next year, and future years if necessary, until the assets are fully written off. But you *must* elect the write-off the year the assets are acquired and placed in service in order to get the carry-forward. Use Form 4562.

5. If an asset is used partly for business and partly for personal, non-business use, the business portion can be written off. However, the following specific assets cannot be written off at all unless used more than 50% for business: vehicles, cellular phones, recreation and entertainment property, and computers (if the computer is used away from your business premises).

6. Vehicles, even if used 100% for business, have a maximum Sec. 179 deduction. See "Limitations on Automobiles" below.

7. Assets converted to business use, owned before going into business, are not eligible.

8. If you sell assets you've previously written off, or convert them to non-business use, you may have to "recapture" the amount you wrote off (add it back into income) the year of sale or conversion, depending on how many years you own the asset. The recapture rules that apply to depreciation also apply here (explained below).

9. You must fill out IRS Form 4562, "Depreciation and Amortization".

Assets ineligible for the Sec. 179 write-off, or in excess of the maximums, must be depreciated. See the chapter "Depreciation" below.

You should also understand that this write-off is optional. If you prefer, you can depreciate some or all of these assets over a period of years rather than write them off the year of purchase. Why would anyone choose complex, multi-year depreciation over this simple, write-it-off-now deduction? Many businesses make little or no profit the first year or two and may not have any use for the additional tax savings the write-off offers. It might be better to depreciate the assets, deducting the bulk of the expense in future years when you can use it to save taxes. You might want to calculate your profit and taxes under both methods to find the bigger tax savings.

You can write off some assets and depreciate others. It is not all-one-way or all-the-other.

DEPRECIATION

Depreciation is a tax term and means that the cost of an asset is spread out over several years; each year, a portion of the cost is deducted. The assets are variously called fixed, capital, or depreciable assets. The same rules apply to both new and used assets.

The assets described above under "Business Assets", equipment, furniture, machinery, etc. are depreciable assets. Major improvements to your shop and major repairs that increase the value or that extend the life of an asset are considered depreciable assets. Buildings and vehicles are depreciable assets.

All office supplies and all inventory, regardless of cost, are not capital assets and may not be depreciated. Inexpensive tools and equipment also should not be depreciated, but should be deducted as an expense the year purchased.

Buildings: If your business is located in a building that you own, you can depreciate the portion of the building being used for business (including your home if you meet the home office requirements). If you rent, the rent is a direct expense; there is no need to compute building depreciation. The land apart from the improvements cannot be depreciated. Land is considered a permanent asset that cannot be expensed until sold. If the cost of land and building are not separately stated, most accountants figure 80% of the cost was the building, 20% the land, but you can use any reasonable allocation.

Antiques: Valuable antiques and art treasures, if used for decoration only, may not be depreciated or written off until sold. Antiques actually used in the business, such as an old desk, may be depreciable. The IRS says no, but the Tax Court says yes. You'll need help here.

Vehicles: Your vehicle can be depreciated if you do not take the Standard Mileage Allowance. But there are limitations, discussed below.

Films and Recordings: Motion picture films, video tapes, and sound recordings—originals, not duplicates for sale or rent—come under a completely different set of IRS rules not covered in this chapter.

Rental businesses: Businesses that rent out equipment can depreciate (or write-off) the equipment just like any other depreciable assets. Video stores can either write off videotapes when purchased (if the tapes won't last more than a year) or depreciate them.

Intangibles: The term "depreciate" applies only to tangible assets (physical assets). Intangible assets, such as patents and copyrights, also come under these rules, but they are "amortized", not depreciated. The two terms basically mean the same thing.

Warning: The Rules Change All The Time

Depreciation rules change almost every year, sometimes dramatically. And with every change, I swear, the rules get lengthier and more complex. Whatever rule was in effect when you purchased an asset (or when you first used it in business if you purchased it before going into business) is the rule you must use for that asset for as long as you own the asset. So if you have been in business and buying depreciable assets for several years, you will be calculating depreciation using several different sets of rules!

The depreciation rules explained below are only for newly-acquired assets, under IRS laws in effect when this edition of *Small Time Operator* was published. These are federal rules only. For state income taxes, some states use the same depreciation rules and some, God bless 'em, require entirely different calculations.

How Much Can Be Depreciated?

You are allowed to depreciate the cost of your depreciable asset. "Cost" is defined as the purchase price and includes sales tax, freight charges and any installation charges. If you bought your equipment very inexpensively, your cost is what you paid, not what the equipment is "worth". When equipment is purchased in installments (on time) the cost is the total purchase price as if you had paid cash for it. Any finance or interest charges can usually be written off as a regular business expense the year paid, completely separate from the cost of the asset.

One exception to this rule: for buildings or equipment that you construct yourself or have custom made for you, if they take more than two years to build or if they are depreciated over 20 years or more, the finance or interest charges must be added to the cost of the asset and treated as part of the asset.

Depreciable assets used in your business that were purchased before going into business can be depreciated regardless of when acquired. These assets must be valued at their cost or at their market value at the time the assets are first used in your business, whichever is less. If some old machinery, or an old computer, which cost you $2,000 eight years ago, was only worth $500 (market value) when first used in your business, you may only depreciate $500.

Depreciable assets used partly for business and partly for non-business can be depreciated to the extent used for business. For example, if you use your tools 50% for business and 50% for personal use, you can depreciate 50% of the cost.

Write Off Period

There are several categories of assets, each with a different write off period (also called a "recovery period"), how many years the assets are to be depreciated. The categories most used by small businesses and farmers are listed below.

3 Year Property: on-road tractor units, hogs, race horses over two years old, all horses over 12 years old, software (but see separate discussion).

5 Year Property: cars, trucks, trailers, aircraft, and buses; most equipment used for research and experimentation; computers, copiers, calculators, and similar office equipment; semi-conductor manufacturing equipment; solar, wind and some other alternative energy property; some electronic equipment; cattle, sheep, goats.

7 Year Property: most machinery, equipment, furniture, fixtures, signs, etc.; railroad track; horses other than those listed as 3-year Property.

10 Year Property: most boats, barges and tugs; single-purpose agricultural and horticultural structures; fruit and nut trees and vines.

15 Year Property: Intangible (intellectual) property such as goodwill, trademarks, trade names, most patents, copyrights, franchises, customer lists, and covenants not to compete. The IRS calls this property "Section 197 intangibles". Gas stations, including their mini-marts.

20 Year Property: all-purpose farm buildings.

27½ Year Property: residential rental buildings, including built-in elevators.

39 Year Property: all buildings other than residential rental property, farm buildings, and gas stations.

Methods of Computing Depreciation

Business assets are depreciated under a system called MACRS, which stands for Modified Accelerated Cost Recovery System. "Cost recovery" is the government's term for depreciation. "Modified" refers to the fact that it is a modified version of an out-of-date depreciation method. "Accelerated" means faster write-offs than other methods (which is no longer true: IRS changed the rules but left the description; some MACRS calculations are "accelerated", some aren't).

Under MACRS, there are four methods of depreciation (in addition to the Section 179 First Year Depreciation explained above). All four methods result in the same tax write-off eventually, but each method involves different amounts that can be written off in any given year.

General Depreciation System (GDS) #1.

This is the most common depreciation system and offers the fastest write-offs: larger write-offs in the first few years, smaller write-offs in later years. Most business assets other than buildings, intangibles, farm assets, and certain "listed property" can be depreciated under this method (see below for the exceptions).

This method is also called the 200% Declining Balance Method. "200% declining balance" is a formula for calculating depreciation that, fortunately, you don't have to learn. The Depreciation Table will help you compute GDS depreciation quickly and easily.

At your option, assets eligible for this method can be depreciated under the other three methods described below. If you already have reduced your taxes down to nothing and don't need any more deductions this year, the other methods will bring larger deductions in future years.

GDS #2.

Also known as the 150% Declining Balance Method. Required for most farm buildings and equipment, and some land improvements. The method is similar to GDS #1 but with smaller write-offs in the early years.

Straight Line.

This method must be used for most buildings (other than farm buildings), and farmer's vines and fruit and nut trees.

The straight-line method distributes depreciation equally over the write-off period. Each year, the same amount is depreciated (except the first year, when only part of a year's depreciation is allowed; more on this later). Straight-line spreads depreciation over the same number of years as the two GDS methods but with a smaller write-off in the earlier years.

Alternative Depreciation System (ADS).

This method is required for certain assets if used 50% or less for business (called "listed property"): vehicles (unless you take the Standard Mileage Allowance, in which case you take no depreciation at all); boats; airplanes; cellular phones; computers (*if* you use the computer away from your business premises); and entertainment and recreation property. ADS is also required for assets used primarily outside the U.S., assets imported from certain trade-restricted countries, and assets financed with tax-exempt bonds.

Under ADS, the write-off periods are different than those shown above, and the depreciation runs over a longer period of years. If you are required or want to use ADS, IRS Publ. #534, "Depreciation", lists the different write-off periods.

First Year Depreciation

Under all of the above depreciation methods, you are not allowed a full year's depreciation the first year. "Year" refers to the calendar year, not to the first twelve months you own an asset.

For assets other than buildings, you are allowed only a half year's depreciation. If you compute your own depreciation, just divide the first year's depreciation in half. At the end of the write-off period, you add the remaining half year's depreciation.

In effect, this "half-year convention" adds an extra year to the write-off period. A 7-year asset, for example, will be depreciated over an eight year period: a half year the first year, a full year

DEPRECIATION TABLE

Year	3 Yr. Assets			5 Yr. Assets			7 Yr. Assets		
	GDS #1	GDS #2	St. Line	GDS #1	GDS #2	St. Line	GDS #1	GDS #2	St. Line
1	33%	25%	17%	20%	15%	10%	14%	11%	7%
2	45	38	33	32	26	20	25	19	15
3	15	25	33	19	18	20	17	15	15
4	7	12	17	12	17	20	13	13	14
5				11	16	20	9	12	14
6				6	8	10	9	12	14
7							9	12	14
8							4	6	7

the second through the seventh years, and a half year the eighth year. If you use the Depreciation Table, the half year is already figured into it.

There is an important exception to the half-year rule. If more than 40% of your depreciable assets (other than real estate) are purchased in the last three months of the year, you do not use the half-year calculation. You must instead group the assets according to which quarter of the year they were purchased and then make four separate computations—which I'm not going to even try to explain. They're very drawn out, and they have to be recalculated every year! If you have to deal with this "mid quarter convention", as it's called, the instructions are in the IRS publications. (Or go back and read "Writing Off Assets The Year Of Purchase").

Buildings: First year depreciation on buildings is calculated building by building using what's called a "mid month convention". Whatever month a building is acquired for business (or first used for business), you are allowed a half month's depreciation that month, and then full depreciation for the remaining months of the year. So if you purchased a building in April, you are allowed 8½ months depreciation the first year. Then at the end of the depreciation period, you get an additional 3½ month's depreciation.

Part Business, Part Personal

Depreciation may be computed only for the business portion of a depreciable asset. If your tools are used 50% for work and 50% for pleasure, you compute depreciation only on 50% of the cost. If you opt to write off an asset the first year rather than take depreciation, you write off only the portion applicable to business.

Special limitations apply to certain "listed property" used 50% or less for business, as mentioned under the ADS method above. Try to keep business use above 50%, and keep detailed records—dates, hours, miles, etc.—to prove it.

Software

Computer software that you purchase can be depreciated over three years, or less if the software has a shorter life (such as a tax program, which is only good for one year); or you can write it off the year purchased, under the First Year Write-off rules explained above.

Software that was packaged with your computer when you bought it is considered part of the cost of the computer. It can be depreciated or written off according to the computer depreciation rules explained above.

If you develop software programs, you can, at your option, write off the development costs as current expenses. This write off is in addition to, not part of, the $17,500 First Year Write-off. You also have the option to depreciate software development costs over five years, using the straight line method.

Limitations on Automobiles

Regardless of the percent used for business or the depreciation method used, automobile depreciation (and the Sec. 179 deduction) is limited to a maximum of $3,060 the first year, $4900 the second year, $2,950 the third year, and $1775 each succeeding year. Dollar limits change from year to year; verify these amounts with the IRS.

Due to this limitation, expensive cars cannot be fully depreciated in the 5 years normally allowed. Depreciation is spread out over a longer period.

Depreciation Table

This table will help you compute depreciation using GDS #1, GDS #2, and straight-line, and to compare the three methods. The fourth method, ADS, can't be included in a simple table because there are too many asset categories. "Year" refers to the calendar year, not to the first twelve months you own the asset. Percentage is the percentage of cost you can write off that year.

This table is only for assets qualifying for the half-year convention (see "First Year Depreciation"). Do not use for assets requiring "mid-quarter" calculations.

Selling An Asset

When you sell an asset that has been written off, or fully or partly depreciated, there may be a taxable profit on the sale. These are known as "recapture rules" and are somewhat complex and depend on how many years you've had the asset, how much depreciation or write-off you've taken, and what method of depreciation you've used. The basic concept: The cost of the asset is reduced by the total amount of depreciation or write-off *allowed* (whether the depreciation or write-off was taken or not!), to come up with what's called "adjusted cost" (or "cost basis"). If the selling price is higher than the adjusted cost, you have a taxable profit. If the selling price is lower, you have a tax-deductible loss.

For example, let's say you bought a piece of equipment a few years ago for $4,000, and you already deducted $3,000 of depreciation. Your adjusted cost is $1,000 ($4,000 original cost less $3,000 depreciation). Let's say you sell the asset for $2,500. You will have a $1,500 taxable profit:

Original cost	$4,000
Accumulated depreciation	(3,000)
Adjusted cost	$1,000
Sale price	(2,500)
Profit	$1,500

Now, let's change the example and say you sold the same asset for $600. You will have a $400 deductible loss:

Original cost	$4,000
Accumulated depreciation	(3,000)
Adjusted cost	$1,000
Sale price	(600)
Loss	$ 400

Sale of a depreciable asset should be recorded on your income ledger the month of sale, but below the regular sales figures for the month. Although the sale may be subject to income tax, it is not a regular business sale and should be shown separately. You should also record the sale on your equipment ledger.

No depreciation is allowed for any asset sold the same year it was purchased.

Discarding or Junking an Asset

If an asset is fully depreciated or fully written off when it becomes worthless/useless/unsalable junk, that's as far as the taxes and bookkeeping go—there is no profit and no loss. But if the asset is only partly depreciated, you can write off the balance of the cost (the undepreciated part of the cost) in full the year the asset becomes worthless.

For example, a piece of equipment cost $3,000 a year ago, and so far you've deducted $800 in depreciation. The thing burns up. This year you can write off $2,200, the undepreciated balance ($3,000 cost less $800 depreciation). This example assumes, besides no selling price, no insurance. If the asset is insured, any insurance payment is treated the same as income from the sale of an asset (see "Selling an Asset" above).

When you junk an asset, no entry should be made to your income ledger, but you should note it on your equipment ledger.

IRS Reporting

IRS Form #4562, "Depreciation & Amortization" can be used to figure depreciation. You must use the form if your business is a C corpo-

EQUIPMENT LEDGER AND DEPRECIATION WORKSHEETS

1	2	3	4	5	6	7	8	9	10	11	12	13	14	15	16	17	18
DATE	DESCRIPTION	METH.	WRITE OFF PERIOD	NEW OR USED	%	COST	BAL. TO BE DEPR.	DEPR. 19__	BAL. TO BE DEPR.	DEPR. 19__	BAL. TO BE DEPR.	DEPR. 19__	BAL. TO BE DEPR.	DEPR. 19__	BAL. TO BE DEPR.	DEPR. 19__	BAL. TO BE DEPR.

ration (not an S corporation); or if you are depreciating or writing off newly acquired assets; or if you are depreciating a vehicle, airplane, computer, cellular phone, or recreation/entertainment equipment. Otherwise, the form is optional.

The Depreciation Worksheet

The combination Equipment Ledger and Depreciation Worksheet will help you keep track of your equipment and other depreciable assets and the depreciation on them. If you use Form #4562 (see above), this worksheet will help you prepare that form. Some people simply photocopy the worksheet and attach it to the tax form.

Use a separate line on the worksheet for each asset. Fill out the columns when you purchase an asset and you'll never have to hunt up the information a second time. Even if you hire an accountant to prepare your taxes, you will save the accountant time, and save yourself money, if you fill out Columns 1, 2, 5, 6 and 7 (the basic information). Enter the information as follows:

Column 1, Date. Date purchased or date first used in business.

Column 2, Description. Be specific enough to distinguish this particular asset from all others. If the asset is your one and only welding torch, the description "welding torch" is sufficient. If, however, you have four welding torches, "welding torch, serial no. 34-15" or some other specific designation is needed.

Column 3, Method. The depreciation method you've selected. If you are writing off the asset instead of taking depreciation, put "W/O" (for first-year write off) in this column.

Column 4, Write Off Period. How many years the asset is being depreciated. If you are writing off the asset instead of depreciating it, leave this column blank.

Column 5, New or Used.

Column 6, Percent Used for Business. 100% if the asset is used solely for business; a smaller percent if partly personal.

Column 7, Cost. See the discussion of cost in this chapter.

Column 8, Balance to be Depreciated. Column 6 x Column 7 = Column 8. This column is the cost adjusted for the percentage used for business. The amount you arrive at here is commonly called the "cost basis." This is the amount that is actually depreciated or written off the first year.

The five sets of paired columns, 9 and 10, 11 and 12, 13 and 14, 15 and 16, and 17 and 18, provide five years of depreciation scheduling for each asset. The first column in a pair is the depreciation for the year, and the following column is the remaining undepreciated balance. Column 9 less Column 10 equals Column 11, and so on.

This ledger may not be adequate for businesses purchasing, repairing and maintaining heavy or expensive equipment. Manufacturing equipment, construction equipment and the like will require separate records for each item. The basic ideas and the depreciation laws are the same.

A Last Word on Depreciation

If you are totally dismayed by this chapter, you are not alone. Depreciation is vastly complex, a real struggle to compute correctly. Few business owners are willing and able to make these calculations, and they usually turn to tax accountants for help. Most accountants now own computer programs that can automatically compute depreciation under all of the different methods, select the correct method for you, compare methods to find the biggest tax savings.

I hold in my hand 1,379 pages of tax simplification.
—Congressman commenting on
last year's tax bill

NON-DEDUCTIBLE EXPENSES

Certain expenses are specifically disallowed by law and cannot be deducted, no way, no how:

1. Business expenses not meeting the "ordinary and necessary" or the "reasonable" test.

2. Federal income tax and tax penalties. State income tax is deductible on your federal return.

3. Fines or penalties for violation of the law. Even though you were parked on business, you cannot deduct that parking ticket. Other business fines or penalties, if they don't involve breaking the law, are deductible.

4. Payments to yourself. The only way you may pay yourself a wage and deduct it as an expense is to incorporate.

5. Loan repayments. The loan was not income when received and is not expense when paid. Any interest on the loan may be deductible, but there are exceptions. See the Interest chapter.

6. Clothing, unless used exclusively for work and unsuitable for street wear.

7. Regular meals at work, but see the Meals chapter for exceptions.

8. Regular commuting expenses between your home and usual place of business.

9. Cost of land, until you sell it. Only the structure on the land may be depreciated.

10. Certain start-up expenses as explained in the Start-Up chapter.

11. Some club dues (see the Dues chapter).

12. Some interest is deductible, and some isn't. See the Interest chapter.

13. Charitable contributions cannot be deducted as a business expense except, with certain limits, by corporations.

SELF-EMPLOYMENT TAX (SECA)

Self-employment tax, also known as SECA (Self Employment Contributions Act), is combined Social Security and Medicare tax for self-employed individuals. Independent business people pay the highest Social Security/Medicare rates of all, and they go up every year. Self-employment tax is based on your taxable profit from the business.

Sole proprietors (including independent outside contractors and freelancers), partners in partnerships, and active owners of LLCs are subject to self-employment tax. (LLC members who are investors only, not active in the business, are

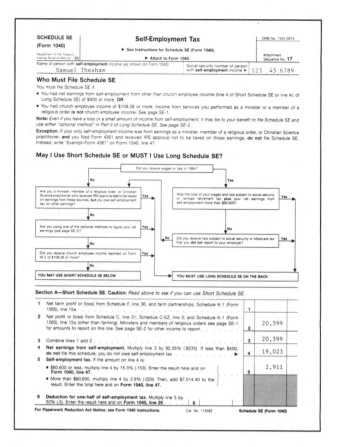

probably exempt from self-employment taxes).

The tax is not imposed on corporations; if you own a small corporation, you are an employee of your business and pay regular Social Security and Medicare instead of self-employment tax. Director's fees not included as part of a regular salary are subject to the self-employment tax.

Only "business income" is subject to self-employment tax. (The difference between business and non-business income is explained in the Bookkeeping Section under "Defining Income"). Also, income from a brief one-shot job that is neither continuous nor regular is usually exempt from self-employment tax.

Self-employment tax is apart from and in addition to federal income tax. You may owe no income tax but still be liable for self-employment tax. Retirement deductions, deductions for health insurance, and the regular personal deductions and exemptions, which reduce income tax, cannot be used to reduce self-employment tax.

Very often this tax comes as quite a shock to new and very small businesses. People, particularly in part-time and sideline businesses, are not making enough profit to worry about income taxes, but they never realize they may have a substantial self-employment tax bill.

Special note, if you business profits are $400 or less: You do not have to pay any self-employment tax and can skip this entire chapter (if you net $401, you pay self-employment tax on the entire $401, not just the dollar over the $400 minimum). If you made $400 or less but want to pay self-employment tax, to increase your Social Security account, the IRS provides an optional method so you can pay into Social Security and Medicare. It is explained on the SE tax form.

Figuring The Tax

For 1997, the self-employment tax rate is 15.3% (combining 12.4% Social Security tax and 2.9% Medicare tax) on profits up to $65,400. On all profits above $65,400, the tax rate is 2.9% (no ceiling). If you have more than one unincorporated business, you combine all the profits (and losses) to figure the tax.

Your actual tax will be lower than the above figures indicate, because of two deductions:

The first deduction reduces the self-employment tax itself. You figure the tax not on your full profit, but on a reduced amount. You reduce your profit by 7.65% (which is half the self-employment tax rate) and figure the tax on the reduced profit. You accomplish this by multiplying your profit by .9235.

For example, if your taxable profit was $30,000, multiply the $30,000 by .9235, which comes to $27,705. The self-employment tax will be 15.3% of $27,705, or $4,239 (pennies rounded). If your business made more than $65,400, the formula is different; see below.

The second deduction is an income tax deduction, taken on your 1040 tax form. Whatever your self-employment tax figures to be, reduce your business profit by half the self-employment tax before figuring your income tax.

Using the same example (a $30,000 profit, and self-employment tax of $4,239). Half the $4,239 is $2,120 (rounded). So you reduce your $30,000 profit by $2,120, to get $27,880, and figure your income taxes on the $27,880.

Understand that the two deductions are completely separate calculations, using different figures. In the example, a business with a $30,000 profit, self-employment tax is figured on $27,705 (the first deduction), and income tax is figured on $27,880 (the second deduction). Some idiot in Washington actually dreamed this up.

Self-employment tax is computed on your regular federal income tax return, using Form #1040-SE. If you have more than one unincorporated business, combine all profits and losses to figure self-employment tax. You file only one #1040-SE.

Businesses with profits above $65,400: You compute self-employment tax and the two deductions differently, because your profit is taxed at two different rates: 15.3% on the first $65,400, and 2.9% on all profits above $65,400. You follow the same procedures, but using two tax rates.

Husband and wife businesses: If a husband and wife operate a business together, who pays self-employment tax depends on how the business is set up. If the business is a partnership, formally set up as such and filing partnership tax returns, or an LLC, both spouses pay self-employment tax. Each spouse files his and her own #1040-SE form. If the business is a sole proprietorship, only one spouse pays self-employment tax—the one who is the primary operator of the business. See "Husband and Wife Partnerships" in the Appendix.

Outside Employment (You Also Hold a Job)

Self-employed people who are also holding jobs where Social Security and Medicare is withheld from their pay should combine the two incomes to arrive at the self-employment tax maximum. You will be in one of these situations:

1. If the combined incomes, outside job and business profit, are under $65,400, nothing changes. You figure self-employment tax (and the two deductions) exactly as described above, but only on your business profit. Your outside wages are subject to regular employee payroll taxes; you do not pay self-employment tax on them.

2. If the combined incomes, outside job and business profit, are over $65,400, you pay a reduced self-employment tax. How you figure the tax depends on several factors:

(a) If your outside job pays more than $65,400, all of your business profits are subject to the lower 2.9%, less the two deductions.

(b) If your outside job pays less than $65,400 (but combined earnings, job and business, are over $65,400), you first subtract the outside job wages from $65,400. The result is how much of your business profit is subject to the 15.3% self-employment tax. For example, let's say you have a job paying $30,000. $65,400 minus the $30,000 comes to $35,400. So the first $35,400 of business profit is subject to the 15.3% tax (less the deductions). Any business profit above $35,400 is subject to the 2.9% tax (less the deductions).

Although the calculations under situation #3 sound confusing, you will find them much easier to do than to explain. And be warned: these figures change every year. Always check with the IRS before relying on any of these figures.

Remember that if your business profit is $400 or less, you owe no self-employment tax regardless of the maximum combined incomes.

For more information, see IRS Publication #553, "Information on Self-Employment Tax."

RETIREMENT DEDUCTIONS

You may invest a portion of your business profit in a special retirement plan and pay no income taxes on the money invested or the interest until you retire and withdraw the funds.

There are several tax-deferred retirement plans available to business owners and their employees. Each plan has different options, different contributions, different deadlines for making contributions, and, most important to employers, different requirements for including your employees in the plans. You can choose just one plan, or you may be able to set up multiple plans. Any contributions you, as the employer, make for your employees are tax deductible.

Individual Retirement Account (IRA)

The simplest plan is the Individual Retirement Account. There are no administration fees or IRS forms to file. Any business owner or wage earner can set up an IRA. The maximum annual contribution is only $2,000 ($4,000 if you have a nonworking spouse) or your taxable earnings, whichever is less. Maximum is reduced if you or your spouse has an outside job that includes a retirement plan. With an IRA, you have no obligation to cover any of your employees. You can set up or contribute to an IRA anytime up to the date your tax return is due, not including any extensions (April 15 of the next year).

Simplified Employee Pension Plan (SEP)

A SEP (SEP-IRA) is also very easy to set up and maintain. Like an IRA, there are no administration fees or IRS forms to file. You can invest up to 13.04% of your earnings every year, up to a maximum investment of $24,000 a year. The law actually says the maximum is 15%, but the convoluted way of computing the contribution works out to 13.04%. You can set up or contribute to a SEP right up to the due date of your tax return (April 15 of the next year, or later if you file an extension), applying the deduction to the previous year's income.

With a SEP, however, you must include all employees over 21 years old who have worked for you for three of the last five years, including any part-time employees if they earned at least $400 during the year. You are not required to cover employees until after five years of employment. You, the employer, pay the full cost of the plan. Whatever percentage of your salary you contribute for yourself, you must contribute an equal percentage for each eligible employee.

"SIMPLE" Plan

Another plan is the Savings Incentive Match Plan for Employees, SIMPLE for short. Unfortunately, the rules are far from simple.

If you have no employees, you can set up a SIMPLE just for yourself and contribute 1% to 3% of your income (the percentage depends on several factors), up to a maximum annual investment of $6,000 ($12,000 if incorporated), and defer income taxes until retirement.

If you have employees, you must include every employee who earns $5,000 a year or more and who chooses to join the plan. Each employee who joins can contribute as much as 3% of their wages (1% in some low-profit years), up to a maximum contribution of $6,000 a year, and pay no income taxes on the amount contributed until they retire. You, the employer, must contribute an equal amount on behalf of each employee. That's why it's called a "match" plan: you match your employees' contributions.

As an alternative, you can contribute 2% (instead of 3%), up to $6,000 a year, for *every* employee who earned $5,000 or more. Under this arrangement, the employees are not required to make any contributions themselves.

	Maximum Contribution	Minimum Contribution	Employees Who Must Be Included	Deadline	Paperwork
IRA	$2,000 (add'l $2,000 for spouse)	none	none	set up & contribute by tax return filing date (no extensions)	minimal
SEP (SEP-IRA)	13.04% or $24,000	none	over 21 & worked 3 of last 5 years	set up & contribute by tax return filing date (including any extensions)	minimal
SIMPLE	$6,000 employer, $6,000 employee	1%-3% can vary	$5,000 or more income, if employee elects to join	varies	minimal for some; more for others
KEOGH profit-sharing	13.04% or $30,000	none	over 21, worked 2 years & 1,000 or more hours a year	set up by last day of year, contribute by tax return filing date (including extensions)	forms & special tax return
KEOGH money-purchase	20% or $30,000	fixed: same % each year	over 21, worked 2 years & 1,000 or more hours a year	set up by last day of year, contribute by tax return filing date (including extensions)	forms & special tax return

Keogh

The Keogh plans (there are several) are more complicated, more paperwork, more forms to file. But the Keogh plans offer larger contributions and different requirements for including employees. For some businesses, a Keogh plan will be more than worth the extra trouble.

The most common Keogh plan, the defined contribution plan, has two options: a profit-sharing plan and a money-purchase plan. Neither has anything to do with profit sharing or purchasing money; they're just terms. You can choose one or a combination of both plans.

The profit-sharing plan's maximum annual contribution is 13.04% of earnings, up to a maximum annual investment of $30,000. The money purchase plan's maximum contribution is 20% of earnings, up to $30,000 (the law says 25%, but the calculation works out to 20%). The money purchase plan, however, requires that you make the same percentage contribution every year; whatever percentage you decide on when you open the plan, you're stuck with it. Under the profit sharing plan you can change the contribution, or make no contribution at all, each year. You must set up a Keogh plan by year-end but you have until the due date of your tax return, including extensions, to make your contribution.

Keogh plans have a different set of requirements for including your employees. You must include and pay for employees over 21 years old who have worked for you two or more years, but only if they work 1,000 or more hours per year. So any employee who works less than half-time doesn't have to be covered under a Keogh plan. Under a SEP, you'll recall, *all* employees who have worked for you three or more years (out of five) must be covered. This is a major factor for many businesses with only part-time help.

There is yet another type of Keogh plan, called a "defined benefit plan." You decide what pension you want to receive after you retire; the contributions are then based on the pension amount. Defined benefit plans usually allow larger contributions and bigger tax deductions than defined contribution plans. But most business owners shy away from the defined benefit plan because it is much more complicated and expensive to set up than a defined contribution plan. There is no easy formula or percentage to figure how much to contribute each year. People who are close to retirement age and just setting up a new retirement plan may find a defined benefit plan very attractive, however, because it allows them to make much larger contributions than the other plans. In effect, it allows them to catch up for lost time.

Keoghs plans can include a salary reduction arrangement similar to the SIMPLE plan. They are called Effective Deferral Plans or, more often, 401(k) Plans. Employees have part of their income withheld from their paychecks. The withheld income is invested in the company Keogh plan, and the employee pays no income tax on it until it is withdrawn, usually at retirement.

More Details: All Four Plans

Under IRAs, SEPs and profit-sharing Keogh plans, you can change the contribution, or make no contribution at all, each year. Although there are maximum tax-deductible contributions, there are no minimums. SIMPLE minimums depend on what your employees want to contribute.

Under all the above plans, you cannot withdraw your money without penalty until age 59½. (IRAs and some SIMPLE plans can be tapped penalty-free for large medical bills).

For self-employed individuals, the income figure you use to calculate retirement contributions is not the full profit from your business. You must reduce the profit by one-half your self-employment tax (the "second deduction" explained in the Self Employment Tax chapter). You also have to include your non-business income and losses in determining total income.

Self-employment tax: Retirement plan contributions for yourself are not deductible for computing self-employment tax. You base self-employment tax on your business profit before the retirement contributions made for yourself.

State taxes: Not all states allow retirement deductions in calculating state income tax. You may still owe state income tax on your full profit.

A final word for employers: If you want to set up a retirement plan just for yourself, without having to pay for your employees' retirement, many insurance companies offer "non-qualifying plans" of all types. But under those "non-qualifying plans" (so called because they do not qualify for an income tax deduction) you must pay regular income taxes on your entire business profit. You are not allowed any tax deduction.

Corporations: IRAs are for individuals, sole proprietors, partners in partnerships, and LLC members. SEPs, Keoghs and SIMPLEs are available to all businesses, including corporations. There are also corporate retirement plans you can set up, different than those described here.

More Information

Most banks and insurance companies offer IRA, SEP, SIMPLE and Keogh plans. The interest will vary with different plans and contribution amounts. Many banks offer free booklets describing all the plans. The IRS publishes two free booklets, Publ. 590, Individual Retirement Accounts (covers SEPs and IRAs); and Publ. 560, Self Employed Retirement Plans (Keoghs).

ESTIMATED TAX PAYMENTS

If your federal tax for the current year, income and self-employment combined, is estimated to be $500 or more, you are required to pay your tax in quarterly installments. The government wants your tax money just like the taxes withheld from employees' paychecks.

The four quarterly installments are due April 15, June 15, September 15, and the following January 15. You do not have to pay the fourth estimate if you file your tax return by January 31 and pay the balance due.

How do you estimate your taxes? You can base your estimate on your prior year's taxes, even if you were not in business then. Whatever your total tax came to last year, divide it by four and send the IRS four equal installments. If your total tax last year (including self-employment) was less than $500, you are not required to make any estimated tax payments. (If adjusted gross income was over $150,000, or $75,000 for married couples filing separately, you must pay 110% of prior years's tax).

You also have the option to estimate your taxes based on your current year's income. Four times a year, you figure your taxable income for that quarter and send in the correct tax. As you can imagine, this is not an easy task. Under this method you may be hit with an interest penalty if you underestimate by more than 10 percent.

When you compute your actual tax at year-end, any overpayment of estimated taxes will, at your option, either be refunded or applied to the following year's estimates.

If you pay very low estimated tax or none at all, and if you are having a profitable year, be prepared when April 15 rolls around. You may have to come up with a lot of cash to pay this year's taxes *and* to pay next year's first quarterly estimate; both are due the same day. You may want to make voluntary estimated payments or set some money aside to cushion the blow.

Estimated taxes are filed on Form, #1040-ES. You file one Schedule ES no matter how many unincorporated businesses you own.

If you are also holding a job where taxes are withheld by your employer, instead of filing a Schedule ES, you can have your withholding increased to cover the additional income and Self Employment taxes. The IRS doesn't care whether it gets your money through withholding or through estimated payments.

Some fine print: The above rules apply to sole proprietors, partners and LLCs. There is a different set of rules for corporations and a third set of rules for farmers and fishermen. If you base your estimates on the prior year's taxes, you must have been a U.S. citizen or resident for the entire previous year. See IRS Publ. 505, "Tax Withholding and Estimated Taxes."

BARTER

"In the beginning, there was no money." But there always was the tax man, and barter does not escape his grasp. Barter transactions are taxable just like all other business transactions.

When you exchange or trade your business goods or services for someone else's goods or services, it is called barter. The "fair market value" of the goods or services you receive must be included in your regular business income and treated just like any other business income.

If the goods or services you receive are to be used in your business, you get a business write-off on your taxes, just as though you paid cash.

For example, let's say you are a cabinetmaker, and you build some custom cabinets for the person who owns the local office supply store. In exchange for the cabinets, you get $1,000 worth of "free" office supplies (or maybe some equipment or a computer). You have taxable income of $1,000. If you use the supplies or equipment 100% for your business, you also have a $1,000 expense you can write off. If any of what you receive in trade is for personal, non-business use, the personal portion is not deductible. The owner of the office supply store also has $1,000 to report as business income. If she uses the cabinets in the store, she has a $1,000 business expense. If she uses the cabinets in her kitchen at home, she does not have a deductible expense.

If the exchange is valued at $600 or more, and if it includes services (not goods), the business receiving the service must report it to the IRS on Form 1099-MISC. This is the same law that applies to outside contractors (see "Hiring Help" in the Growing Up section).

If you are bartering for services, be careful that the person providing the service is not an employee in disguise, one who should be on the books with payroll deductions, worker's compensation insurance and the rest. An employee who gets paid in goods or services, instead of cash, is still an employee. The "fair market value" of the goods or services the employee receives is considered wages, 100% taxable. The contractor-versus-employee tests described in the "Hiring Help" chapter apply here as well.

If you join a barter club (exchange, network), the rules are basically the same. But you must recognize the income at the time you receive the "barter credits" even if you haven't yet "spent" them. And keep in mind that these organizations report all transactions to the IRS.

Barter transactions should be posted to your income and expenditure ledgers (and if applicable, to the equipment ledger) the same way you would post cash transactions.

OPERATING LOSSES

If your business suffers a loss this year, you will owe no income taxes on the business, which I'm sure you know. You may not know that this loss will also offset other income, such as a salary from an outside job or your spouses wages, to reduce this year's income tax.

You can also use this year's loss to offset income, and reduce taxes, from other years. You are allowed to carry back what the IRS calls a "Net Operating Loss" (NOL) to apply against prior income and receive a refund of prior years' taxes, even if you were not in business then. The loss can be carried back three years. And if your taxable income for the three prior years is not sufficient to absorb the entire loss, you may carry the balance forward to apply to as many as 15 future years. At your option, you can forego the 3-year carry-back period and apply your NOL entirely to the 15 future years.

An NOL, like any other tax deduction, is worth more in a high income year. If the three preceding years generated little or no income tax, you probably will do better to forego the carry-back, and apply the entire NOL to future years.

Net Operating Loss is not simply the business loss shown on your tax return. It is a complicated combination of business and non-business income and deductions. I don't include the NOL calculations because they are quite complex, and there's no way to simplify the procedure. Step-by-step instructions are explained in the IRS's *Tax Guide for Small Business* (Publ. 334). Don't be put off by their complexity; the NOL deduction may save you a bundle in income taxes.

TAX CREDITS

Tax credits are special tax deductions created by Congress to stimulate the economy or to

Here's that book you ordered, "Income Taxes Made Easy."

encourage businesses to act in socially or environmentally responsible ways. Tax credits are often allowed in addition to any regular deductions. In other words, they can be a real gold mine for your business.

In the past, there have been credits (sometimes lumped under the heading "General Business Credit") for hiring disadvantaged or handicapped people, for using renewable energy sources, for purchasing electric and other clean-fuel vehicles, for rehabilitating old buildings, for research and development, for investing in equipment.

Unfortunately, tax credits come and go, available one year and not the next. If you fail to take a tax credit you are entitled to, the IRS will not tell you. So you need to do your own research.

Some credits appear on Schedule C or on your partnership or corporation return, reducing your taxable profit. Other credits are on the first page of your 1040 return, directly reducing your taxes. The IRS's Publication 334, *Tax Guide for Small Business* lists the current credits.

TAX SOFTWARE

Computer tax-preparation programs can help organize your ledgers so they match tax-return categories, suggest tax options, ask questions, and prepare your entire tax return. But small business taxes can be quite complicated, as you well know. It would take a clever and sophisticated program (and one without bugs!) to know just the right questions to ask and how to ask them.

I have talked to several tax accountants about tax programs, and every one thinks you'd be making a mistake to trust your business tax return to a computer program, one that may or may not include all the peculiarities of small business tax law. Now, I admit that accountants would loose a lucrative chunk of their income if people started using computers instead of them, but their warnings are valid.

A face to face discussion with a tax accountant is much more likely to turn up tax savings than typing answers to formula questions on your computer. An accountant can spot possible problems you might avoid, by rewording an answer to a question, or relabeling an expense, or maybe by not claiming some deduction that might be a red flag to the IRS. An accountant can also show you how you might do things differently next year, to reduce future tax bills.

FARMERS: Special Tax Laws

"...and the taxes on the farmer feeds us all."
—from an old folk song

Federal income tax rules for small-time farmers are somewhat different from those for other small businesses. Some of the differences are outlined in this chapter but for complete information farmers should obtain a free copy of IRS Publication #225, "Farmer's Tax Guide."

Farmers do not report their profit or loss on Schedule 1040-C. Unincorporated farmers use Sch. 1040-F, "Farm Income and Expenses."

Purchased breeding stock and dairy stock must be treated as depreciable property, just like a tractor or machinery. One exception: the cost of egg laying stock—chicks, pullets, hens—can be written off the year of purchase. Livestock born on your farm cannot be depreciated because there is no purchase cost to depreciate.

The cost of feed, fertilizer, seeds and young plants (except seeds and young plants for tree farms, orchards and timber land) can sometimes be deducted the year of purchase even if they are purchased for future years' use, but only if they do not exceed 50% of current expenses.

The cost of clearing, leveling and conditioning land, purchasing and planting trees (other than certain young plants), building irrigation canals and ditches, laying irrigation pipes, constructing dams and building roads must, in most cases, be depreciated. Some soil and water conservation expenditures that meet government approved conservation requirements can, at your option, be deducted as an expense the year incurred instead of being depreciated. The requirements and dollar limitations are explained in IRS Publication #225, "Farmer's Tax Guide". All expenditures for citrus and almond grove development must be depreciated.

Farmers—and fishermen and women, too—do not have to make quarterly estimated tax payments if your gross income from farming (or fishing) is at least two-thirds of your total estimated gross income from all sources. One estimated tax payment for the entire prior year's taxes is required of farmers and fishermen, due on January 15. And you don't have to make that estimated tax payment if you file your income tax return by the last day in February.

Farmers can use the ledgers in this book, but you will need to make some alterations. Generally, most farm sales are not subject to sales tax, so you probably do not need a sales tax column in your income ledger. I suggest that you delete the headings on columns #3 through #6 in your income ledger and re-title them to suit your needs.

Use a different column for each different type of income, such as livestock sales, produce sales, milk sales, patronage dividends, etc.

In the Expenditure ledger, Column #1—Inventory can certainly be deleted, and probably several other columns. In their place, you may want columns for livestock purchases, feed, fertilizer, veterinary fees or other typical farm expenses.

If your only employees are immediate family members, you are exempt from Occupational Safety and Health (OSHA) requirements.

A few words from the IRS to part-time and "weekend" farmers: "A farmer who operates a farm for profit may deduct all the ordinary and necessary expenses of carrying on the business of farming. The farm must be operated for profit. Whether a farm is being operated for profit must be determined from all the facts and circumstances in each case. However, you will not ordinarily be considered as operating a farm for profit if you raise crops or livestock mainly for use of your family, but derive some income from incidental sales." Such "incidental sales" are subject to income tax, but deductions cannot exceed income (that is, no losses allowed).

The INTERNAL REVENUE SERVICE and You

Small Time Operator is not a manual for beating the IRS at their own game nor is it intended to be another "101 Ways to Reduce Your Taxes." Still, a general knowledge of the Internal Revenue Service and its inner workings may benefit you in your dealings with the agency and may even add to your peace of mind.

Most people, including most small businesses, file their tax returns and never get audited. The IRS audits less than 2% of all tax returns. IRS agents have to earn their keep and they are not going to be nickel-and-diming every little business that files a return. In almost all instances, returns selected for audit are those obviously out of line with the IRS's idea of the "norm". The IRS does sometimes audit a random sample of tax returns, but the number is very small.

All tax returns, big and small, are automatically checked on the computer for errors—addition, multiplication, tax computation. If there is an arithmetical error, you will be notified of the error and any change in your taxes due to it. This is not an audit; and if you make an error, it does not increase your chances of being audited.

Many income tax returns are checked against other documents sent to the IRS, particularly W-2s, 1099 forms, and other "information returns." If your tax return does not include income that was reported to the IRS on a W-2 or 1099 form, you may get an inquiry, or even a tax bill, from the IRS.

All federal income tax returns are entered into the IRS computers and automatically compared to what is known as the "Discriminate Input Function Formula," a computer program of the average American's financial profile. If your return falls within the "DIF" formula, you will be deemed An Honest Taxpayer. Your return will be filed away in the deep recesses of computer storage and will probably never be seen again.

If the computer does kick out your return, flags it for a possible audit, it will be sent back to your local IRS district office. An agent in the local office will review the return and decide whether or not to initiate an audit. Not every tax return rejected by the computer is audited; usually, only those returns the agent feels are potential money makers for the IRS are selected.

When examining a small business, the IRS will probably be looking for some of the following:

1. A reasonable profit, comparing total expenses to total sales. If your sales are $10,000 and your expenses $9,990, you may arouse suspicion that all is not right.

2. Consistency from one year to the next. Large fluctuations or unusual changes from year to year might invite an audit.

3. Unusual or unreasonable expenses. Large expenses not usually found in your type of business will be suspect. Large deductions for entertainment, conventions or travel away from home often invite audits.

4. Estimated numbers. The IRS is very suspicious of round numbers.

5. Whether you've been audited before. If you have been audited in the past and wound up owing more tax, your chances of being audited again are increased. On the other hand, if prior audits did not result in more tax, you probably will not get audited again even if the computer does "kick out" your return.

6. What kind of business you own. The IRS has a "Market Segment Specialization Program" (MSSP) where they select a specific industry, and audit a whole slew of restaurants, or maybe lawyers, insurance agents, or independent cab drivers—often a type of business where "problems" have typically shown up in prior audits. What you write in the "occupation" box on your tax return may affect your chance of being audited.

7. The IRS has an agreement with most states to exchange tax information. If your state tax return was audited, the state may notify the IRS about your audit: the year involved, the reason for the audit and the results. The IRS may also notify your state about the results of IRS audits.

"MOST PEOPLE BRING THEIR ACCOUNTANT."

"You're saying that as a professional writer, your expenses totaled $22,000 more than your income? What kind of way is that to make a living?"

Home Businesses: A lot of people think that home-based businesses (those claiming a home-office deduction and filing Form 8829) are more likely to be audited. This has not been my experience. If you are entitled to a home office deduction, you certainly should claim it.

Business Loss

A loss on your tax return is by no means a sure cause for audit. It is not uncommon for new businesses to show a loss the first year, with high start-up costs and early, slow business.

A warning, however, to people who manage to show a loss year after year: if you do not show a profit for at least three out of five consecutive years, the IRS can declare your business to be a hobby and disallow any losses. The IRS treats any income from a hobby as taxable income, but losses are not deductible. By contrast, a business loss is deductible. (If you breed, train, race or show horses, the IRS hobby loss test is two out of seven years instead of three out of five.)

These are not firm rules, however. A business can deduct losses for several years in a row without ever being challenged by the IRS. In the event of an audit, the IRS will allow the ongoing losses if they are convinced that you are operating a real business and trying, though unsuccessfully, to make a profit. The key issue is *intent*. What are you really doing? Trying to earn some money or just having fun? It will help if your business looks like a business (licenses, ledgers, bank account, business cards, etc.) and if you're devoting time to it in a businesslike manner.

If your business is showing losses in the first year or two, you can keep the IRS from invoking the hobby-loss rule until the full five year period is up, by filing Form 5213, Election to Postpone Determination. The form must be filed within three years of the due date of your first business tax return (April 15 of the fourth year in business). If you don't file this form, it doesn't mean the IRS will audit you. They'll probably accept your return as is, and you'll probably never hear from them. The form is just extra insurance and may be totally unnecessary. I mention it but do not recommend it.

Notice of An Audit

Your first notice of an audit will be a letter from the IRS informing you of the audit and the year or years to be examined. You may be asked to come in person to a meeting with an agent or merely to send in certain written information. They may request to see a specific bill to support a specific item of expense, or they may request your entire set of ledgers. You may be asked to bring or mail in copies of your tax returns for other years that are still open to audit. The auditor may want to visit your business.

If the IRS is doing an audit of your business, it may be a costly decision to face the IRS without an accountant there to help you. IRS agents are trained to ask leading questions in order to get information from you that may increase your tax bill or lead to an expanded audit. A good accountant knows what to expect and can help answer questions, honestly and legally, but in a way that may avoid unnecessary trouble. The accountant can possibly help narrow the scope of the audit, and arrange to meet the auditor at the IRS office or the accountant's office, instead of your own business location.

The accountant, being a professional and used to dealing with IRS agents, can defuse any personal animosity. Business owners often get angry at IRS agents. And IRS agents, being human beings, are sometimes harder on owners who are unable to control themselves. A little politeness can go a long way in helping an audit along.

People will do silly things to avoid taxes.
—J. C. Small, tax attorney, Counsel to the
Director, New Jersey Division of Taxation

You should also realize that federal income tax laws and their legal interpretations fill entire bookshelves. IRS agents must have a knowledge of many different areas of law. Small business law by itself is full of special rules, exceptions to those rules, and Tax Court rulings overthrowing or restricting those rules. IRS agents simply do not know all the small business rules, and they make mistakes. Honest mistakes, I'm sure. But if you don't know the law, you don't know if the IRS agent is right or wrong when he says that you cannot deduct some expense you thought you could. A good tax accountant, one experienced in small business, knows those rules inside and out. I have saved some of my tax clients lots of money by being at the audit, tax books in hand, showing an IRS agent that his ruling is incorrect.

If the audit goes against you, and you still feel you are in the right, the IRS provides all taxpayers an elaborate system of appeals, starting with informal meetings with agents and going right up to the Supreme Court.

Penalties

Generally, no penalties are assessed where there is an honest mistake on a tax return. You will owe only the back taxes and interest, as long as you pay up when the IRS says pay up.

There *are* a large variety of IRS penalties, some mild and some severe, for various offenses: failure to file; failure to pay (the more you owe, the bigger the penalty); "negligence"; "intentional disregard of rules and regulations without intent to defraud"; "willful attempt to evade or defeat taxes" (that means fraud). Where fraud is involved, the IRS can impose both civil and criminal penalties. Civil penalties (fines) can be imposed in the normal course of an audit. Criminal penalties (large fines and/or jail) may only be imposed after full due-process of law, a trial, etc.

If you cannot afford to pay the taxes when your tax return is due, file the return on time anyway. The penalties will probably be less. Quite often, the IRS will waive penalties where failure to file a return or failure to pay the tax is due to "reasonable cause."

Except for special situations, the general statute of limitations—the length of time the IRS has to audit a return and assess back taxes—is three years from the time the return is filed. If you omit more than 25% of your gross income,

the statute of limitations is increased to six years. If your return is "false or fraudulent" or if no return is filed, there is no time limit . Most IRS audits, however, are initiated within 20 months of filing the return. If you haven't heard from them by then, you probably won't.

This chapter is full of vague words: "reasonable cause," "without intent to defraud," "intentional disregard of rules and regulations," "willful attempt to evade," "unusual" this and "unreasonable" that. Many people make their living arguing over these and other godawful terms. As with so many other legal situations, the words often wind up meaning whatever the agent or the judge wants them to mean. This is not an area for amateurs. If you are caught up in an audit involving these issues, your philosophy and your finances will have to dictate your reactions. Good luck.

Failure to File a Tax Return

I would like to cover briefly an area about which I have received a surprisingly large number of questions over the years: what if someone has been in business a few years and never filed a tax return? It's rarely a case of intentional dishonesty. A typical example is a craftsperson who starts out with a hobby. At Christmas, he sells a couple hundred dollars worth of merchandise, and he never thinks of his craft as a business. But now, two or three years have passed, and he realizes that $5,000 or $10,000 a year is going through his bank account, and he's never filed a tax return. Now what?

Contrary to what many people think, the Internal Revenue Service is not all-powerful nor all-seeing. Their computers are not set up for Big Brother snooping—not yet, anyway. The IRS will not know you have earned money unless you or someone else reports it to them. For most Americans, this information comes to the IRS on a Form W-2, report of income of employees.

A self-employed person is most likely to be known to the IRS via something called a Form 1099, report of income paid an individual other than an employee. If you sell your services to another business (not goods, just services) and that business paid you $600 or more during one year, they are required to file a Form 1099, notifying the IRS that you have received this money. Also, if you are an independent sales agent and you purchase $5,000 or more in goods for resale (from one company in one year) that company will report the purchase to the IRS on a 1099 form. In both of the above situations, the business that files the 1099 must also send you a copy of the form. Interest on your bank account is reported to the IRS on a Form 1099.

If you receive a Form 1099, the IRS has your name. If the amounts paid exceed the minimum requirements for filing, you are likely to get a letter of inquiry or possibly even a tax bill.

Forms you yourself file might also alert the IRS to your existence, such as employment reports, sales tax reports, even state tax returns.

If no one reports you, and if you file no reports or other documents, the IRS will probably not know of your existence. Probably. But you are breaking the law, and there is no statute of limitations on how many years later they can come after you.

The law says, and I recommend, that you file returns for all those prior years, pay the back taxes and interest. Some people will just go on their merry way and never file and never be found; we've all heard of someone with that kind of experience. Other delinquent folk may decide that this is the year to file their first return, and let the prior years lie, hopefully, unnoticed.

Although the law specifies penalties for failure to file an income tax return, the IRS often grants "amnesty" (no penalties) to people who file their old tax returns and pay the back taxes and interest due. Even when the IRS finds you, if they haven't formally initiated a criminal investigation, which is a rare situation, you still may be able to escape penalties.

AMENDING OLD TAX RETURNS

There may be gold in old income tax returns. Two facts few people know: (1) Most income tax returns, especially small business returns, have errors no one, not even the IRS, discovered; and (2) You may amend prior years' tax returns and get refunds of overpaid taxes.

The IRS catches glaring and obvious errors on tax returns: mistakes in addition or tax computation, missing forms, entries on the wrong line, improper procedures. Beyond the obvious, unless you get audited—and less than two percent of small business tax returns are audited—your return will be accepted as is, errors and all.

Whenever I get a new tax client, I have a look at the prior year's tax return before I prepare the current one. Over the years, I've found errors and omissions on over half the returns prepared by professionals and on close to 100% of the returns prepared by the taxpayers who do their own returns. In many of the cases, more tax was paid than required by law.

Amended tax returns must be filed within three years from the date you filed your original return or within two years from the time you paid your tax, whichever is later. A return filed early is considered filed on the due date. So for 1996 tax returns filed and paid on time (April 15, 1997) or ahead of time, you have until the next century, April 15, 2000, to amend the return.

How do you know if there is an error or omission on your tax return? If you prepared the return yourself, there's probably an error. The tax laws are so complex, even the experts don't know it all. Unless you studied the tax laws thoroughly, you probably missed something. If you took your taxes to one of those tax chains or storefront tax operations, your return was probably prepared by someone with little experience and brief training. These people do not take the time to look into your business finances in search of tax savings. If the tax preparer took your numbers and asked few or no questions, chances are good your return is not all it could be.

The most common omissions and errors I've found on business tax returns are: not taking tax credits you are entitled to; failing to accrue expenses at year-end (see the chapter Accrual Accounting); overlooking legitimate business expenses that didn't get into your ledgers or your business checkbook, such as out-of-pocket cash payments, business expenses paid out of your personal checking account, automobile expenses, home office expenses, purchases that are partly personal and partly business, bank service charges, equipment and furniture used in your business but purchased prior to starting your business; incorrectly computing depreciation or choosing the wrong depreciation method; miscalculating cost-of-goods-sold.

If you find or suspect an error or omission, ask your accountant about it. If you prepared your own return or if it was prepared by someone of questionable competence, locate an experienced accountant (see Professional Help in the Appendix), and ask the accountant to look over your return. Most accountants will give it at least a glance. Some will catch and correct an error. Others will want to re-do the entire return: they're less likely to make a mistake if they are not working from someone else's mistake.

Tax returns are amended on form 1040-X for sole proprietorships, 1120-X for regular corporations, 1120-S (marked "Amended") for S corporations, and 1065 (marked "Amended") for partnerships and LLCs. Refunds are fairly prompt.

An amended return is more likely to get the once over from an IRS agent. My experience, however, is that amended returns are not more likely to be audited than original returns.

If your federal return was in error, your state return was probably also in error. States have similar procedures for amending returns. Some states require you to amend the state return if you amend your federal return.

FEDERAL INFORMATION RETURNS

Certain business transactions must be reported to the IRS on special "information returns." These reports are not tax returns, and no taxes are paid with them. In most cases, you must also give a copy of the information return to all parties involved in the transactions. Some information returns are covered in other sections of the book, more are covered here.

Large cash transactions. Businesses that receive $10,000 or more in cash (currency), money orders, travellers or cashier's checks (but not personal or business checks) in a single transaction or in two or more related transactions, must report it to the IRS on Form #8300.

Real estate transactions. The person responsible for closing real estate transactions (usually the title company but sometimes the broker) must file Form #1099-S with the IRS.

Royalty payments. If you pay $10 or more in royalties to one person in a calendar year, report the payment to the IRS on Form #1099-MISC.

Dividend payments. Corporations paying $10 or more in dividends must report each payment to the IRS on Form #1099-DIV.

Interest payments. If you pay $600 or more in interest in any calendar year on a business debt, report the payment on Form #1099-INT.

Owners or operators of fishing boats report all payments to crew members on proceeds from sale of catch, on Form #1099-MISC.

*Interest receive*d. If your business receives $600 or more of mortgage interest from an individual in a calendar year, report the income to the IRS on Form #1098.

Lenders. If you lend money in connection with your business, and in full or partial satisfaction of the debt, you acquire an interest in property secured for the debt, you must file form 1099-A.

Stock brokers. Report sales of stocks, bonds commodities, etc. on Form 1099-B.

Rent. Businesses paying $600 or more a year in rent (for business premises, machinery or equipment, etc.) must file Form 1099- MISC.

Tips. Restaurants with more than 10 employees earning tips, must file Form #8027.

Outside services. Businesses paying $600 or more a year in fees, commissions or prizes to non-employees and outside contractors, must file Form 1099-MISC. See the Growing Up section.

Independent sales agents. If you make direct sales of $5,000 or more of consumer products to outside sales agents in any one year, you must file Form 1099-MISC.

Medical coverage. Businesses paying $600 or more for health insurance, or paying $600 or more directly to a physician for an employee's medical expenses, file Form 1099-MISC.

Fish resellers. File 1099 if you buy more than $600 of fish from fishing boats.

The present system will not be abolished untill all the members of Congress are forced to fill out their tax returns alone, without the help of an accountant.—Columnist Nicholas Von Hoffman

FEDERAL EXCISE TAX

Most small businesses are not liable for federal excise taxes. Businesses that are required to file excise tax returns must have an Employer Identification Number (EIN) even if you are not an employer. Use Form SS-4 to request a number.

Some states call their corporate income tax an excise tax, not to be confused these excise taxes.

Regular excise taxes are imposed on manufacturers of trucks, truck trailers, truck parts, tires, inner tubes, fishing equipment, outboard motors, bows, arrows, firearms, ammunition, coal, gasoline and gasohol, lubricating oils, and cars that do not meet fuel economy standards; on businesses operating aircraft; on businesses using fuel in inland waterways; on retailers of heavy trucks and trailers; on retailers of diesel, gasoline substitutes, noncommercial aviation and marine fuels; and on retail sales of new automobiles over $32,000. The excise tax is payable quarterly on Form 720, Quarterly Federal Excise Tax Return. Excise taxes are also imposed on brewers; on wholesale and retail beer, wine and liquor dealers; on manufacturers of stills; on tobacco; and on importers and dealers in firearms. These excise taxes are paid on Form #11. For more information on the above taxes, ask the IRS for a free copy of Publication #510, "Excise Taxes."

A highway motor vehicle Federal Use Tax is imposed on owners of large highway trucks, truck trailers and buses. Form 2290 must be filed annually. For more information, see IRS publication #349, "Federal Highway Use Tax."

STATE INCOME TAXES

As of last year, every state had some form of income tax on resident unincorporated businesses except Alaska, Florida, Nevada, New Hampshire, South Dakota, Tennessee, Texas, Wyoming and Washington, though Washington has a "gross receipts tax" and New Hampshire has a "business profits tax" (see below).

Most states compute state tax as a percentage of your federal income tax, or based on a percentage of the income shown on your federal return. Five states have income tax rules just different enough from the federal rules to require separate calculations: Alabama, Arkansas, Mississippi, New Jersey, and Pennsylvania.

State income taxes, like federal income taxes, are based on your net income (net profit). Total (gross) income less deductible expenses gives you net income. Generally, states allow businesses to deduct the same expenses as the IRS allows with a few important exceptions: you may deduct state income tax on your federal return but not on your state return (in most states; you should check your state's laws on this); you may not deduct federal income taxes on your federal tax return, but several states allow a deduction for federal income taxes; some states do not make allowances for Net Operating Loss carry-back and carry-forward; many states have different years allowed for NOL carry-back and carry-forward; self-employment tax is a federal tax only, although some states allow a deduction for it; not all states allow the same nontaxable retirement contributions the IRS allows. Many states offer tax credits, reducing state income taxes. Some of these credits are similar to federal credits, some are completely different.

Most state income tax returns for calendar-year taxpayers are due April 15, the same due date as the federal returns. Six states have later due dates: Arkansas—May 15; Delaware—April 30; Hawaii—April 20; Iowa—April 30; Louisiana—May 15; Virginia—May 1.

Corporations: The above due dates are for unincorporated businesses. Corporate due dates vary considerably from state to state. Many states require corporations to file income tax returns a month earlier (often March 15).

STATE GROSS RECEIPTS TAXES

A gross receipts tax is a tax on total business receipts—sales, income—before any deductions for expenses. The tax is in addition to any income or sales tax. Some states call their sales tax a gross receipts tax, but the tax referred to here is not a sales tax. Sales tax is collected from your customers. Gross receipts taxes are paid out of your own pocket. As of last year, the following states had a gross receipts (or other unusual) tax:

Alaska has a gross receipts tax on the fishing industry.

Delaware has a gross receipts tax called a "merchants and manufacturers tax". Amounts vary depending on the kind of business: $25-$75, plus 0.09% to 0.72% of gross receipts in excess of $3,000-$35,000 a month.

Hawaii. Called a "general excise tax". Varies from 0.5% to 4% depending on type of business.

Indiana. Called a "gross income tax." 0.3% for most businesses, 1.2% on some.

Michigan has a special state "Single Business Tax", 2.3% of net profits (*not* gross receipts), but only after a $45,000 deductible. This tax is in addition to the sales and income tax.

Nevada has a flat tax on businesses, called a "Business Privilege Tax", of $25 per employee.

Nebraska has a "Litter Tax" based on gross receipts, for some businesses.

New Hampshire has a "Business Profits Tax". 7% of the profits on your federal tax return if your business grossed more than $12,000. New Hampshire also has a Business Enterprise Tax of 0.25% of the business' tax base, but only for businesses grossing $100,000 or more or having a tax base (value) of $50,000 or more.

New Mexico has a gross receipts tax on vehicle leasing businesses: 5% plus $2 per day.

Oklahoma has a 0.1% "Tourist Promotion Tax" on some businesses.

South Dakota has a 2% "Excise Tax" on some contractors.

Washington has a gross receipts tax called a Business and Occupation Tax. The rate varies, depending on type of business, from less than .01% to 3.3%. Washington has an Enhanced Fish Tax, a gross receipts tax on the fishing industry. Washington also has a Compensating Tax on personal property (6.5%) and car rentals (5.9%).

OTHER STATES TAXES

The list of state taxes on businesses is virtually endless. Many (but not all) states tax:

Manufacturers, wholesalers and retailers of alcoholic beverages, fuels, tobacco, motor vehicles, boats and airplanes.

Mining, logging, forest land, and real estate dealings.

Admissions on theaters, amusement parks, clubs, music halls, etc.

Freight, delivery, transportation and tour bus companies.

Chain stores, for businesses with more than one location.

Hotel rooms and restaurant meals.

Grain handlers and processors.

Financial and investment businesses.

Some states have state business licenses and annual fees (often called a "business privilege tax").

You should make an effort to find out about your state's tax laws on small businesses. Call state offices, ask other business owners, ask your accountant. You don't want to be caught by surprise or hit with some whopping penalty for failure to file a tax return you didn't know about.

LOCAL TAXES

Counties almost always impose property taxes (also called ad valorem taxes) on real estate. Some counties also impose a property tax on other business assets such as equipment, furniture and tools. This is called a "personal property" (or ad valorem) tax, and it could be quite high if your assets are assessed at a high value. You should examine this tax bill, and make sure retired or sold assets are not included, and that older assets are not overvalued.

Some counties impose an inventory tax (sometimes called a "floor" tax), a property tax on business inventory on hand at a given date, or based on an average inventory over the last twelve months.

Some large cities impose income taxes, gross receipts taxes, and/or sales taxes on businesses. These taxes are usually in addition to any similar state tax. A few large cities impose a flat "Business Tax" or "Business Registration Fee," which is in addition to the regular business license. Your business may have to pay special sewage or disposal fees.

You should contact your county or city offices to inquire about business taxes, on general and specific types of businesses. Don't be caught by surprise, and find out too late about a tax you didn't know about and can't afford.

With the exception of some income taxes, business taxes are tax deductible.

It is our Patriotic Duty to keep as much money out of the hands of our government as we can.
—*Philosopher Walter Camp*

The best thing Congress can do is go home for a couple of years.
—*Will Rogers*

He says we're free.

Section Five
APPENDIX

"Mercy!" Scrooge said. "Dreadful apparition, why do you trouble me?"

The same face; the very same. Marley in his pigtail, usual waistcoat, tights and boots. The chain he drew was clasped about his middle. It was long, and wound about him like a tail; and it was made of cash boxes, keys, padlocks, ledgers, deeds, and heavy purses wrought with steel. His body was transparent; so that Scrooge, observing him, and looking though his waistcoat, could see the two buttons on his coat behind.

"You are fettered," said Scrooge, trembling. "Tell me why?"

"I wear the chain I forged in life," replied the Ghost. "I made it link by link and yard by yard. I girded it on of my own free will, and of my own free will I wore it. Is its pattern strange to you?"

Scrooge trembled more and more. "But you were always a good man of business, Jacob," faltered Scrooge.

"Business!" cried the Ghost, wringing its hands again. "Mankind was my business. The common welfare was my business; charity, mercy, forbearance, and benevolence, were all my business. The dealing of my trade were but a drop of water in the comprehensive ocean of my business."

—excerpted from "A Christmas Carol" by Charles Dickens

HOW TO BALANCE A BANK ACCOUNT

The balance on your bank statement will rarely agree with the balance in your checkbook. But you know that. What you may not know, if you've never balanced a bank account, is that the difference is almost always easy to locate and reconcile. The difference is due to one or more of the following:

1. Checks you have written that have not yet cleared the bank; called "outstanding checks."

2. Deposits not yet posted by the bank; called "deposits in transit."

3. Interest earned or bank service charges you have not recorded in your checkbook and any return (bounced) checks that you still show as deposits; called "reconciling items."

4. Someone's error, usually yours; called "oops".

If you follow these procedures, balancing your bank account will take only a few minutes each month (hopefully):

1. Sort the canceled checks returned with the bank statement into numerical order.

2. Match each canceled check with the corresponding entry in your checkbook. Put a check mark next to your checkbook entry so you'll know the check has been canceled. It is also a good idea to compare the amount on the canceled check with the amount you wrote in your checkbook. Too many of you speedy check writers will write a check for $15.16 and post it in your checkbook as $16.15. It is known as "transposition" and is an occupational disease of even the best bookkeepers. There will most likely be several checks you have written that have not cleared the bank yet.

3. Match your checkbook record of deposits with the deposits recorded on the bank statement. Check off the deposits in your checkbook. And again beware of transposition errors. Unlike checks, deposits should clear the bank immediately. Electronic deposits usually take two days, mailed deposits take two to three days. Any real lag in a bank recording of deposits may mean a lost deposit. Contact the bank at once.

4. Look for any unusual items returned with the bank statement: notice of a bounced check or a check printing charge or some other bank charge. Also examine the statement itself for any bank charges or service fees. They will be listed along with the checks with a reference number or letter next to the amount. Somewhere on the statement is an explanation of what it means. By the way, if they hit you for a bank charge you don't think is proper, call the bank and complain. Quite often, the bank will cancel the charge. They would rather keep your business and your good will than get a $2 fee out of you. If your account pays interest, the amount is usually shown as the last item on your bank statement.

Now that you've checked off everything and marveled at all the little entries buried here and there on the bank statement, you are ready to reconcile. With pencil in hand and a blank piece of paper, or the back of the bank statement:

1. Write down your checkbook balance.

2. Add up the checks you have written that have *not* cleared the bank, the ones without a check mark next to them. These are your "outstanding checks". *Add* this total to your checkbook balance.

3. *Subtract* from your balance any deposits you have recorded that have *not* cleared the bank. These are your "deposits in transit."

4. *Subtract* from your balance any of the extra charges the bank included in the statement.

5. *Add* to your balance any interest paid.

6. If you made any errors recording check or deposit amounts adjust your balance.

The final figure you come up with should equal the bank balance on the statement. It doesn't? Darn. Let's try to isolate the problem.

Repeat the reconciliation, and check your

addition. If you don't have an adding machine, this may be a good time to read the chapter on adding machines in the Bookkeeping section; at least it will be a good excuse to get away from these numbers for a little while.

Still computes the same? When you checked off the canceled checks and the deposits, did the amounts all agree? Are you sure?

At this point, the error is 99 percent certain to be in your running checkbook balance. Sometime during the month, you wrote a check and recorded the correct amount but subtracted it incorrectly from the balance. Go back and re-subtract each check from the balance, check by check. You are bound to find the error.

No luck? Did you lose one of the canceled checks? Add up the number of canceled checks and compare with the total number of checks listed on the bank statement.

Still can't find the difference? At the bottom right hand corner of each cancelled check you'll see a computer-generated number. This is the amount the bank deducted from your account. This number should be the same as the amount of the check and the amount posted to your checkbook. You may find your error here.

What else? Examine the bank statement: the beginning balance should be the same as last month's ending balance. Was there a reconciling item on last month's statement you forgot to post to your checkbook? Did you balance last month's bank statement? (I'm still trying.)

I think that it is impossible to go through all these procedures and not locate the error. But if you've done the impossible, I suggest two more things: (1) Just put it all away for a few days and forget it. Later, when you're in a better mood, repeat these procedures, from scratch. Don't look at your old calculations; if they are wrong they will throw you off. AND IF THAT DOES NOT WORK, then (2) take your checkbook and the statement and the canceled checks and all down to the bank and get them to help you.

The one solution I failed to mention is the easiest: forget it. Assume you've made a mistake somewhere, correct your balance to agree with the reconciliation, and forget it. But that's just not my nature, so...

If you do have an error or if there are reconciling items such as bank charges, you must correct your books as follows:

Error in addition: Adjust the most recent checkbook balance up or down to correct the error. Make a note in the checkbook as to exactly what you are doing.

Error in check or deposit amount: Adjust the most recent checkbook balance and write a note of explanation. If you recorded a check or deposit incorrectly, make sure you didn't make the same mistake on your expenditure or income ledger.

Bank charges: Record them in your checkbook the same way you record a check, reducing your bank balance accordingly. Remember also to post the charges to your expenditure ledger in Column Two—Supplies, Postage, Etc.

BALANCE SHEETS

A balance sheet, also known as a "statement of assets and liabilities" or "net worth statement", is a listing of your assets, liabilities, and net worth (equity) at any given point in time. Balance sheets are required on some partnership and corporation tax returns. Most banks will ask to see a balance sheet when considering business loans. Audited corporate financial statements must include comparative (current year and prior year) balance sheets.

All balance sheets are made up of three sections: (1) Assets—the property you own; (2) Liabilities—money you owe; and (3) Equity—the net worth of your business, the difference between the assets and the liabilities.

Assets

Assets are broken down into two categories:

Current: Cash, and assets that will be used or sold in the normal course of business within a year. Current assets usually include accounts receivable (also simply called "receivables", the money your customers owe you), less an allowance for uncollectible bad debts; notes and loans receivable (money owed to you other than regular credit accounts) due within one year; inventory, valued at cost or market, whichever is less; prepaid expenses (beyond a year) such as next year's insurance. Current prepaid expenses such as rent or this year's insurance are not included.

Bear Soft Pretzel Co.
as of December 31

Assets

Current Assets

Cash		$375
Accounts Receivable	$140	
Less allowance for bad debts	($20)	
		$120
Prepaid insurance		$150
Inventory (at lower of cost or market)		
Pretzels--hot	$25	
Pretzels--stale	$1	
Flour, sugar, salt	$75	
		$101

Other Assets

Equipment, at cost	$2,300	
Less accumulated depreciation	($450)	
		$1,850
Total Assets		$2,596

Liabilities

Current Liabilities

Accounts Payable	$120
Loan payable, portion due within one year	$250

Long-Term Liabilities

Balance of loan payments	$750
Total Liabilities	$1,120
NET WORTH (owner's equity)	$1,476
	$2,596

Other Assets: Cost of fixed assets such as equipment, vehicles, furniture and buildings less the accumulated depreciation; cost of land; intangible long-term assets such as patents; notes and loans receivable that will not be collected within one year.

Long-term notes and loans receivable that are payable to you in installments over several years should be split between "current" and "other." The amount coming due within one year should be shown as "current"; the balance should be listed under "other assets."

Liabilities

Liabilities are divided into similar categories:
Current: Accounts payable (your unpaid bills: money you owe your vendors and suppliers); notes (loans) payable due within one year; unpaid taxes; unpaid wages.

Long-term: Any loans or other liabilities due after one year. Loans payable in installments over several years should be split between "Current" for the amount due within 12 months and "Long-term" for the balance.

You should also include under liabilities any "contingent" liabilities you know about. Contingent liabilities are crystal-ball suppositions about the future: liabilities that may or may not materialize. If the IRS is auditing you or you are being sued, for example, and there is a possibility you will owe money, some dollar estimate of the liability must be included on the balance sheet. Contingent liability estimates should be clearly labeled as such and should be explained fully.

Balance sheets can be simple or quite complicated. A balance sheet prepared for your bank when requesting a loan need not be elaborate. The audited financial statements required of large corporations, however, include fully detailed and footnoted balance sheets. Any basic accounting textbook will include a chapter on balance sheets. One easy way to learn about balance sheets is to study the published financial statements that most corporations put out. You usually can get them free on request.

PROFESSIONAL HELP:
Accountants and Attorneys

This book should help you with most aspects of beginning and operating a small business without need of an accountant. But the time may come when your finances are getting a bit too complicated, or you may need help incorporating or setting up an LLC. Anyone buying a going business or a franchise should get an accountant's help. And then there's income taxes. It's a rare business owner who has the time and inclination to study and understand tax laws.

How do you find a good accountant? Locating a good accountant is like trying to find a reliable doctor: you have to ask around. The best people to ask are other business owners. It is essential to find an accountant with small business experience. It is not important what kind of small businesses the accountant works with, because small business tax law is pretty much the same whether it's a grocery store or a photo studio, a computer consultant or carpenter, a big storefront or a home business.

If you do not know an accountant and can't get a reliable recommendation, here are a few suggestions and warnings to help in your search.

Do not pick a name at random from the phone book. There is no way to know what kind of person you will get or how qualified he may be.

Stay away from the storefront tax operations, the ones that open shop every January and promptly disappear April 15. Most of the people who work for these chains have little experience, brief training, and are usually familiar only with Mr. and Mrs. Nine-to-Five and their typical tax problems. These part-time accountants are not trained to handle complex problems nor do they take the time to delve into your business finances looking for tax savings.

Choose an experienced tax accountant, and expect to pay professional prices. It is not necessary to hire a certified public accountant. CPAs may or may not be the best qualified, depending on their experience with small business taxes. There are also Public Accountants (PAs), licensed in some states; Enrolled Agents (EAs), licensed by the federal government (despite the ominous name, EAs are not IRS agents although some of them used to work for the IRS); and individuals who have no official license but who may be excellent tax accountants. Judge the accountant by his or her experience, how many small business clients he or she has, and whether you like the individual or not.

Talk to the accountant personally before you commit yourself. If he or she will not talk on the phone other than in vague generalities, call someone else. Does the accountant seem familiar with your situation and your problems? Most important, does he make sense to you? Beware of the accountant who talks Advanced Sanskrit or IRS code sections. You need an accountant to answer questions. Find one who can speak English.

It's important to understand what an accountant can do for you and, just as important, what the accountant cannot and will not do for you.

A good accountant will prepare your tax return faster than you thought humanly possible, will know all of the tax options you have, and help you make the best choice. A good accountant will show you ways you might reduce taxes by restructuring your business, changing your bookkeeping, timing certain purchases and payments, or making other changes that will help you better deal with taxes. This is the accountant's area of expertise, and you should make the most of it—you're paying for it.

Tax professionals are held accountable for the work they do and the advice they give. They will not tell you how to break the law, and they don't want to hear about any illegal tax maneuvers.

Certainly you can and should ask honest questions—Is this legal? Is this deductible? Must this be reported?—but expect honest answers. Don't put the accountant in a situation he shouldn't be in; you may be causing trouble for yourself and for the accountant.

These warnings don't mean that you and your accountant shouldn't explore questionable areas of the law if you are so willing, and if the accountant feels you have legal ground to stand on. Some tax laws are very straightforward; but many are ambiguous, subject to interpretation, honest disagreement, what we call "gray areas". Some laws are so new and convoluted, no one is quite sure how to interpret them. The best tax accountants know, from experience and from studying tax manuals and court decisions, how to handle those "gray areas" of tax law.

Finally, avoid an accountant who takes your numbers, plugs them into a computer program, hands you a return and a bill. Even if *you* don't know any questions to ask, your accountant should ask at least a few questions and put some personal thought into your return.

If an accountant prepares your entire 1040 tax return, only the business portion (Schedule C and related schedules) can be deducted as a business expense. Partnership and corporation returns are fully deductible.

Bookkeepers

Accountants are not bookkeepers, and at the rates they charge, you don't want them to have to do any of your bookkeeping. Don't show up with a shoebox full of receipts. Don't show up with unposted or incomplete ledgers that need to be added up. If you can't get your ledgers right, if you hate posting that three-month backlog of invoices, hire a bookkeeper. Bookkeepers not only charge a lot less than tax accountants, bookkeeping is what they do every day. To locate a bookkeeper, get a recommendation from your accountant or from other business owners.

The most expensive professional is the one you don't hire when you should.—CPA David Scully

Attorneys

Most small businesses don't need an attorney. Your accountant can handle any tax matter and can probably provide all the help you need in drafting most business agreements. You may need an attorney's help filing legal papers, incorporating or setting up an LLC, but I suggest you check with an accountant first. The accountant will know what requires an attorney's signature and what doesn't.

If you are being sued or are suing someone, this is beyond the accountant's domain. But your accountant can probably recommend an attorney who specializes in business litigation.

It is more vital than ever that you assume greater responsibility for your financial future. You ought not to rely exclusively on paid advisors. You should be knowledgeable enough to raise good questions and evaluate answers when you deal with a professional. The informed client gets the best advice.   —Tax attorney Julian Block

---

Marc Savoy, accordion maker, Eunice, Louisiana: "I always prided myself with enough common sense to know the difference between superior and inferior, good quality versus poor quality, but I was soon to learn that this one commodity was found lacking in the general public. I think that every artist, craftsman, musician, anyone who produces anything, is working under two forces, the first being that of his own personality, which expresses itself onto his work. The second is that of the general public or potential buyers, whose taste and demands exert pressure on the artist to the extent that he may decide to cater to the majority so that he may have a market or recognition for his work. This second pressure can be very detrimental to expressing the artist's true art form and also limiting the quality of his work for the sake of finding a market. I think it takes a very stubborn and hard-headed person who believes enough in his work to be able to disregard the opinion of the majority and cater only to a select minority. An artist must be very careful not to be too influenced by what the general public demands."

HUSBAND & WIFE PARTNERSHIPS

When a husband and wife operate a business together, the business may be a corporation, a partnership, a Limited Liability Company (LLC) or a sole proprietorship. Each of these legal forms requires different paperwork, and each can result in differences, possibly major differences, in income taxes, Social Security, Medicare and fringe benefits.

It's basically up to the couple to decide how they want to structure their business. If a married couple are truly partners in a business, carrying on the business together, the IRS says they are officially in a partnership, whether they prepare a partnership agreement or not.

The couple could just as easily decide that one of them, either the husband or wife, is sole owner of the business, and set up a sole proprietorship. The IRS has ruled that, generally, if one spouse (let's say the wife) is the main operator of the business, the wife is a sole proprietor. The husband, with a lesser interest in the business, is either an employee or has no "official" designation (more on this below).

Some criteria the IRS uses in determining the status of a husband-and-wife business are (1) does one spouse spend more time than the other operating the business? (2) are the business licenses in one spouse's name? (3) does one spouse have other employment? Generally, the IRS will accept whatever you tell them.

A sole proprietorship is easier to set up than a partnership. A husband-and-wife partnership should have a written partnership agreement, like any general partnership. The partnership must file federal and state partnership tax returns, in addition to the couple's 1040 return.

Income Taxes

The income taxes are exactly the same whether the couple sets up a sole proprietorship or a partnership (assuming they file a joint 1040 return). In a partnership, the couple will share the income, divided equally or divided according to some other arrangement in the partnership agreement. For IRS purposes, the couple combines their incomes, and pays income tax on the total business profit.

In a sole proprietorship, the husband or wife can hire his/her spouse as an employee and deduct the wage as a business expense. The income tax the couple pays on their 1040 return is the same as if they were set up as a partnership.

For example, let's say a husband and wife set up a 50-50 partnership. The business earns a profit (before any draw or wage paid the partners) of $30,000 for the year. Each partner's share is $15,000. The partners file a joint return and pay income tax on the combined $30,000.

Now we'll change the example. The same business is structured as a sole proprietorship with the wife as owner and husband as employee. The husband is hired at a salary of $15,000 a year. The sole proprietorship earned the wife a profit of $15,000 (the $30,000 profit reduced by the husband's $15,000 salary). The couple files a joint return and pay income tax on the combined $30,000, the exact same amount of income tax paid by the couple operating as partners.

Self Employment and Payroll Taxes

You will recall that partners, sole proprietors and LLC members pay self-employment tax, which is Social Security and Medicare for the self-employed. Employees, including a spouse on the payroll, are subject to regular Social Security and Medicare payroll taxes. Payroll taxes and self-employment tax are different taxes, requiring different calculations and different forms and procedures.

A husband and wife who set up a partnership or an LLC will each pay self-employment tax on his and her share of the profits. A wife who sets up a sole proprietorship and hires her husband as an employee, will deduct Social Security and Medicare tax from his paycheck and pay an additional employer's portion. She also pays self-employment tax on her profit.

Using the same examples as above, a business earning $30,000: If the business is a 50-50 partnership, each spouse pays self-employment tax (and gets Social Security credit) on $15,000. If the wife hires her husband as an employee, his $15,000 wage is subject to regular payroll taxes (earning Social Security credit for him), and her $15,000 profit is subject to self-employment tax (earning Social Security credit for her).

Although a couple's income taxes are combined, their payroll and self-employment taxes are never combined.

MAY I HELP YOU, SIR?

Businesses making over $65,400: The Social Security portion of payroll taxes cuts off at $65,400. Only the Medicare portion, which is a much smaller tax, continues above $65,400. If one spouse is a sole proprietor and the other spouse is not on the payroll, the first $65,400 is subject to the maximum self-employment tax rate (15.3%). Any profit in excess of $65,400 is subject to a much lower rate (2.9%). If both spouses are officially part of the business, either as partners or as employer-employee, both of the spouses are subject to payroll or self-employment taxes, each spouse to the $65,400 maximum. Together, they might pay a great deal more in Social Security and Medicare taxes than if only one of them earned all the business income. (1997 figures; look out, they go up every year).

Outside employment: A similar Social Security tax situation exists if one spouse has a high paying outside job and is also the sole proprietor and the only official person in the business. The business profit subject to self-employment tax will be reduced by the amount of outside income (explained in the Tax section under Self-Employment Tax), reducing the self-employment tax substantially. Again, this savings can only be realized if only one spouse has an outside job and also runs the business alone.

Some More Considerations

Another important issue (for some couples, the deciding issue) is health insurance and medical benefits. Putting your spouse on the payroll might enable you to deduct medical expenses you cannot deduct as a lone sole proprietor or as a couple in a partnership. See "Family Employees" in the Health Insurance chapter in the Tax Section for the details. A lot of money may be saved here.

If the husband is an official employee of his wife's business, the business must keep complete payroll records on the husband, issue regular payroll checks, withhold taxes, file payroll tax returns, issue a W-2 at year-end, and comply with state regulations as well.

How about one spouse hiring the other as an outside contractor? What you've created are two separate businesses, two sole proprietorships requiring two Schedule C tax returns. Both spouses pay self-employment tax.

The Easiest Option

Things can be a whole lot simpler than this. The wife can set up a one-person sole proprietorship. The husband can work in the business but not be on the payroll nor otherwise officially included in the business. There is nothing wrong with this arrangement; it is perfectly legal. Under this arrangement, the husband is not subject to any federal or state payroll taxes, and he pays no Social Security or Medicare taxes. No paperwork is required. Any "wage" the husband might take is just money withdrawn from the business. It is not a real wage, and the wife is not allowed a business deduction. Her profit and her taxes are figured as if the husband earned no wage.

This arrangement is by far the least expensive way to set up a husband and wife business. The money the couple saves in payroll costs, Social Security and Medicare taxes, and accounting fees can be substantial. The drawback is that the husband receives no Social Security credit in his own name and is not eligible for employee fringe benefits. The husband would also not be allowed any deductions for travel should he accompany his wife on business trips.

This "unofficial" status is for tax purposes only. If the husband's name is on the bank account, he could write checks that his wife could deduct as business expenses. The husband probably could sign legal documents such as contracts and purchase orders, which would be binding on the wife's business.

In determining how to set up a husband-and-wife business, much more than the taxes and the paperwork needs to be considered. The structure of the business itself can affect the feelings the couple have toward each other, how well they work together, and (alas) how difficult and how fair a divorce might turn out. This could be a particular problem if one spouse is not on the payroll or "officially" part of the business.

One very astute woman pointed out to me, "An unpaid worker is generally an unappreciated worker, causing resentment and possibly a great deal of difficulty in a marriage. Tax savings should not be the number one priority in a husband/wife business arrangement. Mutual respect, sense of responsibility, appreciation, and cooperation are far more important than saving tax dollars." What's more, if the unpaid spouse had to look for another job, it could be difficult to establish a work history or job worth without some sort of salary history.

Employment Taxes, Workers Compensation Insurance, and Retirement Plans

Regardless of whether the business is a sole proprietorship or a partnership or whether a spouse is on the payroll on not, neither spouse is subject to federal unemployment taxes and neither is eligible for federal unemployment benefits. Most states exempt husband and wife businesses from state unemployment insurance and from workers' compensation insurance. Both spouses can participate in a Keogh, SEP, or IRA retirement plan.

Husband and Wife Corporation

If you incorporate your husband- and-wife business, the rules are different. Both spouses as owner-employees of a corporation are subject to the same payroll taxes as regular employees. You are eligible for company-paid fringe benefits, and you can set up a corporate retirement plan for yourselves (which is different from a Keogh plan).

Limited Liability Company (LLC)

For income and self-employment taxes, LLCs are identical to partnerships. A husband and wife in an LLC would be taxed the same as a husband and wife in a partnership.

There is a problem for couples who set up a Limited Liability Company and subsequently get divorced. Most states require that LLCs have at least two owners. Husband and wife count as two people for this law. Should they divorce, the LLC may have to be disbanded if only one spouse winds up owning it. A partnership would have the same problem, but partnerships are easier and much less expensive to set up and to fold.

Two Separate Businesses

If a husband and wife each operate their own businesses, where two complete and separate businesses exist (possibly side by side), each spouse is a sole proprietor, each with his and her own set of ledgers, permits and licenses, and Schedule C tax returns. The husband pays self-employment tax on the profits from his business, and the wife pays self-employment tax on the profits from hers. If the couple files a joint tax return, the profit or loss from the two businesses are combined for figuring income tax.

If the two businesses share any assets, share an office or other business space, or share any business expenses, the expenses and depreciation should be divided between the two businesses, 50-50 if owned equally by both. It is not important which business actually writes the check or which has the equipment or lease or invoice in its name. Just be sure that each business records its share of the expense in its own ledgers.

A Northern California business that provides consulting services is owned and operated by a husband and wife, but the business is in the wife's name only. When I inquired why they structured it that way, the wife answered, "Many of our clients are women who prefer to patronize businesses owned by women. It brings us more work."

HOME-BASED BUSINESSES

I'd guess that on every city block and on every rural road in the United States, someone is operating a business out of a home. Home-based businesses have their own unique problems and rewards, and they are subject to some legal and tax restrictions not imposed on other businesses. Just about everything in this book applies to a home business the same as any other business.

Some businesses are naturally suited to being operated out of a home, and others, of course, are not. Ideal home businesses are those where the location of the business is not a significant factor in the success of the business; businesses that require little physical space; and businesses that do not intrude on neighbors and the character of the neighborhood. So, retail stores, manufacturing operations, restaurants, auto repair shops, and businesses where a lot of customers come to the business premises are usually not suitable for operating out of the home.

The "ideal" home businesses include:

1. Mail-order, unless you must have some huge inventory of goods.

2. Publishing, again depending on inventory.

3. Professionals, consultants, freelancers, designers, writers, computer programmers, bookkeepers, and other office services.

4. Any service business where you go to your customers instead of having them come to you, such as cleaning, home repairs, sales agent.

5. Crafts, as long as the workshop isn't too noisy or smelly, and assuming you deliver your goods to your customers as opposed to having a retail shop or showroom at home.

6. Inventors (don't blow up the workshop).

A home-based business is a good way to get started for a small investment, compared to the cost of leasing, furnishing and maintaining a business premises. It's also an excellent way to test your untested business ideas. I always recommend, whenever possible, that people start a new business with as little money as possible, out of the home, in your spare time, without quitting your regular job. Find out if that business will work, find out if you are cut out to run a business. Some people think they have the world's greatest idea, and maybe they do—but maybe they don't. Some people think they will love being their own boss and find out later they hate it. And everyone makes mistakes, particularly when getting started. A $200 mistake and a $20,000 mistake could be the same mistake. If you start part-time, as cheaply as possible, out of your home, your disasters will always be small ones. You'll also be able to learn your trade and learn business in general in a more relaxed, low-pressure environment.

Some people feel there is a stigma attached to home-based businesses, that such businesses are not well thought of by the public, that they have less credence than conventional businesses, that they're not to be taken as seriously, or they're more amateurish, or some other slight.

Having run a business out of my home for 15 years, I don't subscribe to these views, but I realize that many people do. Many home businesses might benefit by, if not out-and-out hiding the fact that the business is in the home, at least downplaying the fact. You also may not want strangers, salesmen and the like coming to your home, bothering your family or the neighbors.

Post Office Boxes

Some businesses use a post office box instead of their street address to hide their location. Unfortunately, this often backfires because a lot of people, particularly those who don't know you, are suspicious of businesses with P.O. box addresses. Is this a real business, or some scam or fly-by-night operation? It's too easy for you to close the box and disappear.

A lot of suppliers ship by UPS (United Parcel Service) or some similar service. Unless the UPS driver knows who you are and where you are located, you might not get your delivery.

Some magazines and newspapers will not accept advertising with P.O. box addresses. A few states require businesses to put a street address on all advertising, order forms, etc. (a law few people know about and that is rarely enforced).

Some businesses, particularly home mail-order businesses, find they must have a P.O. box. Mail left in a rural delivery box, or on your porch, can get stolen or blown away. And there are still many places in rural America where there is no house-to-house mail delivery available.

Businesses that find they must have a P.O. box often list their street address as well as the box number on stationery, mailing labels, ads, brochures, listings, etc. You might want to discuss this with the local postmaster. The post office is more cooperative than you might think, particularly in rural areas and small post offices; there may be a simple solution to your problem.

Another solution might be a "suite number" at the local mailbox store.

Deliveries

United Parcel Service (UPS) and similar delivery services will make deliveries to your door. You don't have to be signed up with the company to get deliveries. If you regularly ship out via UPS or some other company, and you want them to come to your home for pick-ups, you can sign up with the company. They will come to your business five days a week to see if you have anything to go out. They bill you a flat-rate weekly charge plus the charges for packages you ship. If you only ship once in awhile, you can instead arrange for a pick up only when you request it.

Trucks (common carrier shippers) will deliver freight to home businesses. If you are expecting a large or very heavy shipment, you should discuss the delivery with the trucking company ahead of time. Some trucks can make street-level deliveries; their doors are low to the ground or they have hydraulic lift gates. Many trucks, however, have very high doors requiring unloading at freight docks or with fork lifts. Some truck drivers will help unload freight, and some will expect you to do the unloading. Some trucks will deliver only to the curb or as close as they can drive to your door, and they expect you to haul the stuff inside. Freight companies charge extra, sometimes quite a bit extra, for inside delivery. If the freight charge is coming C.O.D., find out ahead of time if you will need cash or if the trucker will take a check.

Zoning

Home businesses are often subject to restrictive zoning laws. Zoning laws vary considerably from one location to another. Some communities outlaw home businesses entirely (though I still stand by the first sentence in the introduction to this chapter!). Some communities restrict the type and/or size of home businesses, the number of employees, number of visitors, the amount of inventory on hand. Some communities have no restrictions whatsoever. For specific zoning regulations, contact city hall if you are in city limits, or contact county offices if you are outside city limits. Don't tell them who you are; just ask if there are zoning restrictions on home businesses.

Before you get totally bogged down in zoning prohibitions, you should consider the reasons for zoning laws. People do not want a lot of noise, odors, trash, traffic, parking problems and strangers near their homes. They want quiet and peaceful residential neighborhoods. So they banish businesses, which often bring noise, traffic and strangers, to other areas of the community.

If you plan to start a home business where you will be operating noisy machinery in the garage, where you'll be storing stuff outside, or where many people will be coming to your home, or where the sign in the window and the business "appearance" of your home detracts from the neighborhood image, you can expect complaints from your neighbors and problems with the zoning authorities.

But if you have some small office business or some quiet (and odorless) crafts business, and if very few if any customers come to your door, you are not likely to disturb your neighbors, and you are not likely to get in trouble with the zoning authorities, even if you are technically breaking the law. Zoning officials don't go snooping around looking for violations; they almost always act only when they receive a complaint.

The first and foremost zoning law, in my opinion, is: Be Considerate Of Your Neighbors. Put yourself in their situation. How would you feel if a neighbor started a business like the one you plan to start? If it seems appropriate to you, talk to your neighbors and tell them of your plans. Find out, before you start your business, if there will be opposition or bad feelings.

What happens if you are operating a home business and are suddenly visited by an official of the zoning board, advising you that you are breaking the law? Ask if a complaint has been filed, and if so, why? Are you causing a genuine nuisance? Will the zoning people allow you to alter your practices to eliminate the nuisance? Can you file a petition or request a waiver, variance or special use permit that will allow you to continue in business? Your neighbors might help by writing letters or signing a petition in support of your business.

If worst comes to worst, and you are forced to

shut down, can you have 30 or 60 or 90 days to relocate? I am not suggesting that you may have to move in order to run a home business without zoning hassles, but you wouldn't be the first person who did. This is more true of someone who wanted to operate a retail shop or an intrusive workshop as opposed to some office or service type business.

The town of Yellow Springs, Ohio, with a population of only a few thousand, enacted a zoning ordinance restricting home businesses, limiting the number of employees and the number of "client visits per day," forbidding outdoor storage, and adding a host of other regulations the local newspaper described as, "at best useless, at worst potentially harmful to the community." The editor added, "I wrote that hesitantly, because the people who created the law are smart people who intended to create nothing at all like this mess we have. But when you get into the details of defining just what is a home business that does not unduly disturb a residential area, it becomes almost impossible to draw a fair line that will be applicable to all cases. The best defense of the law is that it won't be enforced. But of course it will be; not equally against all home businesses but against some in some neighborhoods, when a neighbor demands it. Home businesses can exist, or not exist, according to their neighbors' preference, mood, personality or whim."

Landlords, Condominiums, Co-ops and Homeowners Associations

If you rent your home, live in a condo or co-op, or live in some type of restricted housing development, be sure the lease, ownership agreement or real estate covenant does not prohibit a home business. Co-ops in particular often have strictly-enforced restrictions on home businesses.

Telephone

Telephone company rules for home-business phones vary from company to company and from state to state. The rules are set either by the company or by the state Public Utilities Commission. Some telephone companies require you to have a business listing if you use your home phone for business. Other companies don't care how you list your phone. Business listings are usually more expensive than personal listings, sometimes substantially more expensive. Installation charges, monthly rates, extra services, and sometimes local outgoing calls cost more.

Many home businesses, particularly when getting started, do not get a business listing. If you are required to have a business listing and do not have one, and if the telephone company finds out (which, truthfully, is not very likely), they may demand that you switch to a business listing. There may or may not be a fine or some other penalty depending on your state's laws. You can keep the same phone number.

Regardless of telephone company rules, it often is useful and profitable to have a business listing, well worth the extra cost for many home businesses. The business listing includes a listing in the white pages and usually a free Yellow Pages entry (a one-line listing; an ad costs extra). Your business is also listed with the directory assistance operator. If your business is not listed, lots of people won't be able to find you.

New suppliers who are unfamiliar with your company will sometimes call directory assistance, just to find out if you are listed, before they sell something to you on credit. The telephone listing is some assurance to people that you are most likely legitimate.

When you do list with the telephone company as a business phone, you can also list your personal name in the white pages and with directory assistance under the same number if you want.

As you get more business (and more income) you will probably reach a point where you want two numbers, one for business and one for personal use; so you can answer one, "Hello," and the other, "Good morning, G.M. Aardvark Adding Machine Repair"; or so you can decide not to answer the business phone in off hours; or so the kids can answer the phone without having to pretend they work for some business. One thing sure to chase away prospective customers and clients is an unbusinesslike phone arrangement.

Many businesses want or need even more telephone lines: a separate line for a fax machine and another for a modem. If your budget (or wiring) is limited, the telephone companies offer multi-purpose products and services to make the most of what you can afford. One possibility is a "distinguishing ring" option, where two different numbers, with two distinctly different sounds, ring on the same line.

You are not required to list an address for a business phone or for a personal phone. So if you don't want people to know where you are located, if you don't want strangers driving up to your home uninvited, you can request that your address be left off your listing.

If your phone is an important link to your customers, make the best use of it. If you will not be available to the phone during regular business hours, hire an answering service or voice mail or at least get an answering machine. If you want to encourage people to leave their names and numbers on your answering machine, keep your message brief. People, particularly when calling long distance, do not want to sit through a musical interlude, a recorded chat and a plug for your product. You may enjoy being the star of your own telephone recording, but to many people the telephone answering machine is irritating to start with. Long messages just increase the irritation and make it more likely a prospective customer will simply hang up. If you get voice mail service, remember how much you hate most voice mail systems, prompts, "Press 1 if you...", and the other joys of not being able to reach anyone, and keep your message short and your system simple.

If you drive around a lot, particularly if you provide urgent services such as a plumber or a locksmith, a cellular phone may be a very worthwhile investment. When someone's water pipe bursts, they need a plumber *now*. If you are not at the phone, they're going to call someone else.

"I just want a device to circumvent recorded phone messages. These gadgets may be fine (though I doubt it) for local business calls, but I do not see why I have to pay for a long distance call that is answered by a recording that informs me the person I am calling is not in. If no one answered the phone I would be smart enough to figure that out for free. I do not want the person I am calling to spend his money calling me, only to learn that I am not in either, even though I thought I would be. This kind of recorded non-communication has been known to go on for days.

"Since it is impossible to convince business people that recorded messages are bad business, why can't someone invent a gadget for a telephone that would prevent a long distance call from ringing when one is not in the office. A caller could hear that the phone is not ringing and hang up rather than having to pay to

talk to someone who is not there. How many millions of dollars do we spend a year to find out we are not in? If common sense will not prevail, why not at least a service business which will make recordings sound natural, if that's possible. Normal human beings can't make a recording that says, 'I am not here' without choking, giggling, or gasping. The humanity in them simply revolts at such a stupid remark."

—Gene Logsden, In Business Magazine

Yellow Pages

Once you have a business listing, it won't be long before a salesperson from the telephone company will call and try to sell you Yellow Pages advertising. A business phone usually includes a one-line listing in the Yellow Pages at no extra cost. Longer listings, bold listings and display ads cost more, sometimes a lot more.

A display ad in the Yellow Pages can be quite valuable if you are selling to the local public, particularly if you are trying to reach local people who don't know you. When people look in the Yellow Pages, they are usually attracted first to the display ads. The smallest business can look big-time with a good Yellow Pages ad.

There is a real skill to designing effective Yellow Pages advertising. The phone company will be of some help, but you may want to consider getting a professional designer to help you (maybe you can find someone who will trade design help for your product or service). If you are designing your own ad, study other ads in the Yellow Pages. Note the ones you like, and emulate them. Note the ones you dislike, try to figure out what it is about them that you don't like, and avoid the same mistakes. Don't put too much writing in too little space. Clutter is unattractive to the eye, and people will not take the time to read your ad. Don't waste valuable space with silly illustrations. Give brief, attention-grabbing information: "We are the only store in town where you can buy live giraffes." "We repair all brands and types of geiger counters." "Same day service." If you want people to come to your location, list the days and hours you are open. If the address is hard to locate, give brief directions: "One block west of Main between 6th and 7th, right across street from the roller rink".

Review the proofs of your ads carefully. Misspelled words and poor grammar will send an unprofessional image to people. One typo in your telephone number will make your listing worthless, or worse: people will call and think you are out of business. Proof, and proof again.

Pick your Yellow Pages category carefully, or consider listing yourself in more than one category. How many times were you unable to find a business in the Yellow Pages because you could not figure out how they were listed? Check to see how similar businesses to yours are listed.

Some businesses have no real use for Yellow Pages advertising. Many manufacturers and wholesalers, businesses that do specialized work for a limited number of customers, mail order businesses, businesses where you already know all your customers, and businesses that will not be seeking customers locally, have no reason to spend money on a Yellow Pages ad.

The term "Yellow Pages" and the familiar walking fingers logo are not trademarked, are not owned by the telephone company. Anyone can publish a "Yellow Pages" directory that may or may not be distributed widely. Be sure the Yellow Pages you advertise in are part of the local telephone company, part of the local telephone book.

Telephones and Tax Deductions

Tax deductions for a home telephone are limited. You may not deduct the basic monthly rate for the first telephone line into the home. For tax purposes, it does not matter to the IRS how the phone is listed, business or personal. The basic rate for the first line into your home is not deductible even if it is listed as a business phone. Expenses beyond the basic rate, such as business-related long distance calls, optional services, and any special business equipment are deductible. Any additional business lines into the house after the first line are fully deductible if used exclusively for business. A second line is fully deductible, regardless of its listing, as long as it is used 100% for business.

Federal and State Homework Laws

If your employees work at their *own* homes (not at the employer's home), the U.S. Department of Labor's Fair Labor Standards Act, and several state "homework laws" restrict some businesses from hiring employees and require

the employer to be certified by the Department of Labor. Contact the U.S. Department of Labor and your state's Department of Labor for details.

Insurance

Most homeowner and home-renter insurance policies specifically exclude home businesses from coverage. Some policies actually void coverage if the home is used as a business without the insurance company's knowledge and approval. If the house burns down and the insurance company finds out you had a home business, you may not get paid at all, even if the business had nothing to do with the fire. If a visitor, business or personal, is injured at your home, your liability coverage may be invalid because of the unreported business. So don't keep your business a secret from the insurance company.

If your home business is a low-grossing sideline, with no employees and no customers coming to the house (what the insurance companies call "incidental business office occupancy") business coverage can be added as a rider or endorsement on your home-owner's or renter's policy.

If your home business is a primary source of income, or if you have employees or customers coming to your house, or if you have valuable equipment or inventory you want to insure, you will probably have to get special commercial coverage for your home business.

You must also have special business coverage for your car or truck if you do any driving on business.

"This Is A Business"

People who work in an office, a store, a warehouse, or any out-of-the-home business location, are working in an atmosphere that is totally business, totally a workplace. For most of these people, the only other people they are in contact with during work hours are co-workers, customers and suppliers. It is an atmosphere conducive to work: you go to work, get your work done, and then you go home.

People who run businesses out of their homes often do not have that clear-cut distinction of a work-space versus a home-space, and work hours versus personal hours. If you have a family, particularly if you have young children not yet in school, the distinction blurs even more. You may set up a separate office, put it in a spare room or the basement or garage, and you may say, "10 to 4 is work time, period," but you will find again and again that others are not cooperating as much as you'd like. "Keep an eye on the kids for an hour, will you, honey, while I run to the store." Friends call or stop by to visit during work hours. People who would never expect you to take a break in the middle of the day if you are at the office will think nothing of it if you are working at home.

What's the solution? Have firm rules that your workspace and your work hours are to be honored—and then be prepared to have those rules broken regularly. Ever try to explain rules to a three-year-old? Or to a tired spouse who needs a break from the kids for an hour? There has been more than one home business that relocated to a separate business location just to get away from the family and the constant interruptions.

The "Home Office" Deduction

The term "Home Office", for this important tax law, refers to any home business space—office, workshop, studio, warehouse, retail store, showroom, etc.—and the expenses directly related to the space such as utilities, insurance, property taxes, etc.

Failure to qualify for the home office deduction doesn't prohibit you from operating your business out of your home. It only means that one possibly large expense is not deductible on your federal income taxes. You can still deduct all legitimate business expenses other than those directly related to the business space itself.

In order to deduct your home office expenses, you must meet some very specific, and downright nit-picking rules. These home-office rules apply to sole proprietors, partners, owners of S corporation, and members (owners) of LLCs. They do *not* apply to C corporations.

"Principal Place of Business"

You will not be able to deduct any expenses for a home office unless it is used exclusively and on a regular basis as your "principal place of business", *or* a place of business used regularly by your patients, clients or customers in the normal course of business. You can have a separate "principal place of business" for each trade or business you operate.

The Supreme Court has defined "principal place of business" as "the most important, consequential, or influential location", with the main emphasis on where you meet with customers or clients. A second, but less important guideline is where you spend the most time. This means that consultants, contractors, plumbers, caterers, musicians, independent travelling salespeople and others who do their income-producing work at customers' and clients' homes and offices, are probably not eligible for a home office deduction. The fact that your home office is essential to your business, or even that it is the sole base of operations, is not enough to make it deductible.

Furthermore, if your business is also operated out of another location such as a storefront, you cannot deduct the cost of a home office unless you normally (not just occasionally) see customers or clients, or generate sales, at your home.

Joe Campbell, who owns Resistance Repair, does his repair work in a rented repair shop but does his bookkeeping at home because there is no extra space in the shop, and because the bookkeeping requires uninterrupted thinking time which is impossible at the shop. All legitimate, for sure, but his home office is not deductible.

Another friend of mine who is an attorney, has her office in downtown San Francisco but also sees her clients on a regular basis in her home. Her home office (as well as her downtown office) is deductible.

A jeweler who has a retail store, but who also spends significant time filling mail orders from a home office, is allowed a deduction for both the rented storefront and the home office.

Separate structure: If your home business is located not in the home, but in a free-standing structure such as a studio, garage or barn, you don't have to meet the above test. You are allowed a deduction even if it is not your principal place of business. But it still must be used regularly and *exclusively* for business; read on.

"Exclusive Use"

To be eligible for the home office deduction, a specific part of your home must be used exclusively for business. It can be a separate room or even part of a room as long as it is used for the home business and nothing else. Period. No television in the room. No personal paperwork at the desk. (No games on the computer?) It can't double as a guest room, or kid's play room, or anything else, even when you are not working.

One exception to the exclusive rule: If your home is your sole fixed location for a retail sales business and if you regularly store your inventory or your samples in your home, the expense of maintaining the storage area is deductible even if it isn't exclusive use of the space.

Child care and day care businesses: The home deduction is allowed only if your business is officially licensed. If the room or rooms (or entire house) is regularly used for day care each business day, the IRS considers it used for the entire day. No need to prorate it for actual hours of use. If, for example, you regularly operate five days a week, you can deduct 5/7ths (five days out of seven) of the area used for the business.

What's Deductible

Deductible home-office expenses include a percentage of your rent if you rent your home, or a percentage of the depreciation if you own your home, and an equal percentage of home utilities, property tax, mortgage interest and insurance. Home repairs, such as a new roof or furnace, are also partly deductible (if they are major, they must be depreciated). The IRS specifically prohibits deductions for landscaping and lawn care, even if done solely to enhance the business (a landscaper could probably deduct the cost).

To claim a home office expense, you must fill out Form 8829, "Expenses for Business Use of Your Home", which attaches to your 1040 along with Schedule C. For more information, see the IRS Publ. #587, "Business Use of Your Home."

Homeowners: A warning. If you are eligible for the home-office deduction, you might run into tax complications when you sell the house. In computing profit on the sale, you are required to reduce your home's cost basis by the amount of the depreciation allowed (*whether you took the depreciation or not!*), which will increase your profit, and possibly your taxes, on the sale. There are, however, tax maneuvers to possibly avoid this problem. Check with an accountant.

Business Loss

If your home business shows a loss, part of your home office expenses are not deductible this year. You may deduct regular business expenses (other than expenses for the office space itself) and may deduct interest and property taxes on the office, regardless of profit or loss. But the remaining home office expenses (including rent or depreciation, insurance, utilities) may be deducted this year only to the extent there is no loss.

For example, assume your home business generated $20,000 in sales this year. Your expenses, not including the home office, were $18,000. The home office portion of rent (or depreciation), insurance and utilities came to $4,000. The home office portion of interest and property taxes was $800. Your allowable deductions are computed this way:

Total sales	$20,000
Expenses (other than office expenses	(18,000)
	$ 2,000
Home office portion of interest and property taxes	(800)
	$ 1,200

Only $1,200 of the additional $4,000 in office expenses are deductible this year. The remaining $2,800 can be carried to a future year and deducted then, again as long as there is no loss.

A second example: Let's say sales were $20,000, non-office expenses were $18,000, home office portion of property taxes and interest came to $3,000, all other home office expenses were $4,000. Now the calculations look this way:

Total sales	$20,000
Expenses (other than office expenses)	(18,000)
	$ 2,000
Home office portion of interest and property taxes	(3,000)
LOSS	$(1,000)

Since you are already showing a loss, none of the additional $4,000 in home office expenses are deductible this year. The $4,000 must be carried to a future year. The interest and property taxes are deductible even though they result in a loss.

Once a month I venture into rush-hour traffic to remind myself of what I'm missing.
—Jeannette Scollard, SCS Manufacturing

IMPORTING AND EXPORTING

Importing and exporting involve an entire world of international laws, special tax incentives, international trade procedures, licenses, duties and tariffs, and various "middlemen" (such as agents, brokers and freight forwarders) that domestic businesses never encounter. You must be familiar with U.S. Customs and U.S. Commerce Department laws. You need to learn about standard payment terms, currency conversion (and the stability of foreign currencies), shipping terminology, and shipping methods.

Import and export businesses must also abide by the same regulations, tax laws, etc. that apply to regular domestic businesses. Just about everything in this book will be applicable to you.

IMPORTING

Most of the people who get started in small-time importing are travellers, people on a trip or vacation overseas. They discover some handcraft or fabric or clothing that's attractive and inexpensive, or some clever invention or electronic marvel. They see some business potential in the products, and start figuring out how to bring the products back to the U.S. And "figuring out" is something you really must do carefully.

Customs, Duties, Quotas

You cannot just up and buy a few cases of whatever sparked your imagination, and expect to bring it back to the U.S. without going through a maze of rules, customs, duties and paperwork. It is critically important that you have your paperwork in order. If your paperwork isn't done properly, Customs can confiscate and even destroy your merchandise. The U.S. Customs Service has a book thicker than the New York City telephone directory, listing quotas and duties on hundreds of different products from dozens of different countries.

Some imports are subject to quotas: so many pairs of men's shoes from Honduras per year, for example. Many countries have formal agreements with the U.S., called "quota visas", limiting the quantities of each item they are allowed to export to the U.S.

Many imports are also subject to duties, which

are taxes you the importer must pay before Customs will release your goods to you. Duties vary, from insignificant amounts on handcrafts and electronics, to approximately 34% on clothing and textiles, and on up to as much as 90%, 100% and even 110% of your cost on some restricted items from restricted countries.

Politics, and things like "most favored nation" status play a major factor in determining how easy and how expensive it is to import different goods from different countries. Strong U.S. industries like clothing manufacturers fight imports, so the duties on clothing are much higher than those on, say, handcrafted items and other goods that are not made in the U.S. by large, influential corporations.

Shipping

Beyond the Customs regulations, probably the most important consideration is shipping. How will you get your merchandise into the United States? Will you bring it back with you on the plane? Will you ship it air cargo, and how easy will that be? Can you send it by sea mail, where the Post Office delivers it to your door and collects duties when it arrives? How cooperative and reliable are the shippers and postal agencies in the exporting country? A friend of mine, an experienced importer who regularly travels overseas in search of worthwhile merchandise, always says that the first step is to ask, "How can I ship it?" She feels that carefully planned shipping is your *real* secret to success.

You can get more help from the U.S. Customs Service, or from a licensed Custom House Broker. Customs brokers are in business to prepare and expedite your paperwork and to help get your merchandise through Customs. You can locate them in the Yellow Pages of any major port city, or through a trade organization.

Finding Goods to Import

If you don't like to travel, you can often find goods to import by going to trade shows and gift shows. Most industries have large annual or semi-annual shows where manufacturers and distributors, including those from foreign countries, exhibit their wares. Sometimes you can close a deal and arrange all the details of shipping right at the show. Be sure to examine actual goods before you order. I've heard of importers being very unhappy with merchandise ordered from specifications and illustrations.

One reason many people are attracted to importing is because goods manufactured overseas are so very inexpensive compared to U.S. made goods. Part of the reason some products are so cheap is because workers in some parts of the world are paid criminally low wages and required to work long hours in dangerous and unhealthy workplaces. So, don't hesitate to look for a great deal, but as Jiminy Cricket said, "...always let your conscience be your guide."

EXPORTING

Export regulations are entirely different than import regulations. Exporters don't have to deal with U.S. Customs duties or quotas. The U.S. government encourages exports and is eager to help you sell overseas.

Export Licenses and Documents

Most businesses can export goods without any formal permission. An export license is usually not required. Licenses are required for certain "strategic" goods (usually those with military uses), and goods shipped to certain "restricted" countries. You may also have to prepare a shipping document called a Shippers Export Declaration (SED).

To find out more information, you should contact the Bureau of Export Administration (the BXA), which is part of the U.S. Department of Commerce.

Letters of Credit

If an overseas buyer decides not to pay you, it may be difficult for you to collect what's owed you. Many exporters require an "irrevocable letter of credit", where the overseas buyer's bank guarantees payment.

A letter of credit is very much like a contract. The wording must be precise, particularly the details of what's being shipped, the time deadlines, and the point where ownership passes hands. If the letter of credit specifies an exact weight or an exact count, or specifies a firm shipping date or a firm delivery date, the exporter could lose everything if he is off by a pound or a day. If the letter of credit states that payment is due when the goods are safely in the customer's warehouse rather than when the ship leaves port, the exporter may never get paid if the ship sinks, if the foreign customs inspector rejects the shipment, if the customer claims the goods are damaged or are not what was ordered.

Some exporters obtain export or marine insurance to provide additional protection.

Exporting often requires travel to foreign countries and a knowledge of other cultures and customs as well as tariffs, foreign import regulations, and shipping options. It's a good idea to approach exporting one country at a time.

Like importing, you can avoid all the international headaches by going through intermediaries, export brokers or others who will either arrange all the paperwork for you or simply buy your products and then export them themselves. You can locate these people by asking other exporters or through a trade organization.

The Commerce Department's Export Counseling Division, Washington D.C. 20230, can help you find overseas buyers, explain shipping options, and even help you get paid. The Commerce Department and the SBA sponsor seminars, trade shows, and overseas trade missions where you actually visit potential overseas customers.

The Small Business Administration offers special loans to export businesses through its export assistance offices. These loans are different from the regular SBA loans.

I don't know the key to success, but the key to failure is trying to please everybody.
—Bill Cosby

BUYING A BUSINESS

Buying a going business is certainly a fast way to jump right into the deep water. Instant business. Such a purchase will require a good deal of careful research. You should certainly take your time considering this major, major purchase.

(This chapter is not about franchises or so-called "business opportunities". They are covered in a separate chapter).

Why buy a business someone else started? When you start your own business, it can be a year or more before it produces enough income to pay yourself a decent wage. When you buy a going business, you have an immediate income stream. The very next receipt is yours.

Another reason for buying is that someone else has done all the hard work: identified a need, set up the business, found the customers, worked through all the problems, and proved that it can be successful. Anything that can go wrong probably already has.

A third reason for buying is availability of financing. Investors and bankers are much more receptive to an "acquisition". A proven business is much less risky than a brand new, untested one. The seller may help finance it as well.

How do you find out what businesses are for sale? There may be an ad in the paper, or you might just hear about one. More likely, you will have to ask around. Bankers, accountants, local business people, and people active in community affairs are likely to know who has a business for sale. I know of businesses that sold just because someone walked in and asked the owner if he had any interest in selling.

Real estate agents and, if you live in a big city, professional business brokers will know about businesses for sale. But when an agent or broker helps put a deal together, they collect their fee, usually a percent of the sale price, and it will likely increase the price you pay for the business. Keep in mind, too, that brokers and agents are working for the seller and get paid only if the deal goes through. Don't rely on them for advice or anything other than just locating the business.

There are three basic factors to consider when buying a going business: (1) Is the business worth buying? (2) Is the price right? (3) Are you the person to take over this business? Let's consider the last factor first.

Is This The Right Business For You?

If the business you want to buy is successful, busy, rolling down the track like a fast freight, are you—the new owner, manager, clerk, employer, bookkeeper, and trouble shooter—ready to handle such an enterprise? Do you have the experience and the knowledge to jump right on and keep the business rolling smoothly? Or will your on-the-job training cause disruptions in the operation, possibly displeasing customers enough to lose them?

If the business depends on the owner's personality, or on the owner's training and experience (such as repair shops and service business), taking over that business and keeping the customers might be difficult. Customers get used to certain stores. They expect a certain level of competence, service, convenience, courtesy, from a store they frequent. They expect certain merchandise to always be in stock—the former owner always had it in stock—or they expect a service to be performed within a time period they are accustomed to. If you can't get in sync with the way the business is already running, almost immediately, the customers may have little patience for you.

Quite often, the buyer of a business will train with the seller, the two working in the store together for a period of time, so that the transition is smooth. Discuss this during negotiations with the seller, and whatever decision is made, include it in the written purchase agreement.

Is This Business Worth Buying?

Once you've decided you are the person for the job, you must determine if this particular business is worth buying. Here are some important questions to ask:

Who owns the business? If it is a sole proprietorship, there is one owner, and that is who you want to deal with. If the business is a partnership, be sure all partners have agreed to sell, and that the partner you are dealing with has written authority from *all* partners to negotiate and close a deal with you. If the business is a corporation or an LLC, again make sure that the person has the legal authority to sell the business.

Why does the owner want to sell? Is she or he simply tired out? A lot of business owners, particularly in retail businesses, wear themselves out after five or ten years, working every day. They just want to quit, take a rest, do something else. Is the owner old or ill, and wants or needs to retire? Is a divorce forcing the sale? Is the owner in some sort of trouble and needs the cash? Make sure the trouble is not directly related to the business, and be sure to get legal help with this. Is the business starting to fail? Does the owner know some troubling future prospects for the business—problems with the neighborhood, or a tough new competitor about to move in, or some other upcoming development that will be detrimental to the business—and wants to bail out?

How profitable is the business? Ask to see the ledgers and tax returns for the last few years. Tax returns are an excellent source of information since no one tends to overstate income or profit on a tax return. If the owner declines to show you income and expense figures, something may be wrong, and you may want to move on. Quite often, however, business owners are very reluctant to show *anybody* their ledgers and tax returns, including a prospective buyer. You will have to decide, based on other factors, whether you want to continue investigating this business.

Tuli Kupferberg

If you do get to examine the ledgers and tax returns and if you don't understand the numbers, hire an accountant to help you. Do the numbers make sense? Income as shown on bank statements, sales tax reports, ledgers, and tax returns should have some correlation. Don't pay an inflated price for revenues the owner claims he has been hiding from the tax man.

Are the profits on the increase, or on the decline? Is there enough income to provide you a living wage and to eventually pay off the cost of buying the business? Don't forget that the profit from a sole proprietorship or partnership will not include any salary for the owner. The profit *is* his salary. If it's a corporation, how much of a salary is the owner taking? If the business has a hired manager or employees who won't be needed if you buy the business, eliminating their salaries may improve the profit figure significantly. Be sure to figure in federal and state income and self-employment taxes. Taxes will reduce those profit figures considerably.

Is the business in a good location? Can you assume the lease? How many years are left on the lease? To buy a business with no lease or a short-term lease means that the landlord can, on a whim, evict you, triple the rent, Lord knows what. Find out if there are any city plans for rezoning that may affect your location.

What is the condition of the assets? Is the building in need of repair or remodeling? Is the equipment in good shape, or will it need to be repaired or replaced soon? Is the computer system functioning smoothly? Will you have to sink a lot of money into the business to fix it up the way you want, or possibly to meet a building or health code requirement? Building inspectors sometimes tend to leave old businesses alone but suddenly notice all sorts of code violations when a new owner takes over.

What is the competition like? Is it growing? Are the competitors doing better than this store? Can you determine why?

How reliable are the suppliers? Are any closing their doors, moving away or making other major changes? If you will be dependent on the same suppliers, talk to them and make sure they'll do business with you.

Will you inherit obligations or problems?
Are there outstanding guarantees or warranties to customers that you will have to honor? Are there contracts with customers or suppliers that you must fulfill? Are there lawsuits or threats of lawsuits? Are there obligations to current or former employees? Are there contamination problems you might inherit?

The present owner of the business can probably answer all of the above questions, though you shouldn't expect unbiased answers. If you spend some time and study things closely, you will most likely find your own answers to the questions.

Observe the store, the customers, how much business is being conducted. Does what you see relate to the sales figures in the ledgers? Walk around the neighborhood, see for yourself if there is any nearby competition, and how well they are doing. Talk to other business owners in the area, particularly close neighbors. Tell them your plans and ask their opinions. I guarantee you will get an earful of valuable information.

Customers and suppliers are another vital

"Well. Now that your family company is part of our family of companies, we've decided to let you go."

source of information. Try also to locate former customers and suppliers. I'm sure they can tell you a *lot* about the business. So can the employees; talk to all of them.

You should also become Sherlock Holmes with the present owner's figures. If this is a sales business, check month-to-month purchases as some indicator of how fast the inventory sells once it's in stock (called "turnover"). It also may indicate if the business has seasonal cycles—slow at one time of year, busy at others. Does the owner keep any of the purchases for himself?

Check the inventory carefully. It may be much larger or smaller than the owner tells you, and it may be damaged or obsolete or simply unsalable. How much dust is on it?

Be suspicious of any recent legal fees. What were they for? If you see loan or interest payments, ask about them. If you won't be assuming a loan, you won't be making those payments.

How Much Should You Pay?

Finally you come to the most difficult question of all. Despite what the seller may tell you or what the textbooks say, there are few real guidelines and no reliable formulas when it comes to such a large, unique, emotion-laden transaction as the purchase of a going business. The bottom line, always, is that a business is worth no more than what a buyer will pay for it. The seller may *have* to sell this business; but you, the buyer, do not have to buy it. It is up to you to determine what you are willing to pay for it, and then find out if the seller will accept your offer.

You should realize that the seller has probably never sold a business before, certainly not this particular business. He probably knows what the business is worth, but he really has no idea what he can expect to get for it. A business is not like a used car, or even a house, when it comes to figuring out what price it will fetch. Comparisons are difficult, and prospective buyers are usually few. So, the seller is in the dark himself when setting a price. Quite often, the asking price is no indication at all of what the business will actually sell for. Businesses will often sell for half or even a third of the asking price.

The actual value of the inventory and equipment—what the present owner can sell it for if the business is closed and liquidated—is usually the bottom-dollar value of a business. A surprising number of successful businesses actually sell for close to this amount. So, first you must determine this value. The seller's original cost is a guideline, but you must also consider age, wear, damage, and possible obsolescence.

Then, you can be sure the seller will want, on top of the value of the assets, additional money because the business is successful, established, earning a profit. Some people call this intangible value "goodwill," and they attempt to put a price on it, some dollar figure they pull out of the air (which is probably why this is also called, in business jargon, "blue sky"). Often, the seller will ask for the equivalent of one or two years' profits. Again, throw out the formulas. It is entirely up to you the buyer to decide if you want and can afford to pay for some or all of this "blue sky."

Many small businesses are bought on the installment basis, with the seller extending most of the credit. It is usually to your advantage to have the seller help finance the business, as he or she is much more likely to want to help you be successful. Most sellers, however, would greatly prefer to get the cash and be done with it, and are usually willing to reduce the price considerably if you can finance the purchase yourself.

Keep in mind that the purchase price of the a business is just a start. You will still need money for working capital (day to day expenditures, overhead, new inventory, etc.) and possibly for repairs, remodeling or sprucing up.

When you consider buying a going business, also consider how much it would cost to set up, from scratch, a new, similar business at a different location. Why buy someone else's expensive business if you can start your own a lot cheaper?

Purchase Contract

Once the buyer and the seller agree on the purchase price and payment terms, you will probably need an experienced accountant's help to draft the purchase agreement. Everything should be in writing. The precise legal wording can affect how the sale is taxed, how the assets are valued for tax purposes, and how much of the purchase price will be deductible.

You, the buyer should be careful that you will not unknowingly inherit old business debts, liabilities, lawsuits, or other problems you should not be responsible for. Make absolutely sure all creditors are notified that the business is being sold, and that old liabilities will not be the responsibility of the new owner.

This is particularly important if you are buying a corporation. If you buy the corporation's stock, you are the new owner of an old business, a business that may have old legal and contractual obligations that you may be stuck with. Often it is better to purchase the assets, the lease, the business name and whatever else goes along with the deal, from the old corporation rather than buying the corporation itself. A buyer often gets a much better tax break by buying assets instead of the corporation itself. As you can see, this will require the help of an accountant or a lawyer.

Tax Deductions

The costs of investigating and buying a businesses come under a variety of IRS rules. Costs incurred before you pick a specific business you want to buy, such as travel and general research, are usually not deductible at all. Once you are trying to purchase a specific business, the costs you incur are considered "capital" expenditures. (Whenever you see the word "capital" in tax law, it usually means you won't be able to write off your expenses right away.) If you do not finally buy the business, you have a "capital loss" that may be deductible. If you do buy the business, the costs must be capitalized according to the "Start up" rules explained in the Tax section.

The Seller

A final word to the seller: Once the business is sold, notify all state and local agencies that you deal with (the sales tax people, the department of employment, etc.), your suppliers, your landlord, and others with a legal or financial connection to your business. Let them know the business has a new owner and that you are not responsible for any future problems. Some state agencies can hold a former owner liable for the actions of a new owner if the agencies do not receive official notification of transfer of ownership. Some localities even require you to get a "Going Out of Business" permit. You may also have to file employee W-2s and payroll tax forms early.

It's easy to find a lousy firm you can afford.
—Larry Hammons, Rational Technology Inc.

FRANCHISE BUSINESS

A franchise is an individually owned business operated as though it was part of a large chain. Midas Muffler, McDonalds and H&R Block are examples of well known national franchises. Under a franchise, services and products are standardized. Trademarks, advertising and store appearance are uniform.

With a franchise, your own freedom and initiative are limited. You lose a lot of autonomy, a lot of the feeling of being your own boss. The name on the store is not yours. But a well known franchise gives you instant recognition. The goods and services of the franchisor are proven and trusted. Or as an old Holiday Inn ad read, "No surprises here." (Hopefully no surprises here: Many of the old Sears Catalog stores were franchises, purchased by individuals who were forced to close their businesses when Sears decided, with absolutely no warning to any of its franchisees, to shut down the entire catalog operation).

How Franchises Work

Most franchises work this way: For a fee, the supplier (the franchisor) gives you (the franchisee) the right to use the franchisor's name and sell its product or service. The franchise agreement may require you to purchase your supplies or equipment from the franchisor, at their prices, even if you can get better prices from local suppliers. You may have to pay the franchisor a percentage of your gross sales (that is, a percentage of your total sales before deducting any expenses) whether you are making a profit or not. You may have to pay for a portion of the franchisor's advertising. There may be special marketing fees or charges for contract renewals. Franchise agreements are always lengthy and full of requirements.

There are hundreds of franchise companies in the U.S., some well known but some completely unknown, some with a good, profitable history, and some struggling like any other business. Their appeal to franchisees seems to be two-fold. One, they offer what they call a "turn-key" operation, a complete ready-to-run business (all you have to do is turn the key in the door) that includes training, management support and even some customer leads.

The second aspect is that franchisors often help with financing. Franchisors have their own loan sources; a few even own their own finance companies. But be warned: the franchisor will require you to put up a chunk of your own money, and they may even want a second mortgage on your home to guarantee their loan. Just because it's a franchise, even a well-known franchise, there is no guarantee that you, or it, will be successful. If you can't make your payments, the franchisor will not hesitate to foreclose, and re-sell the franchise to someone else.

Investigating a Franchise

Before signing a franchise agreement, investigate the franchise thoroughly. There is simply no shortcut for this. It involves homework, legwork, phone work and pencil work.

The FTC requires franchisors to give prospective franchisees a copy of what's called a Uniform Franchise Offering Circular. This UFOC includes information on your potential earnings (though these numbers are easily manipulated and should not be trusted), the costs, the company's history and financial standing, and terms of the agreement. The franchisor must give you a copy of the UFOC at least ten business days before you sign any contract. But you should get and study this document long before those last ten days, before you've got so much time and money invested in researching this franchise. (Gasoline companies, auto manufacturers, and some franchises offered to experienced business people are exempt from this law.)

When you investigate a specific franchise, try to get a complete list of all of their franchisees and contact as many as you can. Find out how they are doing and what they think of the franchise. Ask each franchisee, "If you had to do it over again, would you invest in this franchise?"

Are there any lawsuits against the franchise? The Federal Trade Commission can tell you if any complaints have been filed against the franchisor. Contact the people who are suing the company and get their side of the story. Ask the franchisor for a list of former franchisees, call them up, and find out what happened to them. Also check with the Better Business Bureau.

Ask if you'll have territorial rights, and for how long. Territory (called "encroachment" in the contracts) is a major issue with retail franchises, and one of the most common rifts between franchisors and franchisees: How many Subway, or Burger King, or Quick Lube franchises in your town, or within so many miles of each other?

How much of the company's advertising money will be spent in your area? And is it just a promise, or will this be in your contract?

Can the franchisor cancel your franchise, and essentially put you out of business, if the franchisor chooses to do so? Is the contract binding for the life of your business, or can the franchisor revise it, possibly to your detriment, in a year, or five, or ten? Will you be required to meet sales quotas, and what happens if you don't? Can you sell your franchise to someone else if you want to get out of it?

Just like starting any business, do your own market research. Even if you are convinced you are buying into a franchise that is well structured and well managed, make sure there is a local market—customers—for the product.

Once you've done all the investigating you can do on your own, then be sure to have a lawyer or an accountant review the contract with you and explain to you *exactly* what you're getting into.

Give serious thought to whether a franchise is really the best route for you to start a new business. Certainly, a restaurant on the interstate called McDonalds will most likely do better than one called Ralph's Diner. A Best Western Motel will be more inviting than Ralph's Motel. But if you're starting a local business attracting local customers, will your print shop, or video store, or cleaning service, or real estate office, or even hamburger stand, be more attractive as a franchise instead of as a locally owned, independent business? People will quickly get to know you and your business either way, and it will succeed or fail depending on your service and quality and prices and other important considerations, not on the name of the business or the slick national advertising. Why pay the fees and tie yourself to a franchise if it offers no discernable benefits?

There are several books and directories that list names, addresses and details about hundreds of franchises. Some are updated every year. Check your local library or SBA office.

"Business Opportunities"

"*Make $1,000 a day, at home, in your spare time, stuffing envelopes!*" Like a franchise, a so-called "business opportunity" is someone else's idea, plan or system to make themselves (oops, I mean, to make you) a fortune. Unlike a franchise, a business opportunity is not a retail store or a famous name. There is no protected territory, no national advertising, no management support. It's often only a manual or audio tape, or a bunch of flyers to photocopy and try to sell to someone else. Business opportunities are often some sort of mail order or multi-level (direct-selling, or networking) distribution plan, possibly where you buy a minimum initial bulk purchase of vitamins, or cosmetics, or who knows—and lots of luck finding customers.

Some business opportunities are legitimate and practical, and some are not. Use your good common sense, do your market research, and remember the old adage, "If it sounds too good to be true, it probably is".

The Customer Is Always Right—but who cares.
—*Sign on the Shady Nook Snack Bar*

I still go by the old rule that the customer is always right, even when he or she is clearly wrong.
—*Business consultant Marilyn Ross*

No one ever wins an argument with a customer.
—*Dale Carnegie*

157

FREELANCERS:
Professionals, Consultants, Independent Artists, Writers, Photographers, and Designers

Freelancers—including professionals, consultants, artists, designers, and other self-employed individuals—are in business for themselves, like all other business people, no matter how reluctant they are to deal with it.

Freelancers are sole proprietors unless you incorporate, form a partnership or LLC. You are responsible for your own business records, licenses, tax returns, and everything else covered in *Small Time Operator*. Freelancers should read the chapter on outside contractors (Growing Up Section). Many freelancers fall into this category.

Royalties

If royalties from creative effort, such as writing, design or art, are a regular and ongoing source of income for you, they are considered self-employment income, business income, handled the same as any other business income with regular business deductions. These royalties are reported on Schedule C (if you are a sole proprietor), and subject to regular business taxes including self-employment tax. This also applies to licensing fees, assignment of copyrights or any other similar income.

If royalty income is only occasional or a one-shot, it is not considered self-employment income. It is reported on your 1040 tax return as Other Income. It is subject to income tax but not to self-employment tax. You can deduct some of the related expenses on Schedule A of your 1040, but only if you itemize deductions.

None of your royalties should be reported on Schedule E even though Schedule E says it is for royalties. The only royalties that go on Schedule E are royalties from coal, oil, gas and other natural resources, what the IRS refers to as "passive income". In fact, in the IRS Code, the term "royalties" refers only to these natural resources. The kind of royalties a writer or an artist earns aren't even called royalties.

The less fixed costs you have, the more survivable you are. —Business owner Kitson Logue

Advances

Freelancers sometimes get cash advances, deposits on work to be performed, advances on royalties. How are these handled? You should first read the chapter "Cash Vs. Accrual Accounting" in the Bookkeeping section. If you use cash accounting, as many freelancers do, the money is considered earned income, subject to taxes, when you receive it. If you refund all or part of it at a later date, you reduce your income at that time (similar to making a sales return).

Accrual basis businesses recognize income when it is earned, not when cash changes hands. Any advance not yet earned is not taxable income until you do the work. This sometimes becomes a problem at year-end, if you have received an advance for work partially completed at December 31. You will have to report at least part of the advance, to the extent earned, on your tax return. This calculation may require an accountant's help. By the way, if a writer's advance on royalties is not refundable—you keep it whether the book sells or not—for tax purposes, it is not considered an advance. It is current earned income, currently taxable.

Reimbursed Expenses

If you have out of pocket expenses that you add to your billings, these reimbursed expenses should be included as part of your total income. You get to deduct the actual expenses on your tax return, so the net effect for taxes is zero.

Artists, Writers and Photographers

Freelance artists, writers and photographers have been blessed with a special IRS exemption from the onerous "uniform capitalization rules" imposed on craftspeople and other manufacturers (covered in the Inventory chapter in the Tax Section). Basically, producers of goods may not write off their production expenses until they've sold the goods they produced.

Self-employed artists, writers and photographers do not have to abide by the uniform capitalization rules. They may write off their expenses the year incurred. These rules apply to individuals who create literary manuscripts, musical compositions, dance scores, photographs, photographic negatives or transparencies, pictures, paintings, sculptures, statues, etchings, drawings, cartoons, graphic designs, or original print editions. The rules do *not* apply to craftspeople, cabinetmakers, potters, jewelers, print makers, film makers, and others in business providing similar products. Obviously, there is fine line here that must be carefully observed.

The Basic Basics of COMPUTERS

Some businesses will find computers essential, a tremendous help and time saver. Other businesses will have little or no use for a computer.

As a bookkeeping tool, a computer can produce ledgers as simple as those described in this book or as elaborate as you want. If you find hand posting ledgers to be a tedious, lengthy, repetitious job, a computer can make the bookkeeping less time consuming and maybe even a little fun.

Financial analysis, such as comparative (month to month, year to year) sales or expense data, broken down into any categories you want, can be quick and easy on the computer. It might be a long job when done by hand. If you prepare profit-and-loss statements, cash flow projections, balance sheets, partners' capital accounts, or any other financial summaries, a good computer program can turn them out for you quickly.

As a management tool, a computer can help a business keep all manner of inventory records: what's on hand, what's ordered, who the supplier is, how long it takes to get an order, what is and isn't selling well. A computer can check your customer's account status (does he owe money?) at the time of the sale. Computers can make payroll calculations and reports almost effortless. Computers can prepare invoices, shipping documents, customer lists, letters, brochures and most any form, file, chart and schedule you want. Computers can help organize your business for you.

A computer is not just another piece of office equipment like a fax machine or a copier. Mastering a business computer and its programs, and getting them to provide accurate information the way you want it will require an initial commitment of time, possibly quite a bit of time.

If a computer will be a great help to the actual day-to-day operation of your business, you may want to acquire one right away. If you plan to use the computer only for bookkeeping, financial analysis, and the occasional letter or file, you may want to wait. You will have your hands full (and your bank account empty) just getting the business off the ground. After you've gotten to know your business, after it is running smoothly, once you know what information you want and need, you are in a much better position to determine what computer and what programs to buy.

Talk to other business owners who use computers. Find out what the owners do with their computers, how useful they are, how difficult the different programs are to master.

Hardware

Computers are comprised of "hardware" and "software". The hardware is the physical equipment, which includes the "processor": the "central processing unit" (CPU), which is the actual computer, the heart and brain of the machine; and the "peripherals", all the equipment that hooks up to the CPU.

Peripherals typically include a monitor, which is the viewing screen; the keyboard, a combination typewriter and adding-machine with additional function keys for computer commands; a printer, to print out your documents on paper; a "mouse" or "track ball", a hand-operated pointer that is used, along with the keyboard, to operate the computer; disk drives that can read and copy computer disks; a CD (compact disk) drive that can read and copy computer CDs; a modem that connects your telephone line to the computer and allows you to go online or to send faxes directly from the computer; scanners that copy documents and illustrations directly into your computer; and tape-backup drives, external disk drives, battery backups, sound cards, and whatever else has been invented in the last few weeks.

Choosing a Computer

If you are buying a new computer, there are two basic choices (called "platforms" in computer-ese): (1) The PC, which is short for Personal Computer, and is also called the IBM-PC, IBM-compatible or clone. This is the most popular type of computer in the world, and is manufactured by IBM and, under a hundred or more other brand names, by a hundred or more other companies. And (2) The Macintosh (the Mac), made by the Apple Corporation. Although the PC and the Mac perform the same basic functions, they are not usually compatible, and their software programs are not interchangeable. You choose one or the other, and that's it. (This is not totally true, as some Macs can run PC software and PC-generated information, but this "cross-platform" stuff often has a lot of bugs).

A few years ago, there was a dramatic difference in the way PCs and Macs operated. Macs were much easier to learn and to use. I think that is no longer the case (though every Mac owner will disagree with me). I found the PC easy to learn and to use. Besides, it is not the computers themselves that are difficult to use. It's the programs that can be difficult, and quite frustrating to use; but more on that later. PC's are faster and more powerful than Macs, and they cost less money. Still, the Macs are wonderful machines used happily by thousands of small businesses. My guess is that you'll be quite satisfied with whichever machine you choose.

Whether you buy a PC or a Mac, make sure the machine has enough memory to operate the programs you want, and to store the amount of information you need.

Some programs are much more elaborate and sophisticated than others and require a lot of memory (megabytes) built into the computer. "Information", also called "files" (customer lists, ledgers, inventory records, the novel you're working on, a record of your high game scores) consume the same memory. The more information you want to store within the computer, the bigger the memory you'll need.

Speed, too, makes a tremendous difference in you computer's performance (and in your own sanity). Many programs operate *very* slowly on older and slower computers. A speedy computer costs a few hundred dollars more than a slow one, and is worth every penny.

The important thing seems to be having lots and lots of data. Information has become synonymous with knowledge and intelligence, and computers have become synonymous with all these terms. There is a dangerous illusion that what a computer generates is scientific or objective.
—Bernard Zilbergeld, San Francisco Chronicle

A little warning: Computers generate heat, and they have built-in fans to cool them down. The more powerful the computer, the more heat generated, and the bigger, and noisier, the fans. Large monitors also have fans; and some printers make quite a bit of noise as well. If you are accustomed to a quiet office, make sure the noise level will be tolerable.

If you know nothing about computers, I highly suggest you purchase your computer from a friendly, reliable, local computer dealer, someone who is willing and eager to help you set it up and to answer the 101 questions you need answered. A new computer can be an intimidating mystery; personal help will make all the difference in the world. Don't count on getting information out of the instruction manuals (the "documentation"). Most of the manuals are almost impossible for a novice to understand. If you are buying via mail order, find a company with not only a reliable machine, but reliable (and toll-free) support.

Buying A Used Computer

You can buy a used computer, along with peripherals and often dozens of programs thrown in, for a fraction of the cost of a new one, but you must be very careful in your choice. Early computers, such as Apple, Atari, and Commodore, are not compatible with PCs or Macs. Neither the computers nor the programs for them are being manufactured anymore. Avoid the first PCs, the 286 models and earlier, as they are probably too small to run the programs you'd like to operate. The next generation, the 386 models, were much faster and are still used by many small businesses, but they may not be able to run today's memory-hogging programs.

Software

Software is (are?) the operating systems and the programs that run the computer. The hardware will not work without software telling it what to do. The software is stored on computer disks, also called diskettes and floppy disks (because the larger 5¼" PC disks, invented before the newer 3½" disks, are thin and quite floppy) or on CDs. Software is also stored inside your computer on a built-in hard drive. Software can be copied to and from the hard drive and from disk to disk quite easily.

The "operating system" software is the basic programming that makes your computer function. Before you can install and use a program that will create ledgers, or do word processing, or design newsletters, or play games, or whatever you want to do, the operating system must be installed first. MACs use the MAC system. Most new PCs use a system called Windows. Almost all computers come with the operating systems already installed.

The real key to how much you will like your computer, how much use you'll get out of it, and how easy or difficult a time you'll have, depends on the programs you use. There are thousands of programs on the market that perform all sorts of tasks, some with great ease, some with great difficulty, some well designed, some with serious flaws. You should research individual programs you are considering. For example, if you want a word processing program, there are a few very popular programs and several lesser-known programs to choose from, and each program operates differently.

If possible, talk to other people who use the programs (and make sure they are using the most current version of the program, as some programs change dramatically from one version to the next, sometimes for the better and sometimes for the worse). Read the reviews in the computer magazines. Talk to the dealers: some companies let you return programs if you don't like them. Most important, I have found, choose a program that has a good reputation for support. A helpful telephone support staff (and one that doesn't put you on hold for 15 minutes every time you call) *will* make the difference between success and failure learning and using a program. I can't overemphasize how confusing and unreadable some instruction manuals can be; a friendly voice on the phone is the greatest help in the entire computer world.

Some of the most popular types of programs include:

Word Processing

You can compose letters, correct and re-word them and get them just the way you want them; then push a key, and the computer prints out your finished letter. You can store the letter on a disk or in the computer, and change it or retype it or use parts of it in another letter, any time you want. You can do the same thing with advertising copy, brochures, newsletters, books, invoices and other business forms, mailing lists, and address files. The word processing program can check your spelling and grammar for you, and help you format and lay out your documents.

Word processing programs are the most popular, and probably the easiest to use, of all business applications. Almost everyone who owns a computer has a word processing program.

Desktop Publishing

Most word processing programs double as desktop publishing (page-layout) programs, letting you select the number and width of columns, margins, size and shape of the letters, and add page numbers, borders, most anything you like. Most businesses will not need a separate desktop publishing program. This entire book was typeset and laid out using only a word processing program.

But if you are working in color, designing elaborate brochures, or working as a professional graphic designer, you should consider desktop publishing program in addition to your word processing program.

Spreadsheets

Spreadsheet programs, basically, process numbers. You can create ledgers, profit and loss statements, balance sheets, forecasts, cash flow projections, and a wealth of other schedules and charts using spreadsheets.

"Spreadsheet" is an old accounting term that originally referred to a piece of ledger paper that had so many columns, it had to be folded over to fit in a binder. Today's computer spreadsheets are not much different. A spreadsheet program resembles a piece of graph paper inside the computer. Each of the graph paper's little boxes, called "cells", is labeled with a column and row designation. You can put numbers, words, formulas, and instructions into the cells.

After using my powerful word processor to write a letter to a friend, I printed it on my state-of-the-art laser printer. What a professional look it had! It didn't look like a letter at all. It looked like a piece of junk mail.   —Columnist Russell Baker

In order to get a spreadsheet to do what you want it to do, you can create your own formulas and instructions (called "templates") if they aren't too complex, or you can use the templates that come with the program, or you can purchase ready-to-run templates from software dealers.

A spreadsheet is much like the ledgers and worksheets in this book, with a built-in calculator. Spreadsheets, however, are more difficult to use and are not as complete and integrated as accounting programs.

Accounting Programs

More and more small businesses are abandoning hand-posted ledgers in favor of accounting programs. The software keeps getting better and easier to use. Accounting programs give you a complete set of ledgers that can be customized to meet your specific needs. Some include check writing and bank balancing as well. Some are for general business use, and some are for specific types of businesses and specific industries.

Specialized accounting programs are available for businesses that need more advanced inventory control, payroll, job costing, accounts receivable, customer accounts, and just about any other business function you can think of. A big problem with specialized programs is finding the right software for the task. Many businesses have wound up with expensive "shelfware" and a lot of time wasted because they picked programs that didn't give them what they really needed.

Database Marketing / Management

Database marketing (database management) programs file, sort and organize mailing lists, customer lists, and any collection of information you have that needs regular organization and updating.

Most word processing programs have simple database marketing functions built in. Many small businesses will find their word processing program to be more than adequate for their database management needs, and will not need a separate database program.

People who want detailed customer profiles, buying habits, demographics and all that fun stuff, will probably need a database program.

Insurance and Taxes

Your regular insurance policy may or may not cover your computer. Many insurance companies offer insurance policies just for computers.

Business computers can be depreciated or expensed (see Business Assets and Depreciation chapters in the Tax section). A computer purchased before going into business that you are using for business, can also be depreciated. If you use your computer only partly for business, you must keep a log (dates and hours) of the usage.

Back Up Your Work

Make duplicate copies of all your files onto disks, and store the disks at a separate location. So when—not if—the information inside your computer is lost or destroyed, you'll have most or all of it saved on disks.

You can push the wrong button and wipe out hours of work. You can delete (erase) stuff that later you wish you hadn't. Computers occasionally, without any warning, "crash": freeze up, refuse to work until they are shut down and restarted, almost always resulting in lost information. Eventually, I'm told, all computer hard drives fail and have to be replaced. And when they die, the programs and files on the hard drive can vanish without a trace.

FILING YOUR BUSINESS RECORDS

Complete records and a good filing system are as important as a complete bookkeeping system. Every transaction, every meeting, every action involving employees should be documented and kept for reference or for proof if you get audited.

Here is a list of documents you should keep:

1. Articles, by-laws, partnership agreements, DBA (fictitious or assumed name) statements, and other documents that establish and define the business. Keep as long as the business exists.

2. Names, addresses, Social Security numbers and other pertinent data for all owners and stockholders including date joined and date departed. Keep as long as the business exists.

3. Record of owners' contributions and with-

drawals and all other financial transactions between owners and the business. Keep as long as the business exists.

4. Minutes of board meetings. Keep as long as the business exists. You'll find yourself going back to the old minutes many times. If owners ever get in a dispute, old minutes will often provide ready answers.

5. Permits, licenses, insurance policies and leases. Keep as long as they are in force but, for IRS purposes, keep at least three years.

6. Loan papers. Keep as long as the loan is outstanding but, for IRS purposes, keep at least three years. Actually it's a good idea to keep loan papers for as long as the business exists. Though a loan may have been paid off several years ago, you may want to show a bank a record of the old loan when you apply for a new one.

7. Invoices, bills, receipts, credit memos and other day-to-day business documents. For IRS purposes, keep at least three years. If your sales documents include customers' names and addresses, you may want to keep them longer should you decide to do a mailing or other promotion.

8. Complete data on all current and past employees: names, addresses, Social Security numbers, date hired, wage rates and dates of raises, payroll withholding, W-4 exemptions, injuries

and workers' compensation claims, evaluations, date employment ended and why. Keep as long as the business exists. It is rare but it does happen that some government agency or court will ask you to produce 15-year-old employment records. If this happens, be sure you are legally required to produce the records and are not violating a law or an agreement of confidentiality. Get a written statement from the employee, or get professional advice.

9. Bank statements, deposits and canceled checks. For IRS purposes, keep at least 3 years.

10. Annual profit and loss statements. Keep as long as the business exists. Monthly and periodic financial statements probably should be kept two or three years. It is useful to compare monthly profit and loss statements for two or three consecutive years to see if there is a pattern, a cycle, of business activity.

11. Tax returns. Keep income tax, payroll and property tax records for as long as the business exists. Keep all other tax returns, such as sales tax, excise tax, etc., at least three years.

12. Ledgers. Keep as long as the business exists.

Lucky 13. Don't throw out the paper in the waste basket for two days. "Oh no, I threw it away!"

TRADEMARKS, PATENTS & COPYRIGHTS

Trademarks (including service marks, trade names and trade dress), patents, and copyrights are known as "intangible property" or "intellectual property". You cannot see or touch them, but they exist and they are quite valuable.

The IRS calls patents, trademarks (service marks, etc.) and copyrights "Section 197 Intangibles". Their costs may not be written off when incurred. They may be amortized (depreciated) over 15 years. See the Depreciation chapter in the Tax Section for more information.

TRADEMARKS

A trademark is a word, name, brand, slogan or expression, a symbol, shape, design or logo, a color or combination of colors, a unique sound, or some combination of these, adopted by a business to identify its goods and distinguish them from goods manufactured or sold by others. Trademarks are not functional. They serve no useful purpose other than to identify goods or services.

A different term, "trade dress", refers to a product's image: its appearance or packaging, how it's "dressed up". It is basically no different than a trademark. A third term, "service mark", applies to services instead of goods, but the rules are the same. All references in this chapter to the term "trademarks" also include trade dress and service marks.

There is an important distinction between a design or logo that identifies your products or services (which can be trademarked), and original artwork such as a poster or T-shirt design (which can be copyrighted but cannot be trademarked). If the artwork you are selling *is* your company's logo, then it can be trademarked *and* copyrighted. These are two different procedures with two different sets of laws.

There is also a distinction between a trademark, which identifies your products, and a "trade name" which identifies your company. For example, a company called "General Motors" (a trade name) sells a product called "Cadillac" (a trademark). Sometimes the trademark and the trade name are the same. A company called "Ford" (a trade name) sells a product called "Ford" (a trademark). A trade name cannot be federally registered unless it also functions as a trademark, but you still have some legal protection for trade names.

Acquiring a Trademark

You acquire a basic trademark right, with limited legal protection, simply by creating and using your trademark. You must actually use your trademark in order to own rights to it.

You acquire exclusive legal rights to a trademark by registering with the U.S. Patent & Trademark Office. You may apply for a trademark up to 3 years before actually using it or any time after you start to use it.

Generally, federal protection applies to trademarks that are used in interstate commerce. You must be doing business across state lines or your product must cross state lines in the normal course of business. Many states offer in-state trademark protection for businesses not involved in interstate commerce. A state trademark, however, gives you no legal protection outside your own state (a state trademark is not necessary if you are getting a federal trademark).

You cannot usually get a trademark for your own name, or for a geographical name, such as "Southwest". You cannot trademark words that actually describe your product (a window manufacturer cannot trademark the name "Windows" for its windows, but obviously, a computer company can trademark its software "Windows"). You cannot trademark expressions already in common use, such as "Have a Nice Day". You cannot trademark words or expressions that are deceptive or misleading, or that are too similar to another trademark, possibly confusing people.

Registering a Trademark

The government charges a $245 fee to register a trademark. The Patent & Trademark office will then conduct a trademark search to see if anyone else owns the trademark. If it is already owned, you forfeit your application fee. You can avoid this problem by doing your own trademark search at one of the public search libraries around the country (ask the Patent & Trademark Office for locations) or via computer if you have an on-line service offering trademark searches; or by hiring a lawyer or trademark search company to do the investigation for you.

You should also check trade directories, product catalogs and other business listings, looking for unregistered (but still valid) trademarks.

The initial registration remains in force for ten years, but you must file a Declaration of Use statement between the fifth and sixth years. The trademark may then be renewed every ten years, for as long as you like. For more details, write the Patent & Trademark Office, U.S. Department of Commerce, Washington DC 20231.

The familiar ® symbol means that a trademark or service mark is officially registered with the U.S. Trademark Office, and full legal protection has been secured. The equally familiar ™ symbol (or "SM", for "service mark") is a formal notice that you are claiming ownership of a trademark but have not registered it. The ™ or "SM" symbol can be used even if no federal trademark application is pending. Using this symbol, however, does not provide the full legal protection accorded a registered ® trademark.

Now that you know all the work and money involved in getting a trademark, do you really need one? If yours is a small local sales or service business, and you plan to stay small and local, I don't think you need to protect your identity with a trademark. If, however, you are making a product that will get widespread distribution and get to be well known, at some point a trademark will be a good investment.

Internet Names Vs. Trademarks

Conflicts often occur when someone owns a domain name on the Internet (the World Wide Web) and someone else owns the trademark to that same name. Owners of registered trademarks can usually stop someone else from using the trademark as a domain name. But if the trademark is not officially registered, or if the trademark was registered after the domain name was claimed by someone else, Internet policy (which is not governed by any U.S. laws yet) gets a bit hazy and unpredictable. You may or may not be able to force someone else to abandon their domain name. This is a growing problem that will probably be resolved in the near future by new laws or court rulings on current laws.

Protect Your Business Name

Whether you have a trademark or not, the best way to protect your company name is to make it well known and easy to find. Get listed in every business, trade, association, and phone directory that offer free listings (plenty do; don't pay for a listing). Get publicity. Make it as hard as possible for new businesses not to have heard of you. People don't maliciously steal business names, they just don't know you're there.

PATENTS

Patents apply to inventions. A patent prevents others from making, using or selling your invention without your permission.

The most common type of patent, the "utility patent", may be granted to the inventor or discoverer of any new and useful process, machine, device (gadget), or composition of matter, or any new and useful improvement of such. Some software can be patented, although most software comes under copyright, not patent, law.

A utility patent will not be granted on a useless device (the government's definition of useless, not mine), on printed matter, on an idea, on a method of doing business, on an improvement in a device that would be obvious to a skilled person, or on a machine that will not operate. The government says it never has and never will issue a patent on a perpetual motion machine.

A patent will not be granted if the invention was in public use or on sale more than a year prior to filing the patent application, or if the invention was described in a publication more than a year before filing the application.

A "design" patent covers the appearance of a product—the way it looks, not the way it functions or is constructed. Design patents are similar to trademarks, and may not be necessary if your design is protected by trademark.

"Plant" patents are for new plant varieties.

Products that have federal patent protection from the U.S. Patent & Trademark Office, are said to be "patented". A different term, "patent pending" (or "patent applied for"), means that a patent has been applied for but not yet received. It is a formal notice issued by the Patent Office, and offers some legal protection. (Some people use "patent pending" even though they haven't applied for *anything*, either to try to scare off imitators or to impress customers; this is illegal).

A utility patent is good for 20 years, starting with the date you filed for the patent. The 20 years includes the time it takes for the patent to be approved, which itself can take anywhere from several months to several years. So the actual time your patent is valid may be a lot less than 20 years. (Design patents come under other rules). The patent may not be renewed or extended. Anyone can use an invention after the patent expires. To keep a patent valid, you must also pay periodic government maintenance fees.

Applying For a Patent

Applying for a patent can be a lengthy and expensive procedure, and may require help from a patent attorney or agent. The government charges filing, issuance, and maintenance fees, and sometimes fees for printing and claims work. But any dedicated inventor who is willing to study the laws, do the research, and struggle through the forms, will be able to patent his or her own invention at a fraction of the usual cost.

A patent, however, is not a sure-fire guarantee of anything. Few inventors make money from their patents. Marketing is a much more difficult obstacle to overcome than getting a patent. I suggest that you talk to other people who own patents and people in your field, and get some idea whether a patent is the best method to accomplish your goals.

Inventors who are unsure that their invention justifies the work and cost of going through the regular patent process have another option. They can file a Provisional Patent Application (a PPA), which is a temporary form of patent-pending. A PPA requires a lot less time, money and paperwork than a regular patent application, yet offers full patent-pending protection for one full year. By the end of the year's time, if things are looking promising, you can apply for regular patent-pending status. But you have to start the patent application process all over again. The PPA itself does not lead to a patent. Should you decide to proceed with the patent, you are spending more time and money, because you took the additional step of filling a Patent Pending Application. But you do get an extra year's protection. You get the full twenty years, in addition to the PPA's year.

For more information, write the U.S. Patent & Trademark Office, Washington, D.C. 20231.

COPYRIGHTS

A copyright protects the work of a writer, illustrator, artist, designer, or composer. Literary, dramatic, musical and artistic works can be protected by copyright. Ads, brochures and promotional materials can be copyrighted. The work can be on any tangible or electronic medium: paper, videotape, cassette, CD, computer disk, fabric, etc.

Writing, illustrations, musical compositions, movies and videos can be copyrighted. Software can be copyrighted (some software can also be patented). Clothing and jewelry designs can be copyrighted. Ideas and concepts cannot be copyrighted, nor can names, titles or things. Names and titles can be trademarked, things can be patented. A description of a machine could be copyrighted as a writing, but this will not prevent others from making or using the machine.

The owner of a copyright has exclusive rights to print and copy the work (including the right to make photocopies or to scan it into a computer); to sell or distribute copies of the work (including the right to broadcast it on the Internet); to dramatize, record or translate the work; to perform or broadcast the work publicly. A song played on a jukebox in a tavern, or even performed by the local bar band, technically requires permission from the copyright holder.

The owner of a copyright may or may not be the creator of the work. The creator should be very cautious when selling some or all rights to his or her work, and should also be aware of "work for hire" laws, which automatically give all rights to the employer, none to the creator.

Acquiring a Copyright

Copyright protection automatically exists from the moment a work is created. You are not required to put a copyright notice on the work, although the U.S. Copyright Office strongly recommends that you print a copyright notice anyway: the word "copyright" or the symbol ©, the year, and your name. This will eliminate the possibility that someone will innocently reprint your work, thinking it isn't protected. (For many years, an old copyright law, now repealed, required a copyright notice or you would lose your exclusive rights to your work).

To receive maximum legal protection, a work (and any updates or revised editions) must be registered with the U.S. Copyright Office. You fill out a simple form, pay a $20 fee and send the Copyright Office two copies of the work. It's that simple. The copyright is good for your lifetime plus 50 years; it's not renewable. For information and forms, write the Register of Copyrights, Library of Congress, Washington, D.C. 20540.

Artists: The Visual Artists Rights Act protects, in certain cases, original paintings, drawings, sculptures and some photographs from being altered or destroyed after the works are sold.

Copyright on the Internet

Copyright laws are the same on the Internet and World Wide Web as they are everywhere else. But it is much harder to protect your copyright in digital space, where anything and everything is so easy and cheap to copy, duplicate and alter. Thousands of people can effortlessly take any copyrighted material from the Internet with little or no concern for having to pay for the privilege. Until technology creates some real protections for copyrighted works (much as scrambled signals were created for satellite television), very little copyrighted material will appear on the Internet. Instead, publishers and writers will continue to "give away" excerpts, first chapters, samples, tables of contents, etc. to entice people to call and buy the entire work.

Inventor Stanley Mason: The big problem is that people who call themselves inventors often do it for their own entertainment. They don't really look at the market to see what's needed. They don't think about how they're going to see their invention before they make it. Just because you've got a good idea doesn't mean it's a marketable one.

PRICING

There is no simple, one-size-fits-all answer to the question every new business owner asks: How to price a product or service? There is no magic formula, no industry standard, no single markup percentage that works for everybody.

Cost Factors

There are many factors to consider when trying to come up with a good price to charge people. The first consideration, for any sales or manufacturing business, is what your inventory costs you: the products you sell, and the parts and materials that go into products you make or repair. These are your "direct costs" of doing business (some people call these "variable costs" because they vary with your sales volume).

Other important, but too often overlooked factors, are your fixed costs and your overhead—the dozens of large and small expenses you must pay whether you are generating income or not: rent, utilities, phone, insurance, office supplies, permits and licenses, advertising and promotion, sales expenses, payroll, and the cost and maintenance of your fixed assets such as furniture, tools and equipment. These costs cannot be tied directly to a product or service, but you must somehow factor them into your pricing.

Taxes must also be figured into your pricing, primarily income tax and self-employment tax. These taxes depend, of course, on how much of a profit you earn, making them difficult if not impossible to calculate in advance, but they are significant costs, at least 15% and maybe as much as 40% of your profit.

So, the first step in pricing is to know your true operating costs. If you cannot recoup these costs from sales, you are in a situation commonly known as "going broke". Sounds pretty basic, right? You'd be amazed how many new businesses lose money because they never consider all the obvious and not-so-obvious expenses.

Profit Factors

The second step in determining a price is profit. How much do you mark up a product or charge for your services to bring in enough income, above and beyond your costs, to pay you for the time you put into the business, to pay you a living wage, to make it all worth doing?

There are several factors to consider:

1. Volume: How many sales do you make, and how many of your working hours are actually generating income? How many hours does it take you to do a particular job or make a product?

2. Where will you be marketing your goods? If you sell to wholesalers or retailers, they must get a good enough price from you to be able to mark-up the goods themselves, typically another 40% to 50%.

3. What are other businesses charging for similar goods and services?

If some of these factors seem difficult or downright impossible to calculate, don't be discouraged. That's the way it is for most new businesses. You don't know many of your costs when you are getting started, and you certainly have no idea of the volume of sales or number of hours you'll be working. It is yet one more reason to try to start a new business on a small, part-time basis and to learn as you go.

How Much Can You Charge?

In addition to cost and profit, there is yet another important factor in your pricing: what your customers or clients are willing to pay. Obviously, you cannot charge more than people can afford. You may or may not be able to charge more than what other businesses are charging. Factors such as how good your product or service is, how reliable you are, how important you personally are to your customers or clients (such as being a highly regarded auto mechanic), or some other important consideration—a hassle-free, money-back return policy—may allow you to charge more than the business down the street.

You also don't want to make the mistake of underpricing yourself. You can actually charge too little for a product or service, and make people suspicious that you have a cheap (that is, lousy) product, or that you are not experienced enough to charge a fair price for your services. Business consultants often refer to this as "perceived value": your customers not only want to get value for their money, they want to feel (perceive) they are getting value for their money.

For many small businesses, the secret to success is not charging the lowest prices they can; but instead charging a higher price and offering something extra—a better service, a friendlier or more elegant atmosphere, whatever it takes. Face it, you can't compete with the Wal-Mart. The secret is, don't even try. Consumers are willing to pay more, in fact they expect to pay more, for quality and value. Ask yourself how much you'd pay for the same product or service.

People selling their services (selling their time) might charge by the hour or by the job. If you are a fast worker, and you have a good idea how long a job will take, charging by the job might earn you quite a bit more. It also takes the pressure off your customer, who knows in advance exactly how much it will cost, and doesn't have to worry if you're taking an extra long lunch hour, or feel the need to secretly keep track of your time.

Pricing is an inexact science. Some business people work hard at the numbers, keep track of the hours, and try to arrive at a logical formula that works all the time. Retail stores often decide on a flat mark-up for every item or for every item in a certain category (sometimes called "cost-plus pricing"). Some people simply charge what everybody else is charging, and hope it will be profitable. Some tradespeople, craftspeople and even some professionals "eyeball" your car and your clothes, or feel out how price-conscious you are, before quoting a price or an hourly rate—the old sliding scale. Don't be afraid to experiment; that's about all you can do anyway.

Federal Laws on Pricing

The federal Robinson-Patman Act prohibits companies that sell wholesale goods from discriminating between customers by offering price discounts or other special terms to one customer but not to another. Even volume discounts (the larger the order, the bigger the discount), very common in many businesses, could be challenged under this law, if the discounts discriminate against smaller stores.

Why do customers switch from one store to another? 14% switch because of price, 15% because of the quality of the product, and 71% because of lousy customer service.

—Author Tom Peters

This law applies only to wholesale goods (parts and finished products sold other businesses for resale). It does not apply to retail goods, and it does not apply to any services, consulting, repair work, contracting, etc.

The Sherman Anti-Trust Act forbids competing companies of any size from entering contracts or other agreements, written or verbal, "in restraint of trade". That means it is illegal to make deals with your competitors about what price you'll charge. This law doesn't prevent you from raising or lowering your prices to match or beat a competitor's price. You can do that any time you want, you just can't consult with the competitor about it.

Watercolor artist Grady Harper "One of my large paintings just never would sell even though it seemed to be the main attraction in my exhibit at all of the shows. After reading a pricing article, I decided to follow the #1 suggestion concerning top pricing secrets. I increased the price from $325 to $750. It was purchased after being on display only a few hours. "

CONTRACTS

Business dealings are more likely to be successful and free of disagreements, arguments, misunderstandings and lawsuits if they include a written contract. This is especially true for someone providing a professional service or doing a multi-faceted project. The issues of who does what, when, and for how much, can get dicey without a written contract.

A contract defines your responsibilities and your client's commitment. A contract demonstrates business professionalism and weeds out insincere clients. It also gives your customers a sense of security. And sometimes the only proof you have of the extent of your obligations is your signed agreement.

Don't think of a contract as a means to win, or to protect yourself against a lawsuit. The main purpose of a contract should be to clarify an agreement, to make sure all parties fully understand the agreement, not to set up the rules for a fight. Nor should contracts be used to keep

crooks in check. If you don't trust the people you're dealing with, maybe you shouldn't be dealing with them at all.

Contracts must be understandable. No whereas's, heretofore's, or legal mumbo-jumbo. Avoid words like he, she and they; it's too easy to confuse who you're talking about. Use your names, or "landlord" and "tenant", "seller" and "buyer".

Contracts should be simple and concise yet include full details. A good contracts tries to answer all the questions before they're asked. Contracts must be signed by both parties—original signatures, not faxed, not photocopied.

You might want to include, in addition to your names and addresses:

1. The duration of the contract.

products and services

sing the deadlines or
t.

metable for payment.
h the contract can be

(handwritten note: EVERY VERY IMPORTANT FOR OUR PRODUCT!)

7. wording to the effect that something of value is to be given, and something of value is to be received. This is legally known as "consideration", and it should be spelled out in the contract. A contract is not legally a contract unless there is an exchange.

8. If there will be out of pocket expenses, the contract should specify who pays the expenses, when and if they are to be reimbursed, and any dollar limit.

Contracts don't have to be formal, legal-looking documents. A letter of agreement, signed by both parties, is a valid contract and may be more appropriate in many situations. Regular, signed purchase orders are also valid contracts.

Avoid oral contracts. There's an old saying, "A verbal agreement isn't worth the paper it's written on." Although some oral contracts are legally binding, the problem is and always will be that everyone remembers the agreement differently. People's memories are mighty short. They honestly think they agreed to something completely different than what you think they agreed to.

Before I write up a contract, I make a list of the things I want to cover. I take a few days, to make sure I think of everything. I also find it helpful to look at other contracts to see how other people wrote theirs. There are books of sample contracts you can buy (or check the library). Trade organizations sometimes have sample contracts. Friends in business might let you have copies of their contracts (with names and numbers scratched out). Your accountant may be able to get you samples of contracts. If you are using someone else's contract, make sure you understand every word. If the legal hocus-pocus doesn't make any sense to you, don't use it, or rewrite it so it does make sense.

A note to designers, artists and others whose work involves intellectual property (writing, artwork, computer programming, etc.): The contract should spell out who owns the rights to your work, and the extent of those rights.

Other People's Contracts

If you are asked to sign someone else's contract, it's a whole different ballgame. Large corporate vendors and purchasers, government agencies, landlords, banks, leasing companies, professional consultants, and independent free-lancers often have their own contracts ready for you to sign, and they probably had talented and expensive lawyers create them.

Make sure you understand and fully agree with every word. Don't be too embarrassed to admit you don't know the meaning of a word. Look it up or ask. Be on your guard: nothing in these contracts is superfluous. Every clause was carefully thought out, to give the best advantage and protection to whoever had the contract prepared. (And look out for the word "indemnify").

Just because the contracts are printed on fancy paper, are formal, technical, legal, and etc. and etc., they are not cemented in stone. You can take out your pen and change them, eliminate sections and conditions you don't agree to. If the contract is important and valuable enough, get a lawyer's help if you feel unsure of yourself. Just don't sign it and hope for the best.

A Warning

I don't guarantee that the contract details in this chapter will make your contract legally binding. Your state may have contract laws and filing requirements, may require some precise legal wording, a witness or notarization. If a lot is at stake in a contract, have it examined by a lawyer. The purpose of a contract is to avoid legal entanglements. Once a contract winds up in court, everybody loses.

Groucho: Now here are the contracts. You sign at the bottom. There's no need of you reading that, because these are duplicates.

Chico: Duplicates?

Groucho: I say they're duplicates. Don't you know what duplicates are?

Chico: Sure. Those five kids up in Canada.

Groucho: Well go ahead and read it.

Chico: You read it.

Groucho: All right, I'll read it. Now pay particular attention to this first clause 'cause it's most important. It says, "The, uh, party of the first part shall be known in this contract as the party of the first part." How do you like that?

Chico: I don't like that part.

Groucho: What's the matter with it?

Chico: I don't know.

Groucho: Look, why should we quarrel about a thing like this? We'll take it right out.

Chico: Yeah, it's too long anyhow. Now, what have we got left?

Groucho: I've got about a foot and a half. Now, it says, uh, "The party of the second part shall be known in this contract as the party of the second part."

Chico: I don't know about that.

Groucho: Now what's the matter?

Chico: I no like the second party either.

Groucho: Well you should have come to the first party. I didn't get home til four in the morning. Now, uh, you just put your name right down there and then the deal is, uh, legal.

Chico: I forgot to tell you. I can't write.

Groucho: That's all right. There's no ink in the pen anyhow.

—Marx Brothers, from "A Night at the Opera"

HOW TO AVOID CROOKS
and How To Collect What You're Owed

There are a lot of con-artists in the world. Naïve small business owners are particularly vulnerable, and every business, I suspect, gets "burned" once or twice. I am not talking about armed robbery or shoplifters or embezzlers. I'm referring to people who offer to buy from you or sell to you or some other business dealing, but are really trying to con you out of goods or money. Pretty quickly you start to recognize these kinds of people, and you learn how to deal, or not to deal, with people you are suspicious of.

In one business I helped set up, which sold books wholesale and retail through the mail, I developed some safeguards for the business that protected us from the rip-off artists as well as from people who seemed suspicious but may in fact have been quite honorable. It is important that any procedures you set up appear to apply to everyone you deal with, so as not to offend people who may turn out to be valuable customers.

The first person who ever "took" us was a man who came by our booth at a book trade show. He was well dressed, in his fifties, and he handed me a nicely printed business card. He owned some distribution company in Arizona and asked us to ship him three cases of books with a bill. And, poof, he was gone. He got the books, and we got a "no such number" recording when I tried to call him to ask when our payment was forthcoming. Today, twelve years and many experiences later, I would be immediately suspicious of the man, the way he approached us, the look in his eye, the too casual dealing.

But suspicious or not suspicious, here is how I suggest handling a new, untested and maybe untrustworthy account. The easiest way, of course, is Cash Up Front. We had a written sales policy, just a sheet of paper we handed out to most prospective (and unknown to us) dealers and wholesalers. It stated, "We request that your first order be prepaid." As an extra incentive, we offered an additional 5% discount for prepayment. Some people offer free shipping for prepayment. This may sound like the end of your problems, period, but of course it isn't. All rules are made to be broken, and you will always find yourself dealing with people who, for any of a thousand reasons, cannot or will not prepay

(maybe they don't trust *you*). Do you do business with them anyway? Do you take a chance? Sometimes that's what business is all about.

Minimize your risk. Like the cardinal rule of gambling, don't ship more than you can afford to lose. Tell them you will send them one case of whatever-it-is, so they can "try it out and see how it does"; and as soon as they use it up or sell it or whatever it is they're doing with it, *and* pay for it, you will be more than happy to ship some more. Emphasize that yours is a small business, and thanks to a lack of red tape and bureaucracy, you can ship reorders very quickly

Here is a warning about shipping COD (cash on delivery). If the shipment is more than one package, make sure each package has a COD tag on it. Check with the post office or your shipper to find out how to mark the COD tags. We once sent a shipment of six cartons COD and put the COD tag, one bill for all six cases, on only one of the cases. They were shipped as one lot, marked 1 of 6, 2 of 6, etc. Well, two weeks later, the case with the COD tag comes back refused, and Lo And Behold, the other five cases do not come back. No payment ever came either.

When you get an order (not prepaid) in the mail from a company you don't know, call Directory Assistance and ask them if they have a listing for the business. No listing doesn't mean the company isn't legitimate (many home businesses are not listed) and, likewise, a business listing does not vouchsafe for it either, but it is an indicator whether you're dealing with reputable people. I am immediately cautious of a company without a business listing; we usually stuck to the written policy and demanded prepayment.

If you do get the company's telephone number, and the order is big enough to warrant a long-distance call, call the company "to confirm the order," maybe inquire how they want it shipped, tell them about your special prepayment offer, and definitely ask if you are going to get paid.

Establishing Credit

When dealing with someone for the first time and extending them credit, be very direct about being paid. Tell them you will be happy to extend credit, but you need their assurance that you will be paid. If you are dealing face to face, look the person right in the eye. And get the person to say, "Yes, I will pay this bill." Sometimes they'll say, "Well, this and that corporation extend us credit, we have an AA#1 Dun & Bradstreet rating, we are an established business, member of the Chamber of Commerce" and various and sundry impressive stuff that is of absolutely no value to you. Just repeat that all you need is their assurance you will be paid. It's a powerful "Yes" when they say it. Even crooks have a hard time going back on their word.

Collecting Past Due Accounts

If a bill goes past due, get on it right away. The longer you wait to try to collect it, the less likely you'll collect. Many people have little money, and they pay as they can until they just call it quits and disappear or file bankruptcy. You want to get paid before this happens, and squeaky wheels get the grease. Write. Telephone once a week. Be friendly and understanding, but be persistent. Don't be hostile or threatening—it gets nowhere, and that's the truth—but be persistent. Let people know they can make partial payments. Many people are unable to pay the entire balance at once, so they let the bill languish, unaware they can make partial payments.

And if it finally becomes apparent that you aren't going to get your money, just drop it and forget it. It's bad enough not getting paid, no sense twisting the knife in your own wound with anger and ulcers. If you've been "conned", there's really nothing you can do. The con artist has moved on. A collection agency, attorney, even the courts are not going to be of any help. Accept the fact that you won't recover the goods or your money, and be done with it.

Going To Court

Should you take a non-paying customer to court? The answer depends on one important factor: can you collect if you win? Does the debtor have accessible assets such as cash or property, and will you be able to get the assets? Otherwise all you have is one more piece of paper that says the debtor owes you money, but you still don't get the money.

Retail Customers

Retail customers are easier to deal with. People don't usually expect to get credit, and they don't usually ask. When we received a retail order in the mail, "Please send one book and bill me," we almost always declined. Even if the person is honest (and most are) it's simply not worth the time, the invoices, the ledgers, writing for payment, etc. We sent an order form and a note saying, "We request prepayment on all retail orders." The word "all" is important because it implies no bias or suspicion towards one person. And try to help the customer, because lack of trust cuts both ways. Offer an unconditional guarantee. "Cash refund if you are not satisfied for any reason at all." No explanations required. Be simple and straightforward; it always sounds the most honest.

We handled retail telephone orders differently. We took VISA and Master Card, and most of the people who called had those cards. But a new business, particularly a home or mail order business, may have a hard time getting to be a credit card merchant. The banks, fearing fraud, are sometimes very selective as to who they will set up as credit card merchants.

For several years, we did not take credit cards and we did bill retail customers when we got telephone orders. A long distance telephone call is more expensive (and a lot less anonymous) than a postage stamp, and less likely to be used by someone who's trying to rip you off. We told every customer that we would mail the merchandise and a bill, and all they had to do was agree to pay when it arrived. They agreed every time, and they paid *almost* every time. Non-payment was rare. If they didn't pay, we would send a reminder note in the mail and then kiss it off. Not worth the $15. Of course, if you take large dollar orders, you may want a less risky policy.

No credit policy should be cemented in concrete. I would not hesitate to extend credit to most large corporations, government agencies or anyone whose title or company suggests that they are likely to pay.

For many types of small businesses, the "credit crooks" are actually rare. And after a few experiences, I tell you, you can spot 'em a mile coming. Something about them always tips you off: maybe their stationery, or lack of it; or the "hustle" in their voice; or their lack of knowledge how your type of business usually operates; or always a red flag for us, some stranger talking large quantities and big dollars. In a way, it's kind of fun, too, sleuthing, feeling the people out—and what great dinner stories. Someday I'll tell you about the guy on the phone from Philadelphia, Mr. Cream Cheese my wife called him. He was a real *pro*.

You go to a coin-operated store to wash and dry your clothes. Then you go to a filling station where you pump your own gas. And on to a fast food restaurant where you carry your own tray. And what is it being called? A service economy.
—*Business columnist Bob Orbin*

Service isn't a department. It's a way of life.
—*Businessman Larry Taylor*

"Service" is the way you treat your customers, something that earns you customers. It's an essential aspect of a business that makes a profit. And it does not come in the form of voice mail.
—*Bookstore owner Sam Leandro*

MANAGING YOUR BUSINESS

Volumes have been written on the subject of small business "management." I put the word in quotes because it is such an all-encompassing term. Just about anything you, the owner, do is labeled "management." And just about every study on small business failures blames over 90% of those failures on "poor management."

"Poor management" refers to everything from sloppy bookkeeping to lousy business location. If you sell clothing, and the fashions suddenly change leaving you with unsalable merchandise, it's labeled "poor management": you should have been aware of the market trends and should have made advance preparations to anticipate them. If you expected your business to show a profit the first year, but you wound up with a loss and not enough reserve cash to keep things going, that's another situation they call "poor management."

Management is an organic part of your business, interwoven into every aspect of business. It isn't like Step One—get a business license, Step Two—manage, Step Three—post the ledgers, etc. Management is something you can learn only by doing, but a few evenings spent with some good management reading won't do you any harm.

Almost every library in the country has at least ten books on business management. Some of the books are excellent, some are shallow; almost all of them go unread. An interesting SBA study of 81 small businesses showed that only one owner in 81 read any management literature. Most of those 81 businesses failed. There are thousands of defunct businesses, gone belly-up because of the same management errors repeated over and over again. I guess it's just human nature to want to learn from your own mistakes.

You will get the most value out of management books if you read them after you've had several months' experience in your new venture. You will understand much better what the books are discussing, and you will quickly spot the information most valuable to you.

Join the trade organizations for your type of business, and subscribe to the trade magazines. Many libraries have reference books listing dozens of trade organizations and journals.

The very best management advice you can get, however, is from other small business people. Businessmen and women, I find, love to talk about business. Business is a large part of their

173

lives, and they love to share their experiences and their ideas. You can't get better advice at any price. No accountant or lawyer or college professor knows half of what the person who's doing it every day knows. Strike up acquaintances, get to be friends with business people, find out about the local merchant's organizations and attend their luncheons. Have a little fun, too.

Management is just common sense. As soon as you read or hear advice or a suggestion, you *know* instinctively that it's right. ("Why didn't **I** think of that?") If it doesn't hit you that way when you hear it, if it doesn't make total sense, don't rely on it. It's probably bad advice, for now anyway; but check back in six months or a year.

Lara Stonebraker, Cunningham's Coffee: "It's important to keep your merchandise rotating in the store, constantly change the position of things. You'd be surprised how many people will say, 'Gee, you've got something new in,' when you know it's been sitting there for two years; you've just moved it from this shelf to that shelf. It has to be displayed in a coherent manner. You have to have all those things that are related together. And you have to give your customers an incredible selection. If you have espresso pots, you have to have them in nine sizes because people will not be inclined to buy if there is only a choice of two or three. Even if you stock only one of these odd-sized items that you know will not be selling, you still have to have it just to fill up your shelf, to give the impression that you have a huge variety.

"People will come to your store because they know you have a large selection. A lot of times I know that it's purely psychological, because I know that I will never sell a 12-cup pot and I know that I will never sell a one-cup pot. But I have to have them there just for the comparison, just so that people will feel that this is a store that has everything, that has all the choices they can possibly get, they don't need to go anywhere else for it. I've seen a lot of coffee stores make this mistake, having only two sizes of something. It just doesn't give you the confidence in the store.

"I do rotating displays on the expensive items every other week. I try to create the kind of display that will make customers stop and look, but not so much that the background will overpower the items you are selling. You can't have too many plants, you can't have things that will distract from your merchandise.

"And you can't have a no-don't-touch atmosphere.

You don't want things looking too pretty because people will be afraid to touch them, they'll feel inhibited. Most important of all, you can't have any bare walls. There was a place in San Francisco that opened and the woman just didn't have enough money to buy another cabinet, so she had one wall, the prime wall for display, just blank. Mr. Peet came in and said, 'Oh, that's a lovely wall; are you selling walls?'"

Marketing

Small Time Operator is about getting a new business successfully off the ground. Keeping a business successful, however, requires ongoing marketing: promoting your business every day, trying hard to satisfy and keep the customers you already have and find new ones.

Marketing will always be experimental. Bounce your ideas off other people. Talk to everyone who is interested. Don't hire a consultant.

Advertising may or may not work depending on the type of business you have and how talented you are at designing ads. Word of mouth may be your best advertising, and that means always making sure you have satisfied customers.

Think like a customer. Forget how great your business is, and put yourself in the shoes of your customer. What would you want as a customer?

Most important, take all complaints seriously. Most customers don't complain. ("How was the meal?" "Fine.") They just walk away and never come back. And while they don't say anything to you, you can be sure they tell all their friends. So if only one customer complains, you can figure at least ten others have the same complaint. If you can solve that customer's problem, not only will you keep that customer (and make him or her one of your best boosters in the bargain), you'll probably keep many of the others you would have otherwise lost.

The Internet

The newest opportunities for marketing are on the World Wide Web. The Internet is perfect for the small-time operator because it is still in its infancy, still somewhat experimental, and still wide open to entrepreneurs willing to experiment.

Right now, most people surfing the Internet are looking for entertainment and information.

They don't yet view it, may even be critical of it, as a commercial medium. But if you can pass on genuinely useful (and entertaining) information and slip in a plug for your business in the process, you may have some success. Big corporations cannot get away with this because they're so blatantly commercial.

I suggest that you don't spend money on a Web site right at first. For starters, just get on the Internet and see what's there. If you have a specialized niche market (such as a business that sells unusual collectibles, or caters to a small but die-hard group of hobbyists, or sports buffs, or music fans, or the like) you will probably find their section of the Web, and you can make your presence known. It's definitely time consuming, something you want to do for the fun of it as much as for any income it might bring your way.

When you are ready to try your own Web site, be sure to include good reasons for people to visit it: valuable, free one-of-a-kind information; links to other sites; fast and easy-to-load (minimal graphics). Before you promote your site, test and fine-tune it for a few months. And then include it on all advertisements, business cards, etc.

There is another excellent reason to go online. Businesses are using the Internet to share ideas. It's like a merchant's luncheon without going out to lunch, and you get to "talk" with people all over the country and the world.

Many trade, professional and small-business organizations have Web sites where people within your trade or profession discuss business, answer each other's questions, and share information. For general business information, tax information, etc., the Internal Revenue Service, the Small Business Administration, many business and legal publishers and magazines and newsletters have Web sites, all loaded with useful information for small businesses.

Harvey Mackay, author of "Swim With The Sharks": "I am a firm believer in superior information. Find people who have done exactly what you want to do. Ask them what they would do differently if they had to start over again. Get a mentor if you can. Read everything there is to read. If you get only one good idea from every book or article, it's time well spent."

THE FUTURE OF SMALL BUSINESS

Since the dawn of economic time, a person with the right idea at the right time and any degree of competence could make a go of small business. Today, even in our shaky economy, with giant corporations getting more and more of the consumer's dollars and with chain stores driving independents out of business, small businesses can and do survive and thrive. Small businesses attentive to local and neighborhood needs and small businesses attentive to customers' personal needs will always have an edge over large, faceless corporations. This is particularly true of service businesses where "the personal touch" is still very important.

Small business owners themselves can help, by patronizing other small and locally owned businesses. Not only does it help the small business environment in general, it keeps the money in town, to be re-spent again in town. What's more, you might meet other local business owners, and exchange help and ideas.

We small business people, all of us, also have a much greater responsibility. The future of small business is tied directly to the future of this planet and its inhabitants. Every person starting a business should consider along with profits, percentages and mark-ups, whether his or her actions are going to help or to damage this precious dwindling resource called Earth.

Businesses that avoid wasteful packaging, that do not generate a lot of waste in production or advertising, that make and sell products that are recycled or can be easily recycled, and businesses that sell products with genuine usefulness, will be much more appreciated by their customers (and the world). More and more, customers not only want a good product at a good price, they want to feel good about their choices.

You cannot separate business from life.

Good luck to you. I hope this book was helpful.

When we try to pick out anything by itself, we find it hitched to everything else in the universe.
—*John Muir*

No one dies wishing they had spent more time with their business.
—Arthur Lipper III, Venture Magazine

I never seen an armored car in a funeral yet.
—from the song "Life's a One Way Ticket" by Cousin Joe

Section Six
THE LEDGERS

If you were able to examine a hundred different businesses you would probably see a hundred different bookkeeping systems. Every business has its own needs and its own idea how the ledgers should be set up. Some business owners enjoy bookkeeping and like to keep elaborate ledgers. Many owners hate the paperwork and keep books to the barest minimum.

I designed these ledgers to be of use to the greatest number of small businesses, particularly new businesses with no bookkeeping experience. There is nothing elaborate about them. They are basic, but complete. You can use these ledgers as is or change them to fit your needs. I encourage you to experiment with your bookkeeping, to alter the ledgers in any way that will make them more useful to you and your particular business.

These ledgers are samples to use as you want. You are welcome to photocopy them for your personal use. Or you can buy blank ledgers from any office supply store, and set them up using these ledger as a model.

If you use a computer to do bookkeeping, these ledgers can be used as a prototype. When first using a computer, I suggest you keep duplicate hand posted ledgers for at least a month, just to be sure your computer program is error-free and producing correct information.

Your ledgers should be a permanent record. Keep them for as long as you own the business. They will help you prove your figures if you are ever audited. Comparing months and eventually comparing years will help you plan for the future. Lenders, investors and possible future buyers will want to see your old ledgers.

INCOME LEDGER Month of _____

1	2	3	4	5	6	7
DATE	SALES PERIOD	TAXABLE SALES	SALES TAX	NON-TAXABLE SALES		TOTAL SALES
1						
2						
3						
4						
5						
6						
7						
8						
9						
10						
11						
12						
13						
14						
15						
16						
17						
18						
19						
20						
21						
22						
23						
24						
25						
26						
27						
28						
29						
30						
31						
	TOTALS FOR MONTH					

INCOME LEDGER — Year-End Summary

1	2	3	4	5	6	7
	TOTALS FOR MONTH OF	TAXABLE SALES	SALES TAX	NON-TAXABLE SALES		TOTAL SALES
	January					
	February					
	March					
	April					
	May					
	June					
	July					
	August					
	September					
	October					
	November					
	December					
	TOTAL FOR YEAR					

EXPENDITURE LEDGER

DATE	CHECK NO.	PAYEE	TOTAL	1 INVEN-TORY	2 SUPPLIES, POSTAGE, ETC.	3 OUTSIDE CONTRACTORS

4	5	6	7	8	9	10	11	
EMPLOYEE PAYROLL	ADVERTISING	RENT	UTILITIES	TAXES & LICENSES		MISC.	NON-DEDUCT.	

YEAR-END EXPENDITURE SUMMARY

			TOTAL	1 INVEN-TORY	2 SUPPLIES, POSTAGE, ETC.	3 OUTSIDE CONTRACTORS
		January total				
		February total				
		March total				
		April total				
		May total				
		June total				
		July total				
		August total				
		September total				
		October total				
		November total				
		December total				
		Unpaid bills (Acct's. Payable):				
		TOTALS FOR YEAR				
		ADDITIONAL EXPENSES:				
		Return Checks (from your "Bad Debts" folder)				
		Uncollectible Accounts (from your "Bad Debts" folder)				
		Auto expense (if you take the standard mileage rate) Mileage for year _____				
		Depreciation (from Depreciation Worksheet—Col 11, 13, 15 or 17)				

4	5	6	7	8	9	10	11
EMPLOYEE PAYROLL	ADVERTISING	RENT	UTILITIES	TAXES & LICENSES		MISC.	NON-DEDUCT.

EQUIPMENT LEDGER AND DEPRECIATION WORKSHEETS

1	2	3	4	5	6	7	8	9
DATE	DESCRIPTION	METH.	WRITE OFF PERIOD	NEW OR USED	%	COST	DEPR. 19__	BAL. TO BE DEPR.

10	11	12	13	14	15	16	17	18
BAL. TO BE DEPR.	DEPR. 19__	BAL. TO BE DEPR.	DEPR. 19___	BAL. TO BE DEPR.	DEPR. 19__	BAL. TO BE DEPR.	DEPR. 19__	BAL. TO BE DEPR.

PAYROLL LEDGER

Name _____

Address _____

Social Security _____

Pay Rate _____

1	2	3	4	5	6	7	8	9	10	11	12	13
PAYCHECK DATE	CHECK NO.	PAY PERIOD	HOURS REG	HOURS O/T	GROSS	F.I.T.	SOCIAL SECURITY	MEDI-CARE	STATE INCOME	OTHER WITHHOLDING		NET PAY

PARTNERS CAPITAL LEDGER

1	2	3	4	5	6	7
DATE	DESCRIPTION	ACTIVITY	BALANCE	ACTIVITY	BALANCE	TOTAL BALANCE

PETTY CASH LEDGER

Period _____   Page _____ of _____

DATE	DESCRIPTION	AMT.	BAL.
	Beginning Balance		
	TOTAL		

Check Number _____   Posted to Ledger _____

INVENTORY RECORD

Item _____   Supplier _____

DATE ORDERED	QUANTITY ORDERED	DATE REC'D.	QUANTITY REC'D.	QUANTITY SOLD	BALANCE ON-HAND

CREDIT LEDGER

1 SALE DATE	2 CUSTOMER	3 INV. NO.	4 TOTAL SALE AMOUNT	5 DATE PAID	6 MEMO

INDEX

Quality Small Business Books & Software from Bell Springs Publishing

From the author of *Small Time Operator...*

422 Tax Deductions
for Businesses & Self-Employed Individuals
by Bernard B. Kamoroff, C.P.A.

"You get a raise every time you find a legitimate tax deduction." Here is a genuine gold mine, an encyclopedia of tax deductions, **everything the law allows:**

♦ Deductions you never heard about.
♦ Deductions your accountant forgot to ask you about.
♦ Deductions your tax software program failed to include or got wrong (again).
♦ Deductions the IRS chose not to mention in their instructions or list on the tax forms.

Accompanied by 422 quotes, discouraging facts, and bits of tax wisdom to cheer you up while working on such a depressing subject.

Every business owner is looking for ways to reduce expenses without cutting corners, without reducing quality or losing customers. But few look to the one area almost guaranteed to save you money: your tax return.

Many businesses and self-employed individuals are paying more taxes than they have to, letting deductions and write-offs slip through their fingers. The IRS is not going to tell you about a deduction you were entitled to take. It's up to you. The savings can be tremendous.
#02 200 pgs. approx. **Pub. date June, 1997 $17.95**

Marketing Without Advertising
Michael Phillips & Salli Rasberry

Does advertising work? Do you need to advertise? Are there better ways to market your business?

The first part of this startling book argues convincingly and with documented proof that almost all advertising is totally ineffective and an utter waste of money; and that most business owners have been successfully duped into believing that advertising is both necessary and productive in spite of obvious evidence to the contrary.

Marketing Without Advertising is much more than an argument against advertising. Packed into this large book are more than a hundred tried and tested marketing strategies that have worked for all kinds of small businesses. Here is what you need to know to successfully promote your business—at little or no cost.

Possibly the last $19 you'll ever spend on advertising!
#03 240 pages, 8½"x11"   **$18.95**

Getting Into The Mail Order Business
Julian L. Simon

For years we recommended one and only one mail order book, the best we've ever seen: Julian Simon's famous *How to Start and Operate a Mail Order Business*, a $40 textbook published by Mc-Graw Hill. At last, the most important information in this book—everything the beginner needs to know to get started and be successful in mail order—has been edited and distilled into a trade paperback that covers all the basics:

The kinds of products that naturally sell well in mail order, and those that don't. How to locate and test your market and promote your products. Selling through catalogs. How *not* to compete with the large mail order houses. How to create mail order copy that works.

And more: Setting up shop. Where to go for direct mail lists. Handling shipping, refunds, guarantees. How the mail order laws affect your business.
#04 291 pages, 6"x9"   **$14.95**

Make Money From Your Arts & Crafts
Steve & Cindy Long

Artists and craftspeople can fine tune their business, and novices can learn how to turn a hobby into a livelihood. The authors packed 15 years of experience into this large volume:

Product lines. Wholesaling. Consignment. Displays. Shows. Pricing. Effective table layout. Packaging and signs. Discounts. Dealing with show promoters, sales reps, store and gallery owners, employees, difficult customers. Finding new and unusual sales outlets. Licensing. And much more.
#05 230 pages, 8½"x11"   **$17.95**

We Own It: Starting & Managing Cooperatives And Employee Owned Businesses
Peter Honigsberg & Bernard Kamoroff

The only book of its kind, *We Own It* gives you the legal, tax and management information you need to start and operate all types of consumer, producer and worker co-ops. Covers non-profit, for-profit and cooperative corporations, ESOP's, and all other options.
#06 150 pages, 8½"x11"   **$14.00**

Negotiating the Purchase or Sale of a Business
James C. Comiskey

The price of a going business is tremendously negotiable. This thorough guide will help a prospective buyer determine if a business is worth buying. How profitable the business presently is. How good are the location and the lease. How easy or hard will it be for a new owner to take over. How much to expect to pay. How to value the inventory and assets. How much to pay for "goodwill".

This guide will help the seller determine a fair asking price, prepare for the sale, and deal with prospective buyers. Includes legal and tax aspects of a sale, the contract, & common financing arrangements.

#07   137 pages, 40 worksheets, 8½"x11"   **$18.95**

Small Time Operator: The Software
Bernard Kamoroff CPA, Steve Steinke & Emil Krause

For people with a spreadsheet program, here is the same bookkeeping system as the one in *Small Time Operator*, on a ready-to-use spreadsheet file (template).

The disk contains 23 spreadsheets: Income and Expenditure ledgers. Profit and loss statement. Balance Sheet. Payroll. Cash Flow. Net worth. Petty cash. Partners' capital. Credit ledger. Inventory control. Business plan. Invoice form. Mailing list. Loan amortization. Telephone-address file. Includes 184-page manual.

This is not a stand-alone program. You *must* have Lotus 1-2-3, Quattro Pro, Excel, or Works spreadsheet program (Windows, DOS or Mac).

#08   184 page manual & disk. **Specify disk.**   **$29.95**

The Small Time Operator Update Sheet

State and federal tax laws, Social Security and Medicare tax rates, Federal Trade Commission regulations, requirements for employers, Small Business Administration loan information and other government rules change all the time. Most of the changes usually become effective January 1 of the new year.

Each January, I prepare a one-page *Update Sheet for Small Time Operator*. The *Update Sheet* lists changes in tax laws and other government regulations, referenced to the corresponding pages in the book.

If you would like a copy of the *Update Sheet*, send a self-addressed, stamped #10 (business size) envelope and $1.00 to: Small Time Operator Update, Box 1240, Willits, CA 95490.

With the *Update Sheet*, you can keep your edition of *Small Time Operator* up to date, year after year.

SUPPORT YOUR LOCAL BOOKSTORE.

Small Time Operator is available in many bookstores across the country. If you are unable to locate it, or any of our other titles, please order directly from us.

OUR GUARANTEE:

All Bell Springs books and software are fully guaranteed. If you are not satisfied for any reason, return the items for a full cash refund, no questions asked.

Organizations, schools, professionals, businesses:

Small Time Operator is available at substantial discount for quantity orders. Call (707) 459-6372.

TELEPHONE ORDERS

In a hurry? We accept MasterCard, VISA and American Express. We are open 9am to 5 pm Pacific Time, Monday through Friday.

Toll Free 1-800-515-8050
Fax Orders: 707-459-8614

BELL SPRINGS PUBLISHING

51

Mail Order Sales Dept.
Box 1240, Willits, California 95490

Item	Copies	Title	Price	Total
01		Small Time Operator	$16.95	
02		422 Tax Deductions	$17.95	
03		Marketing Without Advertising	$18.95	
04		Getting Into Mail Order	$14.95	
05		Make Money From Your Arts & Crafts	$17.95	
06		We Own It	$14.00	
07		Negotiating Purchase or Sale of a Business	$18.95	
08		Software for Small Time Operator Disk: IBM 3½ ___ IBM 5¼ ___ MAC ___	$29.95	

Book Total $_____

Calif. residents add sales tax   _____

Shipping   **3.00**

Enclosed is check, money order or
credit card authorization for   **$_____**

Name _____

Address _____

City _____ State _____ Zip _____

Credit Card Orders: VISA ___ Master Card ___ American Express ___

Card # _____ Exp. Date _____

Signature _____